Contemporary Perspectives on Families, Communities, and Schools for Young Children

A volume in
Contemporary Perspectives in Early Childhood Education
Series Editors: Olivia N. Saracho and Bernard Spodek

Contemporary Perspectives on Families, Communities, and Schools for Young Children

Edited by

Olivia N. Saracho
and
Bernard Spodek

INFORMATION AGE
PUBLISHING

Greenwich, Connecticut 06830 • www.infoagepub.com

Library of Congress Cataloging-in-Publication Data

Contemporary perspectives on families, communities, and schools for
young children / edited by Olivia N. Saracho and Bernard Spodek.
    p. cm. – (Contemporary perspectives in early childhood
education)
  Includes bibliographical references.
  ISBN 1-59311-185-1 (pbk.) – ISBN 1-59311-186-X (hardcover)
  1. Early childhood education–Parent participation–United States. 2.
Minorities–Education (Early childhood)–Social aspects–United States.
3. Community and school–United States. 4. Home and school–United
States. I. Saracho, Olivia N. II. Spodek, Bernard. III. Series.
  LB1139.35.P37C66 2005
  371.19–dc22

                                                    2004030904

CONSULTING EDITORS

We would like to acknowledge Elizabeth Johnson for helping us with a number of administrative tasks. She is Program Management Specialist in the Reading Center at the University of Maryland.

CONTENTS

Emergence of Families, Communities, and Schools in Early Childhood
Education: Introduction
  Olivia N. Saracho and Bernard Spodek   *ix*

1. Challenges and Realities: Family–Community–School Partnership
  Olivia N. Saracho and Bernard Spodek   *1*

2. The Relationship of Parents to Early Childhood Education
  Through the Years
  Bernard Spodek and Olivia N. Saracho   *21*

3. Young Children Experiencing Divorce and Family Transitions:
  How Early Childhood Professionals Can Help
  Marion F. Ehrenberg, Jacqueline E. Bush, Jennifer D. Pringle,
  Marei Luedemann, and Jennifer Geisreiter   *37*

4. Family Context and Psychological Development
  in Early Childhood: Educational Implications
  Enrique B. Arranz Freijo   *59*

5. Parenting Self-efficacy, Competence in Parenting,
  and Possible Links to Young Children's Social
  and Academic Outcomes
  Priscilla K. Coleman and Katherine H. Karraker   *83*

6. Emotion Regulation: Implications for Children's
  School Readiness and Achievement
  Julia M. Braungart-Rieker and Ashley L. Hill   *107*

7. Young Children's Achievement: Does Neighborhood
Residence Matter?
Rebecca C. Fauth, Tama Leventhal, and Jeanne Brooks-Gunn 131

8. Children as Catalysts for Adult Relations: New Perspectives
from Italian Early Childhood Education
Rebecca S. New and Bruce L. Mallory 163

9. Cultural Beliefs about Childrearing and Schooling in Immigrant
Families and "Developmentally Appropriate Practices":
Yawning Gaps!
Jaipaul L. Roopnarine and Aysegul Metindogan 181

10. Mexican American Families: Cultural and Linguistic Influences
Olivia N. Saracho and Frances Martínez-Hancock 203

11. Involvement of American Indian Families in Early Childhood
Education
Laura Hubbs-Tait, David Tait, Charley Hare, and Erron Huey 225

12. Contemporary Transformations in Families, Communities,
and Schools
Olivia N. Saracho and Bernard Spodek 247

About the Authors 257

EMERGENCE OF FAMILIES, COMMUNITIES, AND SCHOOLS IN EARLY CHILDHOOD EDUCATION

Introduction

Olivia N. Saracho and Bernard Spodek

Early childhood researchers, scholars, and educators have studied and written about the cultural domains of families, communities, and schools independently although they continually impact on one another. The culture of individualism has been identified as a major theme in American society. As a result, the individual person has been studied independent of the family or the community. However, the individuals' socialization within the family has generated individualized personal styles, which have been shared with the community. This community sharing can occur through formal associations, through friendships, through informal networks, and within voluntary organizations. The type and degree of sharing differ across individuals.

Sometimes formal organizations have sponsored collaborative movements. For example, in the late 1980s several communities throughout the state of Missouri established cooperative groups, believing that appropriate

Contemporary Perspectives on Families, Communities, and Schools for Young Children, pages ix–xvii
Copyright © 2005 by Information Age Publishing

teamwork amongst service providers would lead to good services for families and their children (Rozansky, 1997).

Innovative initiatives have emerged to strengthen families and communities. These initiatives have fundamental components that support successful activities in families and communities in a variety of environments. For example, social support for families with young children can reduce the complexity of their problems. The quality of this social support can contribute to the family's potential for reciprocity and social exchange and their survival relies on the quality of their social networks. Frequently, what seem like innovative programs are revivals of old programs (usually good ones) that had been discontinued earlier, though the new initiative has a different name. For example, in Victoria, Australia visiting child health nurse programs were closed at the beginning of the 1990s; a decade later they reemerge under the guise of new outreach programs (Scott, 2001). When good programs are terminated, families and communities may be harmed; because services are removed, valuable staff and professional resources are relinquished, and inter-agency goodwill deteriorates. In spite of these barriers, families and communities can expect favorable outcomes or endure hopeful aspects from such programs, because they provide a basis for optimism.

Families and communities can be rebuilt, strengthen, and supported through partnerships between funding sources, agencies with expertise in delivering services, and researchers who conduct both outcome and process evaluations. There is also a need to make attempts to disseminate successful ventures, and practices that are substantive and effective. Simultaneously these initiatives must have the flexibility to accommodate the needs of different communities and families (Scott, 2001).

Early childhood educators have often focused on the family and community context with their work with young children. Since the Reform Era, parental education and community involvement has been a tradition within early childhood education. While there is often consistency between the values and goals of families, communities, and early childhood educators, differences may also exist in relation to beliefs, expectations, and goals for their children. Children may become confused when these differences create dissonance in children's lives. Early childhood educators need to understand and accept the culture and context of the different family and community groups.

Knowing and accepting cross-cultural differences and being aware of the values children take to school can facilitate collaboration among early childhood educators, families, and community members. For example, immigrant children may bring different cultural patterns to school that are not reflected in the mainstreamed community. Early childhood educators need to understand that all families within a particular immigrant group or across immigrant groups may hold different beliefs about childrearing practices, values, goals, and early education. Furthermore, acculturation may cause some immigrant families to modify their native values to those of the new mainstreamed society and experience some deprivations and as well as benefits in their quality of life.

Research lends credence to the role of families' and communities' involvement in their children's education. Practice in the schools can only be improved when the differences among the families, communities, and schools are narrowed and/or when differences among them are accepted. These and other concerns have resulted in a wide range of research that is relevant to early childhood schools, families, and communities in a variety of contexts. This volume addresses some of these developments. The authors represent different disciplines and philosophical orientations. The objectives of this volume are to (1) provide an overview on the role of families, communities, and schools in relation to young children's education; (2) summarize the relevant research directions and dilemmas concerning the relationships among families, communities, and schools and their impact on the children's education; (3) feature several elements of the families and communities' involvement that go beyond physical presence in the classroom and their children's extracurricular activities; (4) offer a review of the research in a form that is useful to early childhood researchers, scholars, and educators; and (5) place the current research in its historical context.

Early childhood researchers, scholars, and educators need to understand the impact that the family, community, and school have on each other and the challenges that they encounter. An examination of these challenges needs to be disseminated among those who prepare pre-professionals to work directly or indirectly with young children in order that they help them to address these challenges.

Family, community, and school work independently in solving problems that affect each other. They need to develop a partnership to work effectively in solving problems and to prepare for a better future [North Central Regional Educational Laboratory (NCREL), 1996]. Children can profit from before the time they enter early childhood programs until they have left the public schools when a bond between family, community, and school is constructed. It is important to understand the functional synergetic that can be established as we approach the current and opening social controversies that influence children, families, schools, and, finally, the community. In the first chapter titled, "Challenges and Realities: Family–Community–School Partnership," Olivia N. Saracho and Bernard Spodek discuss the intricate and enterprising relationship between family and community. It also describes how this relationship is constantly changing in relation to social capital, efficacy, integrity, and the family's inner patterns of community. The families have been a fundamental constituent of a neighborhood. Since the Reform Era, educators joined forces with other professionals (e.g., doctors, nurses, social workers) to use the family–community relationship as a productive tool to give assistance and services to children. Initiatives from the Reform era parallel those in the Contemporary era. Saracho and Spodek describe those similarities that were identified by Bhavnagri and Krolikowski (2000) between the Reform era and Contemporary Era including poverty, immigrants, society, active volunteerism, and family–community visits.

Parents have not always been considered an important component in early childhood programs. However, since the introduction of the Froebelian kindergarten, work with parents has been a part of early childhood programs, although this work with parents was different in the original kindergarten, the progressive kindergarten, the nursery school as imported from England, the parent cooperative nursery schools and, more recently the Head Start program. In the second chapter titled, "Families and Early Childhood Education in Historical Context," Bernard Spodek and Olivia N. Saracho discuss the relationships between early childhood programs and families. Seeking lessons from the past allows us to make better sense of the current situation and to plan for the future.

In the next chapter, "Young Children Experiencing Divorce and Family Transitions: How Early Childhood Professionals Can Help," Marion F. Ehrenberg, Jacqueline E. Bush, Jennifer D. Pringle, Marei Luedemann, and Jennifer Geisreiter describe the prevalence and impact of parental separation and divorce during early childhood. They highlight factors that may impact on how an individual child's psychosocial and academic functioning may be affected (such as age, gender, economic circumstances, the quality of the parent–child relationships, and the extent of conflict between the parents). They also emphasize that early childhood professionals need to provide support for those young children who are experiencing divorce in their families. Although not possible to uphold in all instances, they also provide early childhood professionals with a set of recommended practices for promoting children's healthy adjustment under changing family circumstances.

The next three chapters focus on educational implications: (1) "Family Context and Psychological Development in Early Childhood: Educational Implications," by Enrique B. Arranz Freijo, (2) "Parenting Self-Efficacy and Competence in Relation to Young Children's Social and Academic Outcomes," by Priscilla K. Coleman and Katherine H. Karraker, and (3) "Emotion Regulation: Implications for Children's School Readiness and Achievement," by Julia M. Braungart-Rieker and Ashley L. Hill.

In "Family Context and Psychological Development in Early Childhood: Educational Implications," Enrique B. Arranz Freijo analyzes the relationship between the family context and psychological development from an interactive, bidirectional, ecological, and systemic perspective. He presents the most relevant research data to show the influence of parental subsystem and sibling subsystem interactions on cognitive and socioemotional development during early childhood. In general, it can be affirmed that a high-quality family context is associated with healthy psychological development, good cognitive development and academic performance, good personal adjustment, and good relationships with other children in other interactive contexts. The data are assessed from an educational perspective, the conclusion being that parents can contribute substantially to improving their children's psychological development if they have been properly trained to provide high-quality parenting. The chapter concludes with a summary of the optimum child rearing conditions for improving cognitive and socioemotional development.

In "Parenting Self-Efficacy and Competence in Relation to Young Children's Social and Academic Outcomes," Priscilla K. Coleman and Katherine H. Karraker present research focusing on parental characteristics associated with the children's positive development that have been plentiful in recent decades. They closely examine one aspect of parenting self-efficacy beliefs that is likely to play a central role in young children's social adjustment and academic performance. They place the study of parenting self-efficacy beliefs within the broader context of general self-efficacy theory and a systems perspective on parenting competence. They review the literature pertaining to the development of parenting self-efficacy beliefs. Coleman and Karraker also discuss research related to associations among parenting self-efficacy beliefs, parenting competence, and child social and academic outcomes. In addition, the authors describe processes by which parenting self-efficacy beliefs might causally influence parenting competence and child outcomes. Then they conclude with suggestions on how early childhood education professionals can assist parents of young children to become more efficacious.

In "Emotion Regulation: Implications for Children's School Readiness and Achievement," Julia M. Braungart-Rieker and Ashley L. Hill focus on emotion regulation and how it serves to mediate linkages between the child, family, and school systems from infancy to early childhood. More specifically, they discuss the major theoretical issues surrounding emotion regulation including how emotion regulation is defined and its developmental course. They also examine potential predictors and correlates of individual differences in the ability to regulate emotions, including factors such as infant temperament, parent–child attachment, and overall family functioning. Furthermore, they examine how emotion regulation relates to various factors that are central to the children's ability to adjust to the demands of school, such as school-readiness and success, behavioral and emotional competence in the school setting, and developing and maintaining social relationships with peers. Finally, they provide suggestions for future research.

In 2000, one in six children in the United States was living below the poverty line. In the chapter titled, "Young children's achievement: Does neighborhood residence matter?," Rebecca C. Fauth, Tama Leventhal, and Jeanne Brooks-Gunn discuss both how and why growing up in poverty can significantly impact a child's readiness to learn upon school entry, as well as ways public policy can help reduce developmental risks for poor children. Early childhood poverty, particularly deep and persistent deprivation, has negative impacts on children's cognitive and verbal development, as well as children's emotional and behavioral outcomes, although these effect sizes are smaller. Fauth, Leventhal, and Brooks-Gunn present two different pathways through which income may impact child development, one emphasizing the role of familial relationships and parenting, and the other stressing the impact of parental investments in resources for children. They specify ways public policy can affect associations among poverty, child development, and early education, focusing on the role of welfare initiatives and early intervention programs.

In the next chapter, "Children as Catalysts for Adult Relations: New Perspectives from Italian Early Childhood Education," Rebecca S. New and Bruce L. Mallory review research findings on early childhood policies and home-school relations in five different Italian cities. They discuss the impact of collaborative relationships among parents, teachers, and members of the community for early childhood. They provide a comparative analysis of the social policies and local practices that characterize Italian early childhood education and care. For more than four decades, Italy has provided considerable human and financial resources to improve the quality of life of young children. New and Mallory briefly analyze the rationales and actions surrounding early education in the United States, vis-à-vis the Italian experience. Their conclusion considers the possibilities and the impact in developing a more respectful and collaborative home-school-community partnerships regarding the early childhood education and care of young children in contemporary United States society.

The following three chapters discuss families from three different cultural groups (immigrants, Mexican American, American Indian) and their cultural influences on early childhood development and education: (1) "Cultural Beliefs About Childrearing and Schooling in Immigrant Families and 'Developmentally Appropriate Practices': Yawning Gaps!" by Jaipaul L. Roopnarine and Aysegul Metindogan, (2) "Mexican American Family Cultural and Linguistic Influences" by Olivia N. Saracho and Frances Martínez-Hancock, and (3) "Involvement of American Indian Families in Early

Childhood Education" by Laura Hubbs-Tait, David Tait, Charley Hare, and Erron Huey.

Research studies point to the diverse beliefs and practices that immigrant parents in the United States employ in childrearing and education. For the most part, immigrant parents from Latin America, the Caribbean, and Asia lean toward teacher-driven educational practices that are more structured, demand obedience from children, emphasize learning the basics, and assign a good deal of homework, all of which collide with "developmentally appropriate practices." In "Cultural Beliefs About Childrearing and Schooling in Immigrant Families and 'Developmentally Appropriate Practices': Yawning Gaps!" Jaipaul L. Roopnarine and Aysegul Metindogan examine the cultural relevance of the National Association for the Education of Young Children's (NAEYC) "appropriate" and "inappropriate" developmental practices designations for the education of children of immigrant families in the United States. Attention is directed toward the consideration of factors that may be key to designing early childhood programs for immigrant children in the twenty first century: hybrid or transnational identity, ethnotheories about social and intellectual competence, the benefits of didactic-instruction versus child-centered approaches, different patterns of immigrant adjustment, parental belief systems about childrearing and early education, and the faces of parental involvement in education.

In "Mexican American Family Cultural and Linguistic Influences" Olivia N. Saracho and Frances Martínez-Hancock provide an introduction to Mexican American families and their cultural influences on early childhood development and education. Mexican American citizens comprise 38% of the population in the United States. Culture in these families is viewed as the foundation for the children's social development, self-identity, and language that transmit their culture. Saracho and Martínez-Hancock advocate that cultural knowledge about Mexican American families and their language (Spanish) of communication must be viewed as an asset for planning curriculum that is culturally relevant and appropriate for them. They define culture as dynamic and holistic that includes values, language, customs, traditions, beliefs, gender roles, and behaviors learned in the context of the family. Saracho and Martínez-Hancock describe the heterogeneity of the Mexican American population in the United States and how families are adapting to socioeconomic circumstances. Early childhood educators are urged to look beyond the negative stereotypes and biases and to get to know Mexican American children and families in their communities. They suggest some curriculum activities that are culturally relevant. Teachers are invited to discover the strengths of the Mexican American culture and to collaborate with families in setting educational goals. They caution readers not to confuse cultural norms with issues of poverty.

Indian-controlled schools and changes in the federal law since the 1960s have led to increased involvement of American Indian families in their children's education. But the legacy of the past, including the displacement of American Indian peoples and the boarding school experience, combined with cultural differences between American Indian families and both the Bureau of Indian Affairs and public-school educators, inhibits greater parental participation. American Indian parents urge the incorporation of Indian culture and values into the curriculum and Indian teachers into the classroom and administration. Research support this request, in that traditional Indian culture, values, and practices of American Indian parents or children are linked to American Indian children's academic success. In "Involvement of American Indian Families in Early Childhood Education," Laura Hubbs-Tait, David Tait, Charley Hare, and Erron Huey provide an overview of the history of the United States' policies concerning Indian education and their impact on contemporary involvement of American Indian families in their children's education. They review studies of (a) roles of American Indian parents and communities in their children's education, (b) involvement desired by American Indian parents, and (c) barriers to involvement by American Indian parents and communities. They also discuss model programs of American Indian family and community involvement in the children's education. They advocate a legacy and continuing cultural differences between American Indian families and educational institutions that inhibit parental involvement in education.

Radical changes in the lives of American families, communities, and school settings have emerged in the 21st century. Although some changes were positive and supportive of families, others were negative and contemptuous. Cities, suburbs, rural, and everywhere families, communities, and schools encountered a socially toxic environment consisting of terrorism (Wright & Heeren, 2002), "violence, poverty, and other economic pressures on parents and their children, disruption of family relationships, depression, paranoia, nastiness, and alienation" (Garbarino, 1995, p. 14). Such radical changes contributed to the flow of trends that developed in connection to the families, communities, and schools. Trends included work behavior, attitudes relating to gender roles, transmission of values across generations, and family situations like schooling, marriage, divorce, child rearing, growth of women in the work force, the increase in child care, and other family practices. Many families became upset and stressed because of these changes, shifting the cultural meaning of family and community life.

In the concluding chapter, "Contemporary Transformations in Families, Communities, and Schools," Olivia N. Saracho and Bernard Spodek describe some of these radical changes such as the family and community's social change, support system, and consolidations of services. Saracho and Spodek also identify new directions in developing links among the families, communities, and schools. They also provide recommendations for future research to provide an understanding the value of the school–family–community partnerships.

Early childhood education has always been an enterprising one. Innovative models that provide connections among the family, community, and school of early childhood will continue to emerge through the years to acknowledge new educational ideologies, new social demands, and new knowledge. The issues addressed in this volume can provide new directions to prepare early childhood scholars, researchers, and practitioners to work as a team in these different settings.

REFERENCES

Bhavnagri, N.P., & Krolikowski, S. (2000). Home–Community Visits During an Era of Reform (1870–1920). *Early Childhood Research & Practice (ECRP), 2*(1). http://ecrp.uiuc.edu/v2n1/bhavnagri.html

Garbarino, J. (1995). *Educating children in a socially toxic environment.* San Francisco, CA: Jossey-Bass.

North Central Regional Educational Laboratory (NCREL). (1996, January). School-community collaboration. *New Leaders for Tomorrow's Schools, 2*(1). Retrieved on November 20, 2003, from http://www.ncrel.org/cscd/pubs/lead21/2-1a.htm

Rozansky, P. (1997). *Missourians working together: A progress report.* St. Louis, MO: Family Investment Trust.

Scott, D. (2001). Building communities that strengthen families. *Family Matters, 58,* 76–79.

Wright, A.E., & Heeren, C. (2002). Utilizing case studies: Connecting the family, school, and community. *The School Community Journal, 12*(2), 103–115.

CHAPTER 1

CHALLENGES AND REALITIES

Family–Community–School Partnership

Olivia N. Saracho and Bernard Spodek

I think that being a kid is the most important stage of your life. It's a time
when you start to develop a personality. It's when you start to learn about who you are
and what you want to do with yourself. Unfortunately, a lot of kids don't have that.
If you don't grow up learning how to be a productive person, then you are going
to have a problem once you grow up.

—Sarah Rose (Bird, 2001, p. 3)

INTRODUCTION

Families, communities, and schools make important contributions to the children's successful development and to their daily lives. The literature on these areas shows mutually exclusive reviews and studies of each, although these institutions differ in several aspects of life (e.g., child rearing practices, values, and education). Regardless of these differences, they are mutually bonded to each other. For example, schools may feel that children must learn to be both obedient and independent, that is, "to submit to rules which protect the rights of others, and to develop a progressive independence" (Johnson 1985, p. 123), while the families and communi-

Contemporary Perspectives on Families, Communities, and Schools for Young Children, pages 1–19
Copyright © 2005 by Information Age Publishing

1

ties may be more nurturing. Families, communities, and schools may agree on some values and educational goals, but differences usually exist in relation to their beliefs, expectations, and goals for young children. It becomes problematic when children are expected to substitute the school's values for those found in the home. It is important to understand and accept the culture and context of the different family and community groups. Nevertheless, a close loyalty seems to exist among families, local communities, and schools. The local community depends on the integrity of the family as a social institution; whereas the families' participation can promote their communities to provide an environment where families can succeed or fail. It is important to consider the intricate relationship between family and community. In the case of the schools, community focuses on the roles of the family to their children's learning. School community suggests that school learning also occurs outside the school, especially by family members and peers. Evidently school community includes (1) family and community elements outside the school and (2) shared values, trust, expectations, and obligations (Redding, 2001).

FAMILIES, COMMUNITIES, AND SCHOOLS

The relationship among the family, community, and school is constantly changing. The family's life cycle, stage, needs, resources, and history within the community contribute to this relationship. In relation to the schools, the term community has been sustained by an amalgamation of studies and philosophies about the family's contribution to young children's learning in the home. Specifically, families contribute to school learning when they engage in joint reading, parent–child discussions related to school and learning, homework and other studies at home, and provide expectations, structures, and routines about work, punctuality, and daily living. Although many families engage in these roles intrinsically, some need to learn how to implement them. The school community can assume a leadership role in educating and supporting families to provide an educational home environment that can guarantee school success. Sergiovanni (1994) suggested a paradigm transformation in relation to the schools, where schools are considered communities rather than organizations. The culture of a school can cultivate trust, cooperation, intimacy, and responsibility. The school community is reflected in the psychologists' assumption that school learning is affected by circumstances outside the school, especially those in the family and peer group. Consequently a school community is usually described as:

1. Extending to the students' families and various community factors outside the school, and

2. Functioning on the principle of shared values, trust, expectations, and obligations instead of tasks, rules, and hierarchies (Redding, 2001).

McAuley and Nutty (1985) show that families with children usually search for profound community bonds. Cobb (1992) stated the following:

> In a community, people take responsibility for collective activity and are loyal to each other beyond immediate self interest. They work together on the basis of shared values. They hold each other accountable for commitments. In earlier centuries, a person was born into a community and a set of reciprocal obligations. Now, those who seek an identity as part of a larger whole must invent community by voluntarily committing themselves to institutions or groups. (Cobb, 1992, p. 2)

Cobb's (1992) definition of community contains the basic elements of responsibility, collective activity, loyalty, working together, shared values, accountability, commitment, identity, and voluntarism. Cobb (1992) focused on individually selected relationships, whereas Sergiovanni perceived it to be organic and collective. Coleman and Husén (1987) identified three phases of family-school relationships that influenced their economic levels:

Phase I: (a) the families live at a maintenance level, depending on the children for work; (b) the families restrict the children's development; and (c) the schools must separate the children from their family and provide opportunities for their growth.

Phase II: In an attempt to improve the children's utmost economic position, a merger takes place within the industrial economy and the goals established by the family-school community.

Phase III: In the post-industrial prosperity parents believe that childrearing is an obstacle in their occupations. They devote a small amount of time and energy to their children's development and delegate this responsibility to the schools. They assume that the school has the responsibility to educate their children. The "hiring of professionals" is implemented to offer programmatic and therapeutic surrogates to nurture and educate extended families and tight communities, which describes the way social capital can decline, even among the educated and successful classes.

In addition, their level of financial investment in the community (e.g., family ownership), participation in organizations (e.g., political and social), and closeness (emotional and geographic) to relatives, friends, and neighbors also influence their relationship. Etzioni (1991) believed that "responsive communities" are distinguished by non-coercive declaration of values. A community should be linked by a clear set of values that are developed by its members. Cohen (1982, 1985) explored how the boundaries to communities are symbolically defined and how people become integrated into a community. He believed that communities are appropriately considered to be "communities of meaning, because community plays a crucial symbolic role in generating people's sense of belonging" (Crow & Allan, 1994, p. 6). "People construct community symbolically, making it a resource and repository of meaning, and a referent of their identity" (Cohen, 1985, p. 118). The existence of community depends on its members' concept of the power of its culture (Cohen, 1985), which is what Putnam (1993) refers to "social capital."

Social Capital

The concept of social capital appeared in the 1990s as a philosophical linchpin in communitarian suggestions in an effort to resolve several social, educational, and economic problems. Putnam (2000) found that between 1960 and the middle of the 1990s there was a drop in participation in face-to-face relationships such as voting, attending church, and volunteering in groups such as Parent Teachers Association (PTA), Boy Scouts, Red Cross, service organizations, fraternal societies, and labor unions. However, Americans joined mass organizations (e.g., American Association of Retired People or professional and political-interest groups) where there was a minimum of contact among members. Putnam (2000) concluded that the shift was due to (a) the women's movement in the labor force, (b) mobility, (c) decrease in marriages, (d) increase in divorces, (e) fewer child births, (f) the multinational corporations taking over locally-owned and operated businesses, and (g) modern technology leading to the privatization and individualization of entertainment (i.e., the substitution of television for the movie theater, like the substitution of movies for vaudeville). His reasoning may have been based on his connection to innovative trends in entertainment, which allowed individuals to only acquire isolated experiences at the sacrifice of social situations. Social capital may have contributed to the relationship between family and community. Putnam (2000) introduced the concept of social capital:

> Whereas physical capital refers to physical objects and human capital refers to the properties of individuals, social capital refers to connections among individuals—social networks and the norms of reciprocity and trustworthi-

ness that arise from them. In that sense social capital is closely related to what some have called "civic virtue." The difference is that "social capital" calls attention to the fact that civic virtue is most powerful when embedded in a network of reciprocal social relations. A society of many virtuous but isolated individuals is not necessarily rich in social capital. (p. 19)

Social capital refers to "the features of social organization, such as networks, norms and trust that facilitate coordination and cooperation for mutual benefit" (Putnam, 1993, p. 1). Communities differ in their degrees of social capital (e.g., accessible community information, opportunities for economic advancement, stability of residence) that contribute to social networks (Brooks-Gunn, 1995). Social capital may also contain accepted norms of parental supervision and appropriate child behavior achieving "collective efficacy," which Sampson, Raudenbush, and Earls (1997) defined as people trusting the community, the residents' sharing of common values, and the parents' willingness to act on these values, such as interventions in public places (e.g., parks, street corners). Sampson et al. (1997) conducted a comparative longitudinal study of Chicago neighborhoods and found that communities with collective efficacy have lower rates of delinquency and violence.

Efficacy

Efficacy can be linked to families' feeling of power in the community. Power in the community can consist of corporate, political, economic, and law enforcement power as well as being able to influence and intimidate individuals. A feeling of power in families can be related to both the power structure of the community and the families' internal feeling of efficacy, a view that they can control, influence, and achieve (Miller, 1994). All families, to some extent, have a feeling of their power, failure, hopelessness, and despair, which affects how families relate to their community as well as their willingness and ability to become involved in the community and use their power to influence the community.

Families who believe that they are without power may have weak relationships with neighbors, which diminishes their social ties with the community (Geis & Ross, 1998). Individuals are always in social relationships from the time they are born and continue to be members of a social network throughout their lives (Burkitt, 1991).

Social Networks

Behavioral scientists define social support as the structure of the individual's social network (or circle of intimates); whereas this networks function is to provide social support. A social network is the individual's circle of intimate peers or those friends, family, or workmates who are important to the individual (Hall & Wellman, 1985). Network support depends directly on network size; larger networks are more supportive (Hall & Wellman, 1985; Vaux, 1988). Network density is based on support utilization; usually more dense, or close-knit networks compared to less dense networks (Gottlieb & Pancer, 1988). Less homogeneous networks help solve difficult tasks such as job searches (Granovetter, 1974).

Nurturing social networks and their reciprocity, trust, and tolerance can strengthen the community as an aim of education, which has been a key question within debates around schooling for community (Smith, 2001). In the last decade, the communities' educational concerns have been the subject of renewed focus among educational institutions (Arthur & Bailey, 2000).

Families need to nurture their community relationships in order to develop tangible neighborly institutions to support them. Communities need to have a continuous interaction with its families to develop and explore successful possibilities. In *Paths in Utopia*, Buber (1996) was attracted to a co-operative and associational society, because he believed that a "structurally rich" society included local and trade dialogues to create democratic relationships. The individuals' lives:

> . . . are characterized by the ongoing conversations and dialogues they carry out in the course of their everyday activities, and therefore that the most important thing about people is not what is contained within them, but what transpires between them. (Sampson, 1993, p. 20)

The most important thing about individuals is what transpires between them to maintain the integrity of both family and community.

Integrity

The integrity of both family and community can be adapted to Erik Erikson's (1963, 1982) concept of integrity, which he identified as the ultimate stage of adult functioning. His final stage that he calls ego integrity versus hopelessness is the fulfillment of successful achievement of his preceding seven stages. Erickson defines integrity as when individuals encounter reality, recognize it, and accept it. Mature individuals form an acceptable self-concept and are satisfied with their role in life and functioning. Erikson's construct of integrity corresponds to the family and community relationship.

The alliance of both family and community designates a relationship between the families' dynamic involvement in community life to fortify the community; whereas communities provide families with valuable and nurturing environments (Miller, 2001). Three phases of Erikson's belief of integrity relate to the integrity of the family and community. First is the individuals' integrity who have the ability to go beyond egoism and to honestly love and care for others. The second is that integrity involves the capacity to engage one's inner self with the social world. Miller (2001) referred to *family integrity* as "the ability of the family consistently to provide its members with the emotional, psychological, social and economic foundations to support their engagement and involvement with the community" (p. 29). Miller (2001) referred to *community integrity* as "the capacity of a community to provide for its families a safe, economically viable and meaningful place to live, with equal justice for all" (p. 29).

Families may not be able to contribute to their community if they believe that they are under siege and cannot find possible economic and social opportunities for them to meet their basic needs. Family and community integrity constructs have a mutual relationship between them: family integrity reinforces community integrity; whereas community integrity cultivates and supports families. Miller (2001) described the facets of family and community integrity as a mutual relationship between a community and its families (see Table 1.1).

Inner Patterns

The family's inner patterns also contribute to the development of the family–community–school relationship. Families embrace a "family paradigm" that systematizes their world beliefs and meaning systems that become what Reiss (1981) referred to as a "community map," which is a spacial image of community that leads family members to invest value in various placements. Cohen (1985) conceived that boundaries may be recorded on a map (as administrative realms) or by physical characteristics (such as a river or road). However, some boundaries may be ambiguous. According to Cohen (1985), "They may be thought of, rather, as existing in the minds of the beholders" (p.12). Each individual in the community may have a perception of this map, since it is a *symbolic* component of a community boundary and is vital in appreciating the way people experience communities (Smith, 2001). Special locations in the community hold symbolic meaning that strengthens a person's sense of self. Neighborhoods and

Table 1.1. Facets of Family and Community Integrity

Family Integrity Includes:	Community Integrity Includes:
1. *A collective, multifaceted loyalty to the community,* which means that many members of the community participate in their community in a variety of ways.	1. *Equal opportunity in education,* which means that local schools will provide children of families from different backgrounds a safe and high quality education, without prejudice.
2. *A flexible internalized community paradigm,* which means that although the communities are constantly unfolding and modifying, the paradigm of the community allows families to continue their fundamental relationship with their community.	2. *Explicit wards and neighborhoods,* which refers to diverse and heterogeneous neighborhoods that are socially and economically homogenous.
3. *Responsibility to the community,* which refers to their essential involvement in the community (e.g., volunteer and civic work, participating in politics, partnership with religious organizations, sending children to public schools).	3. *Safe neighborhoods,* refers to a neighborhood where individuals feel safe regardless of social indicators (e.g., ethnic or racial neighborhood composition, community stories) to engage in a community life that will strengthen its safety.
4. *Family's credence in their own efficacy,* which refers to the families trust in their capacity to have an impact in their local environment.	4. *High-spirited civic associations and unifying rituals,* which refers to civic and public institutions that merge families to the community and public events (e.g., holidays and celebrations of the variant ethnic and racial groups in the community).
	5. *Successful jobs and access to public transportation,* which refers to jobs that provide the facility to commute to them, bypass racial/ethnic discrimination, and offer support services that assist families to work (e.g., child care).
	6. *Respecting diverse families and offering them equal access to power and resources,* which means that diverse families need to be respected and be provided with equal opportunities to maintain the integrity of the community, families, and individuals.
	7. *Productive social networks,* which refers to anything or anyone (e.g., friends, extended families, churches, working associations) that links families with one another and their community to productively manage their vigorous energy outside of the family system.
	8. *Perception of power and efficacy,* which means that families feel a sense of power and efficacy in their community, having the opportunity to be autonomous and effective.
	9. *Flexible identity,* which means that the communities' historical and social events as well as its collective narrative form their identity.

buildings can represent both the enjoyment of the past and the pain of the present (Csikszentmihalyi & Rochberg-Halton, 1981).

Families are also parts of groups within communities (e.g., ethnic and racial groups, social and economic classes, religious groups). The families' social identity with the community depends on how long they have lived in the community as well as their religion and socioeconomic class. Social identity is part of a family's self-generated history in relation to whom they are, their status in the community, their friends and enemies, and how they value living in their community (Miller, 2001). Outstanding exploration of community can focus on it as a cultural phenomenon (Cohen, 1982, 1985).

The family–community–school relationship is thought of as a unified strategy used by early childhood pioneers from the reform and contemporary eras to promote the total development of young children. A review of these pioneers' contributions can provide an understanding of this relationship.

REFORM AND CONTEMPORARY ERAS

Historically, educators joined forces with other professionals (e.g., doctors, nurses, social workers) to use the family–community–school relationship as a productive tool to give assistance and services to children. Usually, the families were a fundamental constituent of a neighborhood. Subsequently, they vigorously supported the development of the community's neighborhoods, because this development affected the children's welfare. Early childhood pioneers saw the total development of young children taking place within their families and communities. They assumed responsibility for the charity kindergarten movement, also referred to as the "Kindergarten Crusade" (Ross, 1976).

Early childhood pioneers (e.g., philanthropists, university presidents, kindergarten teachers) were primarily young visionary women from prosperous families. Their commitment stimulated them to inexhaustibly strive with missionary enthusiasm to convey the philosophy and practices of Frederick Froebel (Bhavnagri & Krolikowski, 2000). Their cause was to "save the children" from the vice, intemperance, sloth, misery, and the hopelessness that their families were encountering in the slums (Ross, 1976). These pioneers also believed that the Froebellian method was an educational approach that would develop the capabilities of these young and teachable children to help them become honest adults who completely become involved in the democracy of the nation (Snyder, 1972). "The more kindergartens the fewer prisons" (Riis, 1892/1970, p.181) was a major assumption at that time. The early childhood pioneers were responsible for the success of the kindergarten movement. The devotion of these "kindergartners" (i.e., kindergarten teachers) earned them the respect, cooperation, and confidence of the community (Ross, 1976). These teachers visited the children's families and their neighborhoods (Shapiro, 1983; Vandewalker, 1908) after school. These visits strengthened the family and community relationship. Indeed, in the United States, the history of parent education as well as the history of early childhood education intertwined. The curriculum of early kindergartens included working with parents as well as activities for children. As a matter of fact, one of the first nursery schools established in the United States was a parent cooperative nursery school (Bhavnagri & Krolikowski, 2000).

Since the 1950s the parent-cooperative nursery schools, a movement which originated much earlier, evolved into a major movement. The purpose of these parent cooperative nursery schools was to have a school with high quality nursery education at a reasonable cost along with increased parent education. Parents owned the parent-cooperative nursery schools and usually participated in the children's educational program. Some schools provided adult classes or parent meetings to discuss child development, child rearing practices, and other relevant topics (Taylor, 1968).

The family and community relationship was promoted in early childhood education during the "reform era," also known as the "social justice movement" (Levine & Levine, 1992). It was initiated approximately with the beginning of "The Free Kindergarten Crusade" until the end of "The Progressive Era" (Shapiro, 1983). The societal conditions influencing the family–community–school relationship are similar for both the Reform Era (i.e., 1870 to 1920) and current era. Bhavnagri and Krolikowski (2000) identified several similarities between the Reform era and contemporary times including poverty, immigrants, society, active volunteerism, and family–community visits (see Table 1.2).

Poverty

The "War on Poverty" called the attention of researchers in both educational psychology, developmental psychology, and sociology to the needs of low income families and communities. As a result, they initiated research to identify the home elements that influenced young children's success and failure in school. Coleman and his associates (1966) described the status of Black families in America and the difficulties their children confronted to gain access to the educational system. Moynihan (1965) depicted the barriers Black families faced in relation to the national programs. Bilingsley (1968) explored the sociology of Black families, whereas Blassingame (1972) created a historical perspective on Black families.

An attempt was made to reduce poverty by altering the families' environmental circumstances. This was especially important for children who were

Table 1.2.   Similarities in the Families and Communities Between the Reform and Contemporary Eras

Similarity	Reform Era	Contemporary Era
Poverty	Premise that the environment was responsible for poverty rather than the individuals' fragile disposition, body, or intelligence.	Child advocates believe environment conditions are responsible for poverty.
	Poor children live in hazardous housing, possess bad health, experience school failure, have a high drop out rate, are more at risk of delinquency.	Poor children live in hazardous housing, possess bad health, experience school failure, have a high drop out rate, are more at risk of delinquency.
	Families had little education and knowledge to foster positive health and developmental growth.	Families had little education and knowledge to foster positive health and developmental growth.
	Rationale is to better serve the poor.	Rationale is to better serve the poor.
Immigrants	Massive arrival of immigrants, primarily from Europe.	Immigrants arriving from different parts of the globe.
	Immigrant children enter American schools.	Alternative approaches to serve the educational needs of immigrant, such as bilingual education and California's Proposition 227.
	Education serves to "Americanize children."	
	Major reforms to meet the needs of the immigrants.	Major reforms that are attempting to be responsive to the immigrants.
Society	American society evolved from a rural agrarian society to an urban industrial society.	American society evolved from an industrial society to an information society.
	Urbanization required better literacy, specialization, skilled labor force, and effective child care for women working in factories and sweatshops.	Industrialization required computer literacy, a technologically sophisticated labor force, and high quality child care arrangements for working women of all classes.
Active volunteerism	Active volunteerism referred to as "Scientific Philanthropy"	Volunteerism was used to enhance the well being of schools, families, and communities.
	Volunteers visited the poor in their homes.	Republicans in Congress, former President Bush's "Thousand Points of Light," and President Clinton's initiative, guided by Colonel Powell, advocated volunteerism.
Family–community visits by kindergarten teachers, residents from settlement houses, and public school visiting teachers	Reached out to neighborhoods to enhance the well being of the schools, children, families, and communities.	Women saw that boundaries extended beyond the classroom.
	Used educational strategies to offer services and child advocacy through home-community visits.	Purpose to transform the neighborhood.

at risk of educational and social failure. During the Reform Era, assuring the War on Poverty, the premise was that the environment precipitated poverty rather than the individual's fragile disposition, body, or intelligence (Bremner, 1956; Handlin, 1982; Holbrook, 1983). The belief was that poverty could be relieved by modifying the environment (e.g., offering satisfactory health care, housing, support services and public welfare). Such educated notions were committed to progress from 1890 to 1920 (Mattson, 1998) and from 1904 to 1920 (Shapiro, 1983), which was considered the Progressive Era. Present child advocates also have the same educated notion that the United States can and must improve the condition of its children by drastically modifying their existing environmental circumstances and by sensible reforms (Bhavnagri & Krolikowski, 2000; Children's Defense Fund, 1997).

The characteristics of poor families and their children are similar both during the reform and during the present eras. Children of poverty have dangerous housing, have detrimental health, suffer from school failure, have a higher school drop out rate, and a greater risk of delinquency than the children from wealthy families. Poor families fail to have the required education as well as the lack of knowledge and resources to foster positive health and developmental results ((Bhavnagri & Krolikowski, 2000; National Center for Children in Poverty, 1990).

Although "welfare reform" differs in the reform and present eras, its general endorsed rationale is consistent, that is, to improve services of the poor. According to Trattner (1992), "conditions in today's inner cities are similar to those in our nineteenth-century ghettos and slums and that current attacks on the poor and the programs established to help them echo many of the sentiments expressed in the earlier dialogue" (p. xii). Poverty and welfare continue to be a source of profound debate and disagreement about the purpose of the communities, government, law, philanthropy, economy, individual responsibility, and personal morality (Bhavnagri & Krolikowski, 2000).

Immigrants

A vast number of immigrants continue to enter the United States (Bhavnagri & Krolikowski, 2000). There were 8.9 million immigrants entering the United States from 1900 to 1910 and 9.5 million immigrants from 1980 to 1990 (Fix & Zimmermann, 1993). From 1890 to 1920 approximately 18 million immigrants from central and eastern Europe migrated to the United States (Hunt, 1976). "The United State Immigration Commission reported that in 1909, 57.8% of the children in the schools of the nation's thirty-seven largest cities were of foreign-born parentage. In New

York City the percentage was 71.5, in Chicago 67.3, and in San Francisco it was 57.8" (Weiss, 1982, p. xiii). A minimum of 54 nationalities attended the New York City public schools (Hunt, 1976). New York teachers stated that the arrival of every ship increased the enrollment in their classes. The immigrants "landed on Saturday, settled on Sunday and reported to school on Monday" (Berrol, 1976/1991, p. 28), although the instant appearance of all immigrant children in the public schools differed by ethnicity (Handlin, 1982; Riis, 1892/1970).

Before this enormous immigration, the public schools were still inefficient, corrupt, thoroughly politicized, and completely inadequate (Berrol, 1976/1991). In New York immigration improved and modified the schools to include kindergartens, high schools, vacation schools, social service programs, and curriculum alterations. The schools' function was to deliver an ordinary experience to these immigrant children from various backgrounds to help them become dependable and democratic individuals, which was supported by Dewey's philosophy. Dewey (1915, 1916) advocated progressive education as the basis for learning how to engage in a democracy. During the Reform Era, the reformers and public school educators concentrated on homogenizing the different ethnic immigrants to assimilate through "universalism," "democratization and Americanization of citizenry through compulsory schooling," and ignored reinforcing individual ethnic identity through "celebrating diversity" and "cultural pluralism" (Bhavnagri & Krolikowski, 2000).

In recent years, the African American and Hispanic populations have been rapidly increasing, suggesting that by the year 2020 these school-age children will be the majority in the public schools (Berliner & Biddle, 1995). The United States Bureau of Census (1997) indicated that the number of immigrant children had been increasing in the American schools, although the immigrants came from different parts of the globe than immigrants of past eras. The present society and the schools continue with the same response to this continuous increase of immigrants, as manifest in their disputed resolutions (e.g., bilingual education, English as a second language, California's Proposition 227). Furthermore, the public schools continue to make major changes to attempt to provide a more effective education to these immigrants.

Society

American society continues to be in transformation. During the reform era, it changed from a rural agrarian society to an urban industrial society; whereas now, it is changing from an industrial society to a post-industrial, information society. An industrial and urban society requires that family members become literate, get specialized, become part of a skilled labor force, and make appropriate child care agreements for lower class women who work in factories and sweatshops. Presently, society demands computer literacy, a technologically citified labor force, and high quality child care arrangements for working women of all social classes.

Family–Community Visits

The kindergarten crusade developed hand-in-hand with the establishment of settlement houses and compulsory public education. These are dominant social justice movements that influenced the development of the family–community–school relationship during the Reform Era (1870–1920). Teachers from philanthropic kindergartens, residents from settlement houses, and visiting teachers from public schools worked for different institutions, but they had the same goal. That is, their goal was to enhance the well being of the children, families, and communities by visiting and helping in their neighborhoods. Early childhood educators continue to use and apply this goal and appropriate strategies to offer dedicated services and child advocacy through family–community visits (Bhavnagri & Krolikowski, 2000). According to Ross (1976), "these women saw the boundaries of their duties extended into the family and the community" (p . 41), because they perceived that their function extended beyond the classroom. In 1886 Constance Mackenzie, (cited in Vandewalker, 1908), described how the kindergarten teachers' family–community visits had transformed the neighborhood. She described the following condition of the neighborhood, both before and after the intervention.

> The touch of the kindergarten upon the family had a humanizing effect which appeared nothing short of remarkable. One short street at that time reputed to be among the worst in the city, was in some respects practically transformed by the family visits and the reflex influence of the kindergarten children. At the time when the kindergarten began, its unobtrusive crusade in that neighborhood, to walk through the street meant to invite an assault upon four of the five senses, as well as upon one's sense of decency. The place and the people were filthy; the conversation was unfit to listen to; the odors were appalling. By and by, however, a change became noticeable. The newspaper's apologetic substitutes for glass disappeared from many broken windowpanes, and old cans, sweet with green things growing, took their places. Chairs were cleaned when 'teacher' was announced, and by and by the rooms were kept brushed up to greet her unexpected coming. After a while the children's work, first discarded as trash began to assume an extrinsic value—the walls must be fresh to receive it. The children insisted upon clean clothes to be worn to kindergarten, and a general if dingy wash fol-

lowed . . . Lessons of cleanliness, thrift, and trust were learned through experience and communicated to the parents through the insistence of the children and the friendly family talks of the kindergartners. (pp. 61–62)

Hill (1941/1972) also described how these kindergartners utilized the community as a resource and were:

> . . . eagerly seeking work for the unemployed parents, space in hospitals for ill mothers, sisters or brothers, searching for physicians who would remove adenoids and tonsils or dentists who would extract diseased teeth, free of charge. This was the most important contribution of the pioneer kindergartners, as at this period the kindergarten was frequently the only social agency offering a helping hand in the rapidly-increasing slums. (p. 75)

The results of the family–community visits led to changes in the labor legislation that promoted children's prospect for education and limited their work. Addams (1910) stated that:

> While we found many pathetic cases of child labor and hard driven victims of the sweating system . . . it became evident that we must add carefully collected information to our general impression of neighborhood conditions if we would make it of any genuine value. (p. 200)

The systematic observations that were recorded during the family–community visits were used as evidence of essential accurate, authentic, and descriptive data to support their argument to legislators to forbid child labor. Furthermore, they inexhaustibly crusaded to modify social policies and supported labor legislation, by visiting and lobbying in the community (e.g., trade unions, benefit societies, church organizations, and social clubs).

CONCLUSION

The realms of family, community, and school have been viewed as isolated cultural domains. Although the family, community, and school have been studied separately, they have perpetually influenced each other. Culture of individualism has been a major theme in American society and in the family, community, and school. The individuals' histories of socialized experiences generated their personal styles of individualism. Community sharing can occur through formal associations, friendship, networks, and voluntary organizations. The type and degree of sharing differs across individuals. Some states have initiated a collaborative movement. For example, in the late 1980s several communities throughout the state of Missouri initiated the establishment of synergetic groups, considering that appropriate teamwork amidst service providers would lead to good services for families and their children (Rozansky, 1997). Cobb's (1992) concept of community includes responsibility, collective activity, loyalty, working together, shared values, accountability, commitment, identity, and voluntarism. Cobb (1992) emphasized separate chosen relationships, although Sergiovanni believed that it was organic and collective.

Researchers and educators need to understand the impact that the family, community, and school have on each other and the challenges that they encounter. These challenges need to be examined to better prepare pre-professionals in the areas to work together to address the challenges. The philosophies of sociologists from the past two centuries and Cobb's (1992) community elements are attempts to cure many of the social afflictions. Throughout the centuries, scholars have considered the community (1) to intervene with the unresponsive intrusion of mass society; (2) to monitor the deficient segregation of the individual directed against a massive mundane equipment; (3) to create a feeling of morality; and (4) to raise the perspectives of the one above the degree of power of family ties (Redding, 2001).

Family, community, and school connections continue to be a disjointed problem. Presently, it is considerably important than ever for families, communities, and schools to function jointly to improve and guarantee their success in the future (North Central Regional Educational Laboratory, 1996). Children can profit from before the time they enter early childhood programs until they have left the public schools when a bond between family, community, and school is constructed. It is important to understand the need to function synergetic with each other to approach the current and opening social controversies that influence the schools, children, families, and finally the community.

REFERENCES

Addams, J. (1910). *Twenty years at Hull House*. New York: Macmillan.

Arthur, J., & Bailey, R. (2000). *Schools and community: The communitarian agenda in education*. London: Falmer.

Berliner, D.C., & Biddle, B. J. (1995) *The manufactured crisis: Myths, fraud, and the attack on America's public schools*. Reading, MA: Addison-Wesley.

Berrol, S.C. (1991/1976). School days on the old east side: The Italian and Jewish experience. In G.E. Pozzetta (Ed.), *American immigration & ethnicity: A 20-volume series of distinguished essays: Vol. 10. Education and the immigrant* (pp. 27–39). New York: Garland. [Reprinted from *New York History*, (1976), *57*(2), 201–213.]

Bhavnagri, N.P., & Krolikowski, S. (2000). Home-community visits during an era of reform (1870–1920). *Early Childhood Research & Practice (ECRP)*, *2*(1). http://ecrp.uiuc.edu/v2n1/bhavnagri.html

Bird, M.E. (2001). Families: Our nation's future. *Nation's Health, 31*(3), 3. [Also in Carnegie Council on Adolescent Development (1995). *Great Transitions: Preparing Adolescents for a New Century.*] Retrieved on January 17, 2004, from: http://www.carnegie.org/sub/pubs/reports/great_transitions/gr_exec.html

Bilingsley, A. (1968). *Black families in white America.* Englewood Cliffs, NJ: Prentice-Hall.

Blassingame, J. (1972). *The slave community.* New York: Oxford University Press.

Bremner, R.H. (1956). *From the depths: The discovery of poverty in the United States.* New York: New York University.

Brookes-Gunn, J. (1995). Children in families in communities: Risk intervention in the Bronfenbrenner tradition. In P. Moen, G.H. Elder, & K. Lusher (Eds.), *Defining lives in context: Perspectives on the ecology of human development* (pp. 467–519). Washington, DC: American Psychological Association.

Buber, M. (1996). *Paths in Utopia* (R.F.C. Hull, trans.). Syracuse, NY: Syracuse University Press.

Burkitt, I. (1991). *Social Selves. Theories of the social formation of personality.* London: Sage.

Children's Defense Fund. (1997). *The state of America's children: Leave no child behind.* Washington, DC : Author.

Cobb, C.W. (1992). *Responsive schools, renewed communities.* San Francisco: ICS Press.

Cohen, A.P. (1985). *The symbolic construction of community.* London: Tavistock (now Routledge).

Cohen, A.P. (Ed.). (1982). *Belonging: Identity and social organization in British rural cultures.* Manchester: University of Manchester Press.

Coleman, J.S., Campbell, E.Q., Hobson, C.J., McPartland, J., Mood, A.M., Weinfeld, F.D., & York, R.L. (1966). *Equality of educational opportunity.* Washington, DC: Government Printing Office.

Coleman, J.S., & Husén, T. (1987). *Becoming adult in a changing society.* Paris: Centre for Educational Research and Innovation, Organization for Economic Co-Operation and Development.

Crow, G., & Allan, G. (1994) *Community life: An introduction to local social relations.* Hemel Hempstead: Harvester Wheatsheaf.

Csikszentmihalyi, M., & Rochberg-Halton, E. (1981) . *The meaning of things: Domestic symbols and self.* New York: Cambridge University Press.

Dewey, J. (1915). *Schools of tomorrow.* New York: E. P. Dutton.

Dewey, J. (1916). *Democracy and education.* New York: Macmillan.

Erikson, E.H. (1963). *Childhood and society.* New York: W. W. Norton.

Erikson, E.H. (1982). *The life cycle completed: A review.* New York: W. W. Norton.

Etzioni, A. (1991). *A responsive society.* San Francisco: Jossey-Bass.

Fix, M., & Zimmermann, W. (1993). *Educating immigrant children: in the changing city* (Urban Institute Report 93–3). Washington, DC: The Urban Institute.

Geis, K.J., & Ross, C.E. (1998). A new look at urban alienation: The effect of neighborhood disorder on perceived powerlessness. *Social Psychology Quarterly, 61*(3), 232–245.

Gottlieb, B.H., & Pancer, S.M. (1988). Social networks and the transition to parenthood. In G.Y. Michaels & W. Goldberg (Eds.), *The transition to parenthood: Cur-*

rent theory and research (pp. 235–269). Cambridge, MA: Cambridge University Press.

Granovetter, M. (1974). *Getting a job.* Cambridge, MA: Harvard University Press.

Hall, A., & Wellman, B. (1985). Social networks and social support. In S. Cohen & S. L. Syme (Eds.), *Social support and health* (pp. 23–42). Orlando, FL: Academic Press.

Handlin, O. (1982). Education and the European immigrant, 1820–1920. In B.J. Weiss (Ed.), *American education and the European immigrant: 1840–1940* (pp. 3–16). Urbana: University of Illinois.

Hill, P.S. (1972/1941). Kindergarten. In S.J. Braun, & E.P. Edwards (Eds.), *History and theory of early childhood education* (pp. 73–77). Worthington OH: Charles A. Jones. [Reprinted from *American Educators' Encyclopedia.*1941, Lake Bluff: The United Educators, Inc.]

Holbrook, T. (1983). Going among them: The evolution of the home visit *Sociology and Social Welfare. 10,* 112–135.

Hunt, T. (1976). The schooling of immigrants and Black American: Some similarities and differences. *Harvard Educational Review, 45,* 423–431.

Johnson, F. (1985). The Western concept of self. In A.J. Marsala, G. Demos, & F.L.K. HS (Eds.), *Culture and self: Asian and western perspectives.* London: Tavistock.

Levine A., & Levine M. (1992). The visiting teacher: Forerunner of the school social worker. In *Helping children* (2nd ed.). New York: The Oxford University.

Mattson, K. (1998). *Creating a democratic public: The struggle for urban participatory democracy during the Progressive Era.* University Park: The Pennsylvania State University.

McCauley, W.J., & Nutty, C.L. (1985). Residential satisfaction, community integration and risk across the life cycle. *Journal of Marriage and the Family, 47,* 125–130.

Miller, J. (1994). A family's sense of power in the community: Theoretical and research issues. *Smith College Studies in Social Work, 64,* 221–241.

Miller, J. (2001). Family and community integrity. *Journal of Sociology and Social Welfare, 28*(4), 23–44.

Moynihan, D.P. (1965). *The Negro family: The case for national action.* Washington, DC: United States Department of Labor, Office of Policy, Planning, and Research.

National Center for Children in Poverty. (1990). *Five million children: A statistical profile of our poorest young citizens: Summary report.* New York.

North Central Regional Educational Laboratory (NCREL). (1996, January). School-community collaboration. *New Leaders for Tomorrow's Schools, 2*(1). Retrieved on November 20, 2003, from http://www.ncrel.org/cscd/pubs/lead21/2-1a.htm

Putnam, R.D. (1993). The prosperous community, social capital and public life. *The American Prospect, 4*(13). Retrieved on January 18, 2004, from [On-line]: http://epn.org/prospect13/13putn.html

Putnam, R.D. (2000) *Bowling Alone. The collapse and revival of American community.* New York: Simon and Schuster.

Redding, S. (2001). The community of the school. In S. Redding & L.G. Thomas (Eds.), *The community of the school* (pp. 1–24). Lincoln, IL: Academic Development Institute.

Reiss, D. (1981). *The family's construction of reality.* Cambridge, MA: Harvard University Press.

Riis, J.A. (1970/1892). *The children of the poor.* New York: Garrett. [Original work published in 1892]

Ross, E. (1976). *The kindergarten crusade.* Athens OH: Ohio University.

Rozansky, P. (1997). *Missourians working together: A progress report.* St. Louis, MO: Family Investment Trust.

Sampson, E.E. (1993). *Celebrating the other: A dialogic account of human nature.* Hemel Hempstead: Harvester/Wheatsheaf.

Sampson, R.J., Raudenbush, S.W., & Earls, F. (1997) . Neighborhoods and violent crime: A multilevel study of collective efficacy. *Science, 277,* 918–924.

Sergiovanni, T.J. (1994). *Building community in schools.* San Francisco: Josey-Bass.

Shapiro, M.S. (1983). *Child's garden: The kindergarten movement from Froebel to Dewey.* University Park: The Pennsylvania State University Press.

Smith, M.K. (2001). Community in the encyclopedia of informal education. http://www.infed.org/community/community.htm Last updated: September 08, 2003.

Snyder, A. (1972). *Dauntless women in childhood education 1856–1931.* Washington, DC: Association for Childhood Educational International.

Taylor, C.W. (1968). *Parents and children learn together.* New York: Teachers College Press.

Trattner, W.I. (1992). Introduction to the transaction edition. In R.H. Bremner (Ed.) *The discovery of poverty in the United States* (pp. xi-xxvii). New Brunswick, NJ: Transaction.

United States Bureau of the Census. (1997). *Statistical abstract of the United States, 1997* (117th Edition). Washington, DC: Author.

Vandewalker, N. (1908). *The kindergarten in American education.* New York: Macmillan.

Vaux, A. 1988). *Social support: Theory, research, and intervention.* New York: Praeger.

CHAPTER 2

THE RELATIONSHIP OF PARENTS TO EARLY CHILDHOOD EDUCATION THROUGH THE YEARS

Bernard Spodek and Olivia N. Saracho

INTRODUCTION

We generally think of working with families and working with young children as closely intertwined. This has not always been the case. In studying the history of early childhood education, we find times when the education of young children has been closely related to working with families and times when educating young children is conducted in isolation from parents and families. In this chapter we will trace the development of the relationship between children's program and family programs within the United States.

Schools for children were established in the United States during the colonial period. These common schools were not organized by grades and it was not unusual for children as young as 3 or 4 to be included in classes with older children. Before that time each family was responsible for providing an education for their children. Parents, and often fathers were

Contemporary Perspectives on Families, Communities, and Schools for Young Children, pages 21–36
Copyright © 2005 by Information Age Publishing
21

responsible for teaching children to read—a religious imperative in Puritan America. However, by 1646, a Massachusetts Colony law required that towns establish schools for young children. Often children as young as three and four attended these schools, spending the day trying to learn to read along with older children. It was only in the mid-19th century that such young children were excluded from school as minimum ages for attendance were established. While parents often supported these schools, buying textbooks for their children, and often contributing in kind for the support of these schools, they were not included in the educational enterprise in any serious way (May & Vinovskis, 1977).

MODELS OF EARLY CHILDHOOD EDUCATION IN THE EIGHTEENTH AND EARLY NINETEENTH CENTURY

The first truly early childhood program to be established in the United States was the Infant School, established first by Robert Owen in 1816 in New Lanark, Scotland. Owen's idea of school for poor and working class children was disseminated through his books, which were available in America, as well as through his personal visit to New England and the Middle Atlantic portions of the United States. Infants Schools were established in New England and in the middle Atlantic states. When Owen visited the United States, he established a communitarian community in New Harmony, Indiana that was modeled on the community he established in Scotland. An infant school was also established there (Harrison, 1968).

Owen's school—the Institute for the Formation of Character—was part of his scheme to reform society. The lower section of the Institute was called the Infant School. Many educators in England, America and elsewhere adopted the idea of the Infant School considering it mainly as a school reform rather than as part of a broader social reform. Owen's school was designed to train students in good practical habits, most important of which was to make their companions happy. In addition, the children were taught reading, writing and arithmetic. In addition, the children were taught to make rational judgements on any subject (Owen, 1857). The method of instruction used in the Infant School was based upon kindness. Children were neither rewarded nor punished for their actions but were shown the consequences of their actions. Education here was based upon love and a mutual concern for happiness (Owen, 1824). There was little concern for the education of parents in this school or for any form of parent involvement. Parents, in the original school, often worked in the local mills during the day and Owen provided his school as a way of keeping young children out of employment in these mills.

Probably the best know advocate of the infant school was Bronson Alcott, a social reformer and father of the author, Louisa May Alcott. He ran an infant school in Boston and wrote extensively on childhood and infant education (Alcott, 1830). Alcott and other Infant School educators focused essentially on children, without great concern for the educational roles of parents and families.

The infant school movement was short-lived in the United States, partly because it was competing with the common schools of the time, partly because it did not include religious education, and partly because it did not provide a role for mothers, who were venerated by the clergy, many of whom saw "fireside education" as more appropriate for young children.

The Fireside Education model was a model of family reform through parent education. Parents would maintain a safe haven for children in the home, keeping them away from the secular influences found outside the home. Mothers would educate their children at home, on their knees at the side of the fireplace, at least metaphorically.

There were three themes to fireside education: the home, the woman and the child. The advocates of this approach to education saw the home as a haven, protecting young children from the influence of secular life on the outside. They saw women's roles as mothers and cultural arbitrators, endowing women with superior moral character and moral insight. Women's identity was intertwined with the proper discharge of their responsibilities as mothers, nurturing and educating their children (Strickland, 1982). While such a role for women was possible for middle class women in affluent, two-parent families, it was not possible when mothers were working outside the home, for whatever reason. While the fireside education movement provided a model of parent education, it separated the parent from all outside influences on the education of their children, especially the school. This was to be the case until the advent of kindergarten education in the last half of the nineteenth century.

The Kindergarten

Freidrich Froebel opened his kindergarten in 1837 in Blankenburg, Germany. His work was influenced by German philosophers such as Hegel, Kant, Fichte, and Schilling and by educational reformers such as Rousseau and Pestalozzi. Froebel's kindergarten curriculum was different from any early childhood program that was in existence. It included a set of manipulative materials, called gifts, craft activities called occupations, and dancing and singing activities using his mother songs and games. There were also nature study and work in language and arithmetic. Froebel's kindergarten activities were a form of symbolic education where each set of materials or activities represented ideals related to the relationship among man, God and nature (Spodek, 1972).

Early Models of Early Childhood Education

Strickland (1982) identified three models of early childhood education in the period before the establishment of the kindergarten in the United States. The first model was sending children to the "common" school. These were schools that were established in different districts to provide basic education to young children. Often children as young as three and four attended these schools, spending the day trying to learn to read along with older children. There seem to be a belief at that time that the educational needs of young children were no different from the needs of older children. Often these schools were criticized for enrolling young children. Some were concerned that these schools served mainly as a child minding facility in regards to young children, providing temporary relief for parents concerned with the care of their young. Others, however, were concerned that forcing academics on children so young was not in their best interest. It was only in the mid-19th century that such young children were excluded from school as minimum ages for attendance were established. While parents often supported these schools, buying textbooks for their children, and often contributing in kind for the support of these schools, they were not included in the educational enterprise in any serious way.

The second model that Strickland identified was the Infant School. This school was first established by Robert Owen in 1816 in New Lanark, Scotland. Owen's idea of schools for poor and working class children was disseminated through his books which were available in American as well as through his personal visit to New England and the Middle Atlantic portions of the United States. Owen was concerned with the impact of the Industrial Revolution on workers and their families. He created a model community for his workers, part of which was the Institute fo the Formation of Character. The lower level of the institute was labeled the infant school. Owen established a communitarian community in New Harmony, Indiana that was modeled on the community he established in Scotland.

Owen's infant school was not a place for custodial care, rather it provided an education to young children influenced by the educational reformers of his time. However, for many the infant school was seen not only as a place to educate young children, but also to provide care for them while their parents—mothers—could seek employment. Again here, there was little place for parents in the education of their children.

The third model, Strickland identified, has been labeled "fireside education." This movement was concerned with reforming the family through parent education. Talented women and clergymen joined together in publishing books to counter the secular view of the world of that time. These books were on topics such as marriage, home management, and the education of young children at home—at the fireside. These reformers saw the role of women as supporting the home and supporting children through active motherhood. They tried to establish the home as a safe haven from the outside world for the young, providing love, warmth and intimacy as the basis for rearing and educating the young. Women—especially mothers—were seen as the guardians of morality and this morality was to be transferred to their children. Parent educators viewed the education of young children as consisting of moral education and such things as teaching literary and intellectual activities were to be postponed until later, The result of this movement was to foster a strong role for mothers as the primary educator of young children within the protected home environment and suggesting that a school was not the proper place for young children. Thus, while parent education was nurtured, the movement served to sever the relationships between parents and the schools.

Kindergarten Education

The first kindergarten was established in Blankenberg, Germany in 1837 by Freidrich Froebel. Froebel's work was influenced by the German philosophers such as Hegel, Fichte, Schilling, and Kant as well as by educational reformers such as Rousseau and Pestallozi. Froebel's education was designed to help children understand the basic relationships between man, God and nature. His kindergarten curriculum consisted of several parts which were symbolic representations of ideas Froebel wished to instill in children. It included the gifts—a set of manipulative materials that children were to use in prescribed ways, the occupations—a series of craft project using various materials, and the mother songs and games—a series of songs and games children engaged in. In addition there was nature study and work in language and arithmetic. Each part of Froebel's curriculum symbolized an element of Froebel's philosophy. Play was considered an important part of kindergarten activities as well (Spodek, 1973).

The kindergarten arrived in the United States with German immigrants who were trained in kindergarten procedures. The fist kindergarten—a German language one—was established in Watertown, Wisconsin in 1857. The idea of the kindergarten spread with the help of Elisabeth Peabody, Susan Blow, and other pioneers in the field. Many of the developing kindergartens were private enterprises, either designed to serve children of affluent families or to provide a service as part of a variety of charitable causes. Kindergarten education was first introduced into the public schools of St. Louis in the 1870s and slowly, over the next century, became a significant part of public elementary education. While the first kindergartens served children between the ages of three and seven, the kindergarten ultimately became a program for 5-year-olds here.

Froebel himself envisioned women as teachers in his kindergarten. He combined women's interest in emancipation and their abilities as mothers with the needs of children, entreating them to become better educated as mothers and later as kindergarten teachers (Lascarides, & Hinitz, 2000). Thus, when kindergartens came to America, they included the education of mothers as well as the education of young children.

Many mothers who were reluctant to send their children to school, adapted kindergarten methods for their homes and kindergarten educators offered lectures on the theory and practice of kindergarten education to women in afternoon and evening classes. It was quite common for the free kindergartens (philanthropic kindergartens) and others to have teacher work with the children in the morning and with mothers in the afternoons. Often basic child rearing, cooking and housekeeping skills were taught to immigrant mothers. In Elizabeth Harrison's kindergarten, a Chicago Mothers' club was established in the 1890s to teach Froebel principals as well as methods of child study (Beatty, 1995). Only with the entrance of kindergartens into public schools and the financial limitations and space shortages that ensued, did kindergarten become half-day programs with a single teacher working with one group of children in the morning and another group in the afternoon (Shapiro, 1983).

As kindergarten movement continued to grow, it was heavily influenced by American progressive education. The Progressive philosophy transformed kindergarten education by the end of the first quarter of the 20th century as kindergartens sloughed of their German origins and were transformed into American institutions.

The Nursery School

The first nursery school was established in the slums of London, England by Rachel and Margaret McMillan. It was originally conceived as an institution for children ages two to seven and was designed to supplement the child rearing environments of the poor. The nursery school was as concerned with the health and nutrition of young children as it was with their education. Their key educational idea was "nurturance." We might translate it today as "dealing with the whole child."

The McMillans placed high value on the education of the imagination and the school placed heavy emphasis on expressive activity, play, at and movement. A great deal of activities occurred in the outdoors. The McMillans also wanted to help parents improve their child rearing practices, providing observations and seminars for parents. Eventually they hoped that parents would become capable of becoming their own children's nursery teachers (McMillan, 1919).

Nursery schools were established in the United States beginning about the time of World War I. They were primarily private schools or university laboratory schools. Some of the laboratory schools, like the one at the Merrill-Palmer School were specifically designed to serve parent education as were the nursery schools established in women's colleges at this time and those in the agricultural colleges of land grant universities (Beatty, 1995). In some ways these schools foreshadowed the establishment of parent cooperative nursery schools.

YEARBOOKS OF THE NATIONAL SOCIETY FOR THE STUDY OF EDUCATION

By the 1920s kindergartens and nursery schools were well established in the United States, though they served only a minority of young children. Parent education programs were also firmly established with the creation of the Child Study Association and the National Congress of Parents, later to become the National Congress of Parents and Teachers. The convergence of early childhood education and parent education was clearly revealed in the *28th Yearbook of the National Society fo the Study of Education* (NSSE) in 1929. The *Yearbook* was devoted to preschool and parental education (Whipple, 1929). While the yearbook committee was composed of eminent scholars in the fields of education and child development and an extensive list of associated contributors, the contribution of individuals were not identified.

The *Yearbook* begins with general statements regarding the importance of the first six years of life for the individual and the contribution of parents and the home to the physical growth and mental development of individuals. It asserts that parents have not been successful in meeting their responsibilities to their young children and that this situation could be improved by changing the social conditions affecting the home, by increasing and raising the standards of supplemental educational agencies and by educating parents. Thus, it sees the role of preschools and parents as intertwined.

The *Yearbook* deals with both kindergartens and nursery school education and its relationship to parents. For the kindergarten it suggests that each day parents send to school a report on their child. This would include information on the child's sleep, eating difficulties, bowel movement, emotional disturbance, amount of outdoor play and any abnormal conditions in the home. This report would help the teacher deal with any problems with the child that are manifest in school as well as supporting close cooperation between home and school. It also suggests that the child have a physical examination with the parent present so that any problems identified could be discussed. Finally, it suggests that parent and teacher keep a developmental record of the child which discussed periodically.

In advocating close cooperation between home and school the *Yearbook* suggests regular parent-teacher meetings as well as home visits by teachers. Many of the suggestions made here would be considered intrusive today. In addition it seems that the suggested cooperation is one way, with teachers influencing parents. No suggestion is made regarding parents influencing the kindergarten or its teacher.

The *Yearbook*'s chapter on nursery schools describes fourteen nursery schools that varied by organization, purpose and affiliation. While the existence of mothers' cooperative playgroups is acknowledged, these were not included since there were generally no trained nursery school teachers in charge. All of the schools, it is noted, increased parental responsibility for their children, even ones that served working mothers.

In its survey of parent education programs, the *Yearbook* identified two organizations that grew out of the desires of parents: The Child Study Association of America and the National Congress of Parents and Teachers, the latter organization having grown out of meetings of mothers at Elizabeth Harrison's kindergarten in Chicago toward the end of the nineteenth century. The work of these groups is described as well as that of the American Association of University Women, the Parents Publishing Association, which published magazines and other material for children and parents, and a number of university and other centers for child welfare research in the United States and Canada. Additionally, agricultural extension services, public schools and other social and religious agencies provided parent education. The rest of the *Yearbook* is devoted to research and methods of preschool education as well as methods of educating parents. The research described here was essentially child development research; no research on parent education or on early childhood education curriculum and methods was included. It must be assumed from this that at this time there was little research into preschool education *per se* or into parental education.

Eighteen years elapsed before a second *NSSE Yearbook* addressing early childhood education was issued (Henry, 1947). This *Yearbook* acknowledged that the 29th yearbook was devoted to the beginnings of early childhood education in the United States. Since that time research on child development had been popularized in the media, resulting in an increase in demand for supervised play groups and nursery schools. It noted that the progress of development for kindergarten education had been slowed during this period, both due to the depression of the 1930s and the emergency needs of World War II. These same conditions led to an increase in nursery school programs. The Federal Emergency Relief Agency, and later the WPA, supported nursery schools as a form of work relief for qualified and unemployed teachers from 1933 until 1942. During World War II the federal and state governments also supported child care centers for nursery school age children as well as after-school care for elementary school children in communities impacted by war industries, often sponsored by public school systems (Goodykoonz, Davis, & Gabbard, 1949).

Little attention is given in the *Yearbook* to parent education in early childhood education, although the intimate relationship between the home and the school for young children is acknowledged. Among the forms of parent relationships noted were parent visits to their children's school, parent-teacher conferences, organized study groups, and parent teacher association's planned educational meetings (Anderson, 1947).

The difficulty of providing parent education in rural areas is also noted in the *Yearbook*. While a dearth of cultural materials for education in rural areas is noted here, the belief is stated that parents need to learn to better use the rich educational resources of rural areas, including both the natural environment and the human activities related to rural life (Hoppock, 1949).

PARENT COOPERATIVE NURSERY SCHOOLS

While the *28th and 46th Yearbooks* note the existence of parent organized playgroups, neither mentions the development of parent cooperative nursery schools. The cooperatives were an important grassroots movement in that it changed the relationship of parents to early childhood programs. The yearbooks and other literature of its time spoke of parent education and reporting to parents. The relationship of parents to teachers and schools was a one-way relationship; schools were either telling something to parents or trying to change them somehow through education. The cooperative changed this relationship to one of equity.

The first parent cooperative nursery school was established in 1916. Through the 1920s and 1930s the parent cooperative movement grew slowly. By 1950 it was reported that there were 295 parent cooperative nursery schools in the united States. In 1941 the Seattle public schools began training parents to operate cooperative nursery schools (Taylor, 1954). Today the parent cooperatives continue to thrive and are represented by an association: the Parent Cooperative Preschools International.

While cooperative nursery schools were effective parent education institutions, they put parents in a different relationship with teachers. The parents are the owners and managers of these preschools. They take on many administrative responsibilities, including establishing educational policy, finding and maintaining the physical facility, insuring that the various gov-

ernmental regulations and codes are met, setting participation require-
ments and hiring the teachers. In many cooperatives, parents also function
as teaching assistants, working directly with the children in the classroom.
In others, parents take only administrative and maintenance responsibilities. Because they are both the employer and the client of the teacher, their
relationships are different from those in other kinds of schools.

Interestingly, the parent cooperatives were probably the first to be concerned with fathers in relationship to their programs. Parent education
prior to the cooperatives was essentially focused on mothers, helping
women to become more effective mothers. Fathers seldom felt welcome at
"parent meetings," where the programs were geared primarily toward
mothers and fathers seldom felt welcome as participants in the program.
In contrast, Taylor's (1954) book presents an example of a school where
there was little interest in the workbench in a nursery class until a father
came and began working there with the children. While fathers are still
seen here in gender-specific roles, at least they were seen.

PROGRAMS FOR LOW INCOME CHILDREN AND FAMILIES

After World War II, there was an increased interest in early childhood education. The main growth of programs, however, was for middle class children and families (Lazereson, 1972). That changed in the 1960s when
increased attention began to be payed to issues relating to poverty. Even
before the Head Start program was established in 1965, a number of experimental preschool programs had been developed, primarily funded by
major foundations. These programs were designed to test various curriculum models, often based on assumptions different from those underlying
traditional early childhood programs as well as to test various program
delivery systems. While many of these programs had parent involvement
attributes, one of these was specifically designed to deliver educational services to young children through parent education.

The *Parent Education Program* developed by Gordon (1973) taught low
income mothers of children beginning at three months of age. The focus
was on activities to teach their children. It was also designed to enhance
the parents' self-esteem, give them a sense that they could affect their children's lives, help her value educational materials and activities, and expose
them to language and language activities that would increase the children's
verbal facility. The programs were offered in the home and were delivered
by paraprofessional, usually women from the same community of the parents, The program evolved into a Planned Variations model of both the
Head Start and Follow Through programs. Other curriculum models that

included children in center-based programs also included parent involvement activities.

With the establishment of parent cooperative nursery schools and the establishment of the various preschool programs for low income children, the relationship between early childhood programs and parents went from parent education to parent involvement. There was a major shift from educators acting upon parents to educators working with parents in a variety of ways.

The curriculum models were implemented as part of the Planned Variations program of Head Start and Follow Through all included some form of parent involvement. Gordon (1972) analyzed these Planned Variations programs to identify the kind of parent involvement found in each program. All programs were required, by the U.S. Office of Health, Education and Welfare, to have parent advisory boards. In addition, various programs saw parents as clients, had parents teach their own or others' children as well as teach other parents, and had parents share in the decision-making process regarding their child's curriculum, the school's curriculum and/or staff selection.

Parent involvement became and continues to be a stable part of all Head Start programs. Beyond the parent advisory boards, parent function in many ways in these programs. Parent involvement is also a requirement for many of the pre-kindergarten programs for children who are identified as at risk of future educational failure established by many public school systems.

Another form of parent involvement has been established for programs serving young children with disabilities. Public Laws 94-142 and 99–457 made parent involvement mandatory for program serving children with disabilities. These laws mandated program in the public schools for children from age three up with disabilities. The children were to be educated in the least restrictive educational settings. That meant that children from age three up needed to be included in regular classrooms to the maximum degree possible. Since there were few programs fo children below kindergarten age, this was problematic for 3 to 5-year-olds since many public schools do not include programs below kindergarten. Support was also provided for programs for infants and toddlers which were offered primarily ed in the children's homes. In order to plan for these programs parents had to approve the educational services to be provided to their children in Individual Educational Plans (IEPs) for those children from age three up and Individual Family Service Plans (IESP) for infants and toddlers. The younger children would be educated in their homes, with educational personnel working directly with parents who, in turn, would work with their children.

In addition to involvement in educational planning through approval of the IEPs and IESPs, a variety of other parent involvement activities were developed. These included family support programs to support parents in their roles as socializers and caregivers of their children. Schools also became linked to the homes of these children in a variety of way, with teachers reporting to parents in different ways, providing emotional support to parents, exchanging information, and having parents participate in classroom activities. Parents were also encouraged to provide support to each other within the program. In many cases, parent advisory councils were established for these programs.

PARENTS AND CHILD CARE

Child care arrangements are designed to free parents from their caring role for some period of the day. As such child care services seldom have parent programs beyond reporting to parents, either informally when parents pick up their children or formally, through parent conference and parent meetings. This seems to be shifting at present as family-centered child care programs are being developed.

Galinsky and Weisbord (1992) describe the antecedent of family-centered child care as the research on the effects of parent involvement programs on children, as well as research on high quality child care. In addition, the Head Start program was influential in demonstrating how parents can effect program planning and policy.

Family-centered child care views families in the context of their communities and view parenthood as a stage in the adult's life span development. Families are seen as the client of the center rather than just children alone. The family-centered model sees both teachers and parent as experts in different aspects of children's lives. Such a center is also linked to many other services in the community. Within this model, the child care center takes on a range of new roles, placing the care of children in the context of family and community.

FROM THE PAST TO THE PRESENT

Work with parents has been an integral part of early childhood education in America since the introduction of the Froebel kindergarten to our shores. The work that has been done with parent has varied through the years.

Epstein (1995) has categorized parent involvement activities in the schools into six forms. These categories are helpful in identifying how parent involvement has changed over the last century and one half. Epstein's categories are as follows:

1. *Parenting*—helping families establish home environments to support children as students;
2. *Communicating*—designing effective forms of school-to-home and home-to-school communications about school programs' and children's progress;
3. *Volunteering*—recruiting and organizing parent help and support;
4. *Learning at home*—Providing information and ideas to families about how to help students with homework and other curriculum-related activities, decisions and planning;
5. *Decision making*—including parents in school decisions, developing parent leaders and representatives; and
6. *Collaborating with community*—Identifying and integrating resources and services from the community to strengthen school programs, family practices and student learning and development.

These categories do not provide a perfect template for parent involvement programs in early childhood education, but they can help to identify the trends in processes that early childhood programs have used in working with parents.

1. *Parenting.*   From the beginning Froebelian kindergarten programs have worked on educating parents. The earlier kindergarten programs often had the teachers working with the children in the morning and with the parents—primarily mothers—in the afternoon. The programs taught mothers Froebelian philosophy and practices. Many parents purchased Froebelian kindergarten materials and taught their children with them at home. This happened especially when no kindergarten was available in the community. Frank Lloyd Wright, for example, reports in his autobiography that his mother provided him with the Froebelian gifts. And it was this work with the gifts that inspired his architectural vision (Brosterman, 1997).

Kindergartens that were sponsored by settlement houses also worked with the parents to teach them not only parenting skills, but to help them learn to function in American society and to become socialized into the American mainstream culture. Kindergartens that were sponsored by different agencies served different purposes in addition to the education of young children.

With the advent of programs for at-risk children, including Head Start, pre-kindergarten public school programs for at-risk children and for children with disabilities, work with parents increased in early childhood education. Much of this work was designed to help parents establish home environments to support children as learners.

2. *Communicating.*   Early Childhood education programs have always place great emphasis on communicating with parents. Parent meetings and parent conferences continue to be a part of early childhood programs. Most of these programs invite parents to visit when convenient. Teachers may also schedule visits to the children's homes. Very often programs will use newsletters to tell parents about what is happening in the classrooms and will describe activities that the class or particular children engage in.

3. *Volunteering.*   The best example of programs that use parent volunteers is the parent cooperative nursery school. Parents who join such nursery schools are committed to a great deal of voluntary activity. They may be engaged in the school's administration. They may be engaged in maintenance activities, cleaning the facility or building and repairing materials and equipment. They may also be active within the classroom, serving as teachers or assistant teachers.

Volunteering is also emblematic of Head Start programs. Parents may begin by volunteering to participate in classroom activities. As they learn more about early childhood theories and practices, they can become teacher aides, assistants, and, finally classroom teachers.

4. *Learning at home.*   Early Childhood educators have always considered the children's parents to be their first and continuous teachers. Much of the parent education work that has been done over the years has been to help parents interact with their children in more educative ways. The Ira Gordon program model noted above (Gordon, 1973) was designed to educate children through their parents. Similarly, Lombard's (1994) HIPPY program worked through the parents to reach and teach children. In addition, many of the programs for children with disabilities below the age of three are home based programs designed to educate both parents and children together.

One important approach to working to support children through their parents is the family literacy program. Parents are taught skills that they can use to improve their children's literacy development through in home and out-of-home experiences. Studies show that parents contribute to their children's literacy development during story sharing and important parent–child interactions. Researchers use evidence to demonstrate that family literacy is an essential educational and policy issue. They also provide a theoretical framework for developing family literacy programs without invading the family settings (Saracho, 2002).

5. *Decision making.* The two approaches to early childhood education that have involved parents deeply in decision making about programs and policies are the parent cooperative nursery school movement and the Head Start programs. Parent cooperatives have mainly served middle class children while Head Start serves low income families. Thus, parents from all social strata have been able to become involved in decision making in early childhood education programs. Involving parents in decision making does not mean that the professional educator gives up responsibility for these decisions. Parents often must be guided and helped to understand the basis for the decisions they make. Thus, decision making becomes a collaborative activity with teachers helping parents make worthwhile decisions.

6. *Collaborating with community.* Educational programs are embedded in the community they serve. Policies and practices have to be consistent with the values and beliefs of the community. Thus, early childhood educators need to consider the community in which they work. In addition, schools cannot serve all the needs of children and their families. Collaborating with elements of the community can enrich the programs provided to your children. The community can also provide resources beyond those which the school has to better serve children and their families.

As noted, programs for parents and programs for young children have been intertwined for the past 150 years. However, the types of parent involvement and parent teacher collaboration have varied over the years, both in relation to program aspects and parent and child characteristics. Parent programs will continue to be a part of the early childhood field. Parents will continue to be considered as partners with teachers in the education of their children.

REFERENCES

Anderson, J.E. (1947). The theory of early childhood education. In N.B. Henry (1947), *The 46th Yearbook of the National Society for the Study of Education; Part II: Early childhood education* (pp. 70–100). Chicago: University of Chicago Press.

Beatty, B. (1995). *Preschool education in America.* New Haven, CT: Yale University Press.

Brosterman, N. (1997). *Inventing kindergarten.* New York: Harry N. Abrams.

Epstein, J.L. (1995) School/family/community partnerships: Caring for the children we share. *Phi Delta Kappan, 76,* 702–712.

Goodykoonz, B., Davis, M. D. and Gabbard, H. F. (1949). Recent history and present status of education for young children. In N.B. Henry (1947), *The 46th*

Yearbook of the National Society for the Study of Education; Part II: Early childhood education (pp. 69). Chicago: University of Chicago Press.

Galinsky, E., & Weissbord, B. (1992). Family-centered child care. In B. Spodek & O.N. Saracho (Eds.), *Yearbook in early childhood education, Vol. 3: Issues in child care* (pp. 47–63). New York: Teacher College Press.

Gordon, I.J. (972). An instructional theory approach to the analysis of selected early childhood programs. In I.J. Gordon (Ed.), *The 71st Yearbook of the National Society for the Study of Education; Part II: Early childhood education* (pp. 203–228). Chicago: University of Chicago Press.

Gordon, I.J. (1973). Reaching the young child through parent education. In B. Spodek (Ed.), *Early childhood education* (pp. 275–280). Englewood Cliffs, NJ: Prentice-Hall.

Henry, N.B. (1947). *The 46th Yearbook of the National Society for the Study of Education; Part II: Early childhood education.* Chicago: University of Chicago Press.

Hoppock, A. (1949). The education of young children in rural environments, In N.B. Henry (1947), *The 46th Yearbook of the National Society for the Study of Education; Part II: Early childhood education* (pp. 340–349). Chicago: University of Chicago Press.

Lascarides, V. C. & Hinitz, B. F. (2000). *History of early childhood education.* New York: Falmer.

Lazerson, M. (1972). The historical antecedents of early childhood education. In I.J. Gordon (Ed.), *The 71st Yearbook of the National Society for the Study of Education; Part II: Early childhood education* (pp. 33–54). Chicago: University of Chicago Press.

Lombard A. (1994). *Success begins at home: The past, present and future of the Home Instruction Program for Preschool Youngsters* (2nd ed.). Guilford, CT : Dushkin.

May, D., & Vinoskis, M. A. (1997). A ray of millennial light: Early education and social reform in the infant school movement in Massachusetts. In T. Harevan (Ed.), *Family and kin in urban communities, 1700–1930.* New York: New Viewpoints.

McMillan, M. (1919). *The nursery school.* London: Dent & Sons.

Ross, E.D. (1976). *The kindergarten crusade.* Athens: Ohio University Press.

Saracho, O.N. (2002). Family literacy: Exploring family practices. *Early Child Development and Care, 172*(2), 113–122.

Shapiro, M.S. (1983). *Child's garden: The kindergarten movement from Froebel to Dewey.* University Park: Pennsylvania State University Press.

Spodek, B. (1973). *Early childhood education.* Englewood Cliffs, NJ: Prentice-Hall.

Spodek, B., & Saracho, O.N. (1994). *Dealing with individual differences in the early childhood classroom.* New York: Longman.

Strickland, C.E. (1982). Paths not taken. In B. Spodek (Ed.). *Handbook of research in early childhood education* (pp. 321–340). New York: Free Press.

Taylor, K.W. (1954). *Parent cooperative nursery schools.* New York: Bureau of Publications, Teachers College, Columbia University.

Whipple, G.M. (Ed.). (1929). *Preschool and parental education: 28th Yearbook of the National Society for the Study of Education.* Bloomington, IL: Public School Publishing Co.

CHAPTER 3

YOUNG CHILDREN EXPERIENCING DIVORCE AND FAMILY TRANSITIONS

How Early Childhood Professionals Can Help

Marion F. Ehrenberg,[1] Jacqueline E. Bush, Jennifer D. Pringle, Marei Luedemann, and Jennifer Geisreiter

PREVALENCE OF YOUNG CHILDREN'S EXPERIENCE OF FAMILY TRANSITIONS

Since the late 1970s divorce rates increased steadily until a peak was reached in 1989. Between 1989 and 1997 the divorce rate leveled off, followed by an additional 5% increase at the beginning of the 21st century. It is now estimated that 36% of first marriages in Canada, and 48% in the United States, will end in divorce (Statistics Canada, 2000, 2002; U.S. Census Bureau, 2002). An additional 17% of couples separate, but never divorce (Castro-Martin & Bumpass, 1989). In the end, more than one million North American children experience their parents' breakup each year. The risk of divorce is especially high for individuals in their late twenties and for couples who have been married fewer than six years. This find-

Contemporary Perspectives on Families, Communities, and Schools for Young Children, pages 37–57

ing is of particular relevance to early childhood professionals as these couples often have young families with one or two children. Based on the most recent statistics available, 15.9% of children born to two-parent families between 1987 and 1988 experienced the breakup of their parents before their 6th birthday (Human Resources Development Canada, 1999).

Approximately 75% of men and 66% of women eventually remarry, such that about half of all children who have experienced their parents' breakup will have a stepparent within four years of the divorce (Hetherington, Bridges, & Insabella, 1998). It is estimated that 28% of all American families are "lone parent" families, usually headed by mothers, and 14% of two-parent families are actually stepfamilies (U.S. Census Bureau, 1992). In the year 2000 approximately 37% of American children under the age of six lived in lone parent families, with the majority of these lone parent families being headed by separated or divorced parents (U.S. Census Bureau, 2002).

Common law marriages and separations are not routinely recorded as a part of the public record, however, from a young child's perspective parental separation is experientially similar regardless of whether the parents were legally married or common law partners. It is noteworthy that the proportion of common-law couples are increasing and, compared with legally married couples, these couples have an even greater risk of breakups. Many children do experience the breakup of their common-law parents, and these situations are typically not reflected in population statistics (O'Connor & Jenkins, 2001). Recent research has also demonstrated significant differences in the prevalence of divorce, depending on neighborhood and type of daycare, preschool and school setting which, in part, reflect differences in socioeconomic circumstances (Ehrenberg, Stewart, Roche, Carter, & Pringle, 2002).

In summary, many young children seen by early childhood professionals will experience the breakup of their parents' relationship. Most of these young children will need to maintain relationships with two parents living in separate homes. Some will also face the challenge of adjusting to stepparents and stepsiblings before they reach eight years of age.

THE PSYCHOSOCIAL MODEL OF THE DIVORCE PROCESS

Guttman's (1993) psychosocial model of the divorce process reflects an integration of current empirical findings and theories that have been used to explain family transitions from the perspective of individual family members, including the children, as well as from the perspective of the family system as a whole. The psychosocial model recognizes that "divorce, like marriage, is as much a complex personal phenomenon as it is a multidimensional social one" (Guttman, 1993, p. 31) that unfolds over a period of time. From this psychosocial perspective social and community supports are instrumental in contributing to an environment in which individual family members feel understood and the changing family system can reconstitute in ways that are supportive and healthful for the children involved.

IMPACT OF FAMILY TRANSITIONS ON YOUNG CHILDREN: PSYCHOSOCIAL FUNCTIONING

Considerable recent research has examined how family transitions affect a child's psychosocial functioning. On average, young children who experience their parents' divorce or remarriage display more adjustment difficulties than children from intact homes (Hetherington et al., 1998). However, young children vary widely in how they adjust to family transitions (Amato, 1994). Some children demonstrate severe adjustment difficulties; some children appear relatively unaffected; some children actually improve in their overall functioning; and still others show a delayed response to family transitions. Researchers have identified several factors that influence how young children adjust to their parents' breakup and subsequent family transitions. Familiarity with these factors may help early childcare professionals to understand (even anticipate) an individual child's reaction to a family transition, and it is hoped this knowledge may facilitate health-enhancing practices and help prevent situations that are likely to compromise adjustment.

Individual Child Factors

Age.   Young children's responses will vary according to the child's particular developmental level (Emery, 1994). Although few studies have examined how infants and toddlers respond to divorce (Whiteside & Becker, 2000), the existing research indicates that infants and toddlers tend to protest and are overtly distressed when separated from their parents (Shaw, Winslow, & Flanagan, 1999). Compared with older children, parental separation may be a greater threat to infants and toddlers who rely heavily on caregivers to meet their basic needs; moreover, separation may disrupt developing attachment and trust between infants and caregivers.

Preschoolers often manifest externalizing behaviors, such as aggression, disobedience, lack of self-control, distractibility, and hyperactivity, in the face of family transitions. They often appear needy and attention seeking as they look for reassurance and stability (Hetherington, Cox, & Cox, 1982; Pagani, Boulerice, Tremblay, & Vitaro, 1997). Divorce is confusing and frightening for preschoolers, who typically lack the cognitive capacity to either understand why their parents are separating or to have anticipated such changes. Moreover, because preschoolers are egocentric in their thinking, they may believe they caused the divorce (Amato, 1994). Preschoolers may also demonstrate regression to an earlier developmental stage (Amato, 1994). Preschoolers require stability and predictability, and transitions between one parent's house and the other's often are particularly difficult for this age group (Amato, 1994). Daycare, preschools and schools can play an important role in buffering young children from the stress of marital transitions (Hetherington, 1989). Schools that are structured, predictable in their expectations, and have explicitly defined schedules that can serve a protective function for children, especially boys with difficult temperaments and children exposed to multiple stressful transitions. Moreover, a stable, positive relationship with a teacher or caregiver can help buffer young children from the potentially adverse impact of family transitions.

Early school-age children are cognitively capable of grasping the significance of a parental separation, and, consequently, are likely to be sad and anxious regarding their parents' breakup (Amato, 1994; Hoyt, Cowan, Pedro-Carroll, & Alpert-Gillis, 1990). Children of this age may long for reconciliation between their parents, and may attempt to bring their parents together. School-age children are somewhat less likely to blame themselves for their parents' divorce, but are more likely to direct anger toward a parent they feel is responsible (Amato, 1994).

Gender.   Findings regarding gender differences in the impact of family transitions are inconsistent, and when gender differences emerge, the effects are small (Amato, 2001). Some evidence suggests that whereas young boys may manifest greater externalizing difficulties, particularly regarding social behavior, young girls may demonstrate more internalizing difficulties, such as anxiety, sadness, and over-controlled "good" behavior (Clarke-Stewart, Vandell, McCartney, Owen, & Booth, 2000; Morrison & Cherlin, 1995).

Temperament.   Young children's adjustment to family transitions varies as a function of individual temperament (Hetherington, 1989). Children who generally have difficulty adapting to changes are at greater risk for developing adjustment problems than children with easy temperaments. In addition, such change-sensitive children are typically less competent at securing support from others, and are more likely to elicit aversive responses from parents and teachers.

Parent Factors

Parent Conflict.   One of the strongest negative predictors of young children's adjustment to parental divorce is ongoing parent conflict (Kelly,

2000). In fact, many studies have demonstrated that irrespective of whether parents have separated, children in high-conflict families show greater adjustment difficulties than children in low-conflict families. High intensity fighting between parents is associated with more insecure attachments and higher anxiety in infants and toddlers. For older children intense interparental conflict has been associated with externalizing and internalizing symptoms (e.g., disobedience, aggression, depression, anxiety, poor self-esteem) in both boys and girls, compared with children experiencing low-intensity and constructively oriented conflict (Kelly, 2000; Shaw et al., 1999). Conflict can have a wide range of influences on children's adjustment, such as through modeling, disrupted parenting, and inconsistent discipline between both parents (Emery, 1994). Moreover, exposure to parental conflict can disrupt children's ability to regulate their own emotions, which, in turn, can increase children's likelihood of engaging in aggressive behavior (Cummings & Davies, 1994).

Children who are put in the middle of their parents' conflicts, through exposure or by being asked to take sides, are particularly at risk for adjustment difficulties (Emery, 1994). Parents who derogate the other parent to a child, press children to reveal details about the other parent and ask children to deliver messages to the other parent increase children's risk for adjustment difficulties. Young children may be more apt than older children to blame themselves for their parents' disagreements, particularly if the conflict focuses on them, and, consequently, may feel pressure to resolve the conflict for the parents; often, this leads to frustration when the resolution attempts ultimately fail.

Of course, parent conflict is often apparent to a child before the actual separation occurs, and children likely will exhibit emotional and behavioral difficulties as a result of such conflict. If the separation decreases intense parent conflict, children's socioemotional functioning will likely improve. On the other hand, divorce may exacerbate young children's functioning if conflicts between their parents are thereby maintained or intensified. Some recent research has suggested that children exposed to low levels of parent conflict before a divorce may be at increased risk for adjustment difficulties (Booth & Amato, 2001). Researchers hypothesize that for children from conflict-ridden homes, divorce may be a relief from the ongoing stress of living in such an environment; on the other hand, for children in low-conflict families, divorce may be a significant new stress without the concomitant benefit of no longer living in a conflict-ridden, and sometimes violent, environment. Amato (2001) suggests that as divorce has become more common and acceptable, parental separation and divorce in low-conflict families have become increasingly common.

Parent Alliance and Cooperation.   Whereas parent conflict is associated with adjustment difficulties in young children, a cooperative parent alliance facilitates positive adaptation to family transitions (Whiteside & Becker, 2000). Parents who are able to develop a positive, supportive post-separation parenting relationship with each other—in which they are able to exchange information, coordinate parenting strategies, such as discipline and rules, and encourage each other's relationship with the child—facilitate children's adaptive adjustment to family transitions. Such cooperative parenting may be more challenging for parents of younger children, because they have had less experience in developing their parenting alliances than parents with older children (Whiteside & Becker, 2000).

Parent–Child Relationships

General. Many of the negative effects of family transitions on young children have been linked to a post-separation decline in effective parenting (Shaw et al., 1999). Divorce often results in a period of disrupted parenting, in which mothers and fathers are less consistent, more controlling, more authoritarian, more rejecting, and less warm than mothers and fathers in intact families. Often daily routines, such as meals and bedtimes, are unpredictable, which can increase young children's anxieties during a period in their lives when they actually need more than the usual structures and supports. Although a decline in parenting typically follows immediately after a divorce, parenting often improves within the two years following the parents' separation (Hetherington et al., 1998). A decline in economic circumstances (a common outcome of divorce) is also associated with a decrease in parenting effectiveness and may result in additional transitions, such as changing schools, neighborhood, and caregivers. Such changes increase the stress faced by custodial parents and their young children and, in turn, lead to less effective parenting (Martinez & Forgatch, 2002). Parents of young children may be particularly susceptible to such changes, because they themselves are relatively young parents and may have had less time to acquire higher education and establish careers with stable incomes (Clarke-Stewart et al., 2000).

Mother–Child Relationships. During the first year following a marital separation custodial mothers tend to communicate less well with their children, are less affectionate, and are less effective at controlling their young children's behavior, than mothers who remain married (Hetherington, 1989). Mother-son relationships appear to be particularly difficult in the immediate aftermath of a family transition, with coercive, angry exchanges typifying interactions between separated mothers and their sons. Young mothers often face great emotional and financial stress and may struggle to effectively parent a young child who is anxious, fearful, and confused. However, as the marital transition stabilizes, mothers become more affectionate and consistent in their relationships with their children. Although these relationships improve over time, mother-son relationships continue to be more turbulent than mother-daughter relationships until children reach adolescence.

Father–Child Relationships.   Although earlier studies indicated that non-custodial paternal involvement was not related to child adjustment, a recent meta-analytic review of current research indicated that fathers can play an important role in facilitating their children's coping (Amato & Gilbreth, 1999). Although frequency of contact between fathers and children is not associated with child adjustment, feelings of closeness between fathers and children and active parenting by the father are linked to positive child outcomes. Children whose fathers help with schoolwork or projects, listen, provide emotional support, and set limits authoritatively demonstrate fewer internalizing and externalizing behaviors than children whose fathers are less actively involved in their lives. In other words, father involvement in the day-to-day activities of their young children is critical to the development of a close father–child relationship. Moreover, such involvement helps fathers to adjust to family transitions, which is also associated with positive child adjustment (Baker & McMurray, 1998). It should be noted, however, that if parent conflict is high, ongoing paternal involvement may exacerbate children's adjustment difficulties (Kelly, 2000).

Even though involved fathers appear to facilitate positive child functioning, father–child contact often decreases significantly in the year following a marital separation (Hetherington et al., 1998). Although fathers may disengage from their children for a variety of reasons, some evidence indicates that fathers may feel shut out of their children's lives (Baker & McMurray, 1998). Divorced fathers have indicated that maintaining an active role in their children's lives is challenging, and they often feel that their parental role is devalued by custodial mothers, and by agencies, such as courts, child care centers, community centers, and schools. For example, studies have indicated that schools and child care centers often neglect to notify fathers of parent-teacher meetings or school outings, and neglect to send fathers regular updates of their child's progress, instead referring fathers to the custodial parent for such information.

In summary, young children respond to family transitions with a variety of behavioral, emotional, and psychological reactions. Various factors (such as age, parenting, number of transitions experienced, economic circumstances, parent conflict, and quality of parent–child relationships) interact to influence the way in which a particular child adjusts to family transitions. In addition to examining children's psychosocial adjustment to family transitions, researchers have investigated how family transitions impact on children's cognitive and academic functioning.

Impact of Family Transitions on Young Children: Learning/Academic Functioning

Family functioning during the preschool years exerts an important influence on any child's academic success. Parents spend a great deal of time with children of this age group, shaping the world that children experience and structuring the opportunities for learning that will promote the development of children's cognitive skills. Given the profound impact that parental separation and divorce can have on young children's psychosocial adjustment, it is understandable that family transitions can also play a role in children's cognitive functioning and school performance. Although most of the research literature focuses on how divorce impacts the academic achievement of middle-school and high-school aged children, the process of marital separation also influences the cognitive functioning of children in the preschool and the early school years (Guidubaldi & Perry, 1984). While national cross-sectional studies have shown that the experience of parental divorce alone is not sufficient to cause cognitive and academic difficulties (e.g., Watts & Watts, 1991), family transitions may expose children to a variety of circumstances that detract from their cognitive development and academic success, particularly in the transition period of two to five years post divorce.

Interfering Adjustment Problems.   Perhaps the most obvious way in which divorce may negatively influence children's cognitive functioning involves the emotional distress caused by the parental separation. As mentioned above, young children lack the cognitive maturity to make sense of their parents' divorces and the associated changes to the family environment (Schwartz, 1992). The emotional strain of family transitions can be taxing to youngsters' cognitive capacities, such that mental energy for academic challenges is limited and normal school-related stresses are heightened (Karr & Johnson, 1991). Children facing divorce may be distracted, irritable, and distressed, resulting in poor attention for school instructions and rules, and disrupted peer interactions. The emotional confusion that young children typically experience after their parents' separation can also be associated with uncharacteristic behavioral problems that interfere with positive functioning at school or at their daycare setting. Immediately post-divorce, children may act out with increasing frequency and intensity, leading to disciplinary consequences that distract them from learning and socializing appropriately with their age-peers.

Instability in the Home Environment.   Divorce usually introduces a flurry of changes in children's home environment to which they must adjust while simultaneously adapting to normal cognitive-developmental challenges presented at the daycare, preschool or grade school. Joint custody and shared parenting arrangements do allow children much-needed interactions with both parents, but the transfers between homes and possibly between schools may introduce conflicting tasks and expectations in each setting, possibly interrupting children's school schedules and study skills. Disagreements between the parents may continue even after the divorce is complete, preventing parents from focusing on their children's needs and disrupting their children's ability to progress through normal developmental challenges. Instability of this nature is usually at its worst around the time of the separation, and in the two to five years after divorce. The more recent a parental divorce has occurred, the greater the overall negative impact it has on children's aptitude and achievement scores (Kinard & Reinherz, 1986).

Financial Strain and Downward Mobility.   Parental divorce in itself does not impede children's cognitive development (Wadsby & Svedin, 1996; Watts & Watts, 1991), but the associated changes in socioeconomic status that often accompanies divorce can negatively impact a child's academic achievement in a number of ways. For example, single-parent families, particularly those that are headed by a female parent, often have limited funds to spare on resources that bolster a child's cognitive development, such as extracurricular activities, educational outings, books, and challenging toys. Families with decreased finances may be forced to remove children from a stimulating daycare environment, or reduce the days per week their child attends preschool. Changes to the family's economic status may also deplete funds that were originally set aside for a child's future education, changing not only the opportunities for their later educational attainment, but also possibly modifying the academic expectations with which they are raised.

Reduced Availability of Parents.   Researchers note that it is difficult to isolate the impact of lowered socioeconomic status from the more general impact of the absence of the non-custodial parent, still typically the father (Svanum, Bringle, & McLaughlin, 1982). In addition to the emotional distress that children often experience from reduced interaction with the non-custodial parent, a child in a single parent home also tends to have fewer stimulating interactions with adults who are invested in their cognitive development. Children of divorce may receive less attention and supervision if their primary guardian must acquire a second job or work longer hours to make ends meet. This inadvertently results in less attention being paid to the development of children's cognitive skills and to their educational progress. Even parents who have frequent, regular contact with their children may be distracted by the divorce proceedings, and thus not as attentive to their young child's learning.

Remarriage might be expected to have a positive impact on children's cognitive and academic functioning, as it reintroduces a second supervising adult into the family and typically increases the socioeconomic status relative to a single-parent home. However, remarriage is unfortunately not associated with better academic achievement, relative to the achievement of children in single-parent households. Jeynes (1999) found that youth from remarried families had lower academic achievement scores than children from both divorced single-parent families and never-divorced two-parent families. It is likely that very young children have similar initial difficulties in adjusting to their parents' remarriages, especially in the early stages of the family's reconfiguration. While remarriage has great potential to provide children with increased security and closeness of a larger family environment, stepfamilies still struggle with many unique transitions and negotiations of their own, many of which can distract children from their learning.

Potential Positive Influences of Divorce on Children's Learning. While much research demonstrates the potentially negative consequences of divorce on children's adjustment, family researchers and practitioners have begun to attend to the ways in which a family transition may offer children benefits and opportunities for cognitive and personal growth. Under some circumstances, parental divorce could exert a positive influence on children's cognitive development, such as by affording children new opportunities for responsibility in the family. Developmentally appropriate chores for preschoolers and young school-aged children can challenge the capacities of a resilient child and encourage the development of skills. As well, children who grew up in an environment of long-standing hostility between their parents may actually be less distracted by family conflict and more able to relax and learn in their individual interactions with their mothers and fathers. Furthermore, separation and divorce can set into a motion a process of positive personal growth in one or both of the parents. It is not unusual for divorced parents, particularly fathers, to make conscious decisions about increasing their involvement in their young children's lives (including more individual reading time and other cognitively stimulating activities). Thus parents and educators of young children are advised not to become discouraged by the potential for negative effects of divorce, as there is also opportunity—less well explored in the existing literature—to use the experience to challenge children's capacities in a positive way.

CARING FOR, SUPPORTING, AND TEACHING CHILDREN IN DIVORCING FAMILIES

The early childhood professional is in an opportune position to contribute to healthy adjustment in young children experiencing their parents' divorces. Early childhood professionals can provide a consistently positive, supportive, and clearly boundaried relationship to young children in

changing family situations. Similarly important, by maintaining constructive, information-exchanging, and inclusive relationships with *both* parents,
the early childhood professional can contribute to relationships between
the divorcing parents that are cooperative in matters concerning the children. This is important for the young child, because cooperation between
divorcing parents is the best predictor of children's healthy adjustment
(Johnston, Kline, & Tschann, 1989). Finally, by creating an inclusive,
accepting and predictable learning environment, the early childhood professional provides young children stability, positive peer interactions, and
self-esteem enhancing opportunities during times of stress and instability
in the home. The following "best practices" recommendations are
intended to assist early childhood professionals in effectively supporting
young children in divorcing and otherwise changing families. The authors
recognize that early child care workers are faced with a diversity of challenging circumstances in their daily work, such that it will not always be
possible to meet the needs of children in divorcing families to the standard
of "best practices."

*Develop and Maintain Positive Relationships with Young Children and Both
Parents.*   The early childhood professional is in the best situation to support young children experiencing family changes when positive relationships with the child and both their parents[2] are well established before the
parents' separate. Regardless of family structure, parents should routinely
be welcomed to participate in the day-to-day exchanges of information
concerning the child. For example, notices for parent-teacher interviews
or other meetings should be clearly addressed to both parents.

In working with young children themselves the early childhood professional, through non-intrusive exercises involving drawing or telling about
members of the family and care-giving network, can learn about the role of
various family members in the child's life. Such exercises—integrated routinely into the early child care and teaching context rather than arising
from the crisis of family change—communicate to the child the early childhood professional's interest and respect for all of the individuals to whom
the child is attached. The early childhood professional may wish to alert all
parents that important events transpiring in the child's life—such as a
change in the family's structure or the loss of a family member—should be
brought to the attention of the early childhood professional.

With such family-inclusive relationships already established, the early
childhood professional is in an effective position to continue constructive
relationships with both parents after a marital separation rather than trying forge relationships within a stressed family system. In the face of family
upheaval, there is always the risk of being misperceived as taking a special
interest or even "siding with" the "other parent" in the context of the parents' separation. Divorced fathers are particularly vulnerable to feeling

excluded from their young children's lives (Frieman, 1998). Research has demonstrated that children with divorced parents benefit from ongoing, positive relationships with both their mothers and their fathers. Early childhood professionals should be particularly sensitive to helping divorced fathers to remain involved in their young children's school lives, by including fathers in all classroom activities and celebrations. If the divorcing parents are unable to manage to be in the same room together, and particularly if their conflicts may be exposed to their young child, that early childhood professional may develop an explicit policy of alternating invitations to classroom activities between the two parents.

Recently separated parents may feel a need to advocate their positions as the "primary parent" and to make a case to others, including the early childhood professional, of the perceived shortcomings of the other parent. The early childhood professional should expect such attempts as normative (and in many instances short-lived) reactions to the immense emotional vulnerability, fears and insecurities that can be set into motion following a marital breakup involving young children. Early childhood professionals should be extremely cautious not to be drawn into the conflicts between the parents. Instead, they should reiterate their primary commitment to the young child and, therefore necessarily, their need to maintain constructive, inclusive and neutral relationships with *both* parents. A parent, who appears unable to respond to more subtle requests to refrain from providing the early childhood professional with negative information about the other parent, may need to be told more firmly that such exchanges are inappropriate and not helpful to the young child. This message should be given very clearly, but can be accompanied by an acknowledgment that angry feelings are common among separating parents and need to be expressed to an appropriate adult, such as a friend or a counselor.

Post-separation and divorce, the early childhood professional should try to ensure that both parents are provided individually with key information concerning the child's learning, adaptation and behavior. In preschool or primary school settings, there may be a need to make administrative arrangements in order for duplicate report cards to be addressed to both parents. Except in the most cooperative circumstances, separated parents sharing a report card or other important document creates situations where parents are left to theorize about why one parent was provided with the materials before the other and, under the worst circumstances, where a young child is expected to take some element of responsibility in making sure that important materials are shared by the parents. If the early childhood professional has a clear and longstanding policy of including both parents, modifications to deal with the practicalities of two parents now living in different homes are easily achieved and accepted by both parents.

In high conflict family situations, the early childhood professional may need to involve their institution's administration in order to secure documentation spelling out the parameters of custody, access and relevant information-seeking and decision-making powers of each of the parents. For a full discussion of legal parameters of early childhood professionals involving non-custodial parents, see Wilcoxon and Magnuson (1999).

Be Familiar with the Risks and Opportunities of Family Transitions for Young Children. As summarized earlier in the chapter, a significant body of literature will help early childhood professionals be aware of how young children might react to family changes. In interpreting this literature, it is important to recognize that parental separation is one point in a series of family changes that unfold over a lengthy period of time. As such, the parent's separation is not a static event to which a child will adjust in a complete sense, but it is more realistically a part of a dynamic process in which the young child will be coping with potentially numerous or frequent changes in living arrangements, possibly reconciliations of the parents, consequences of financial losses, and involvement of new family members such as stepparents and stepsiblings.

By being familiar with the potential psychological risks to young children in divorcing families, the early childhood professional may inadvertently over-interpret normal behavior or misattribute all of the child's problems (e.g., an emergent learning difficulty) to the stresses of family change. Although at times difficult, the early childhood professional is advised to maintain their role as objective observer, noticing both continuity as well as positive and negative changes in the child's behavior. Although the risks of parental separation for young children are well researched, there are undoubtedly psychosocial opportunities for some children in divorcing families that are not yet well understood (see Galambos & Ehrenberg, 1997). For example, following a brief period of adjustment to parental separation, a young child's functioning at preschool may show an overall improvement, which reflects the young child no longer being exposed to overt conflict between two parents prior to the separation. By remaining aware of the risks and opportunities that may arise from changes in family circumstances, the early childhood professional may be in a position to observe and reinforce positive outcomes in addition to tracking and addressing negative outcomes.

Recognize the Daycare, Preschool and Early Grade School Context as Sources of Stability for Young Children. Early childhood professionals are advised to develop a strong awareness of the stabilizing impact their settings may offer to a child faced with parental separation and other family changes. Taking into account the specific developmental phase of a particular child will allow the early childhood professional to emphasize the stabilizing influences that are most helpful to infants and toddlers, to preschoolers, and to early grade school children.

Infants and toddlers are by virtue of normal developmental processes expected to show stranger anxiety, attachments to primary caregivers, and separation anxiety. When faced with changes in family structure, infants are vulnerable to disruption in their attachment to primary caregivers. Depression, behavioral and emotional regression may follow diminished contact with attachment figures. Toddlers may show confusion about where they live and who is in their family, as well as cognitive and linguistic disorganization, and difficulties with reunion upon diminished contact with care giving parents (Gould, 1998). For this youngest age group, the early childhood professional may help by providing a secure attachment base to help the young child manage the disruptions in attachment resulting from family changes. This is not the time, for example, for changes in primary childcare providers or to have alternating staff members caring for the infant or toddler. The infant and toddler will require extra attention, nurturance and sensitivity from their primary caregiver in the child care setting.

Preschoolers need ritual and structure to provide a secure base from which to explore their social and learning environment. This need for routine in the preschool environment will be heightened as home-based structures are disrupted. Their developing language skills allow this age group to express feelings and needs, and their maturing memory capacity allows them to hold parents in memory (Gould, 1998). Regarding parental separation, preschoolers are particularly prone to "magical thinking" and may believe they are somehow responsible for the family disruptions. Being aware of this may allow the early childhood professional to reassure the child and to alert both parents that their preschooler is drawing such conclusions. Children's books concerning divorce-related topics, such as *Mamma and Daddy Bear's Divorce* (Spelman, 1998), provide a nonthreatening medium for communicating developmentally sensitive information.

Preschoolers generally find it difficult to handle transitions between two homes, such that the preschool environment can provide a stable and constructive context through which these transitions can be achieved. The early childhood professional can help the preschooler by being aware of the visitation schedule, even if this must be directly requested from both parents. On days when the child is brought to the preschool environment by one parent but is expected to be picked up by the other parent, the early childhood professional can build in positively framed reminders of this arrangement near the end of the preschool day. Reassurance may be provided by reminding the young child (with a child-oriented calendar in hand) when he or she will be back at preschool and what activities are planned for that day at the preschool.

Early grade-school children normally shift their focus from an almost exclusively parent-oriented worldview, to one that involves friendships and a larger social network. Competency and mastery are additional influences on the developing self-images of children in this age group. Primary school children are likely to respond to their parents' separation with pervasive sadness, anger, distraction at school, and loss of interest in previous social and learning goals (Gould, 1998). As is true of the preschoolers, early grade school children are prone to blaming themselves for their parents' separation and they may take it upon themselves to help their parents to reunite. With increasing self-awareness, the primary school child will be more aware of how their family situation differs from those of their peers. The early childhood professional can be particularly helpful to this age group by incorporating a range of different family types into classroom discussions and illustrations, and by building on this age group's increasing capacity for empathy as a means of enlisting support for a child experiencing difficult family changes.

When family upheaval changes the rules and routines in the parents' homes, early childhood professionals may also be tempted to "bend" their expectations for the child's behavior (Sammons & Lewis, 2000). However, early childhood professionals should be aware that one of the best ways to provide stability is by maintaining developmentally appropriate expectations for young children's behavior. Consistent expectations and limits on behavior will ultimately increase the child's sense of security and curtail acting out behavior.

Create an Atmosphere Inclusive of Different Family Types and Living Arrangements. Early childhood professionals greatly influence the psychosocial environments in their daycare, preschool and early grade school settings. It is particularly helpful to young children in divorcing families, if early childhood professionals help foster awareness and acceptance of diverse family and living situations. Just as books, materials, exercises, and examples can be used to illustrate children's diversity in terms of race and ethnicity, early childhood professionals can add an element of diversity to how "families" are portrayed in their setting. Most important, this demonstrates to young children in divorcing families that they are not alone in their experience. Furthermore, such efforts contribute to an atmosphere of inclusion, where young children are accepting of peers with families that look different from their own and where constructive connections between children experiencing similar family circumstances can be made.

Provide Opportunities for Young Children with Divorcing Parents to Express their Feelings. We do not suggest that early childhood professionals take on therapist-type roles with young children. However, early childhood professionals can provide opportunities for young children to express feelings of sadness, frustration, fear and anger concerning their changing family situations. For young children the medium of play can be a nonthreatening way for children to express themselves. Allowing young children in difficult family situations to use play-dough, paints, dolls/figures, sandbox and physical activity to work through their feelings can be very helpful. Particularly during the early stages of parental separation, the child may have less opportunity for using play to express the strong emotions that may be disturbing to their already distressed parents. The most appropriate role for the early childhood professional when the child is playing or otherwise expressing important feelings is to act as a listener, a non-directive and nonjudgmental observer, and to allow the child to control the play or flow of conversation. Exercising control, within reasonable parameters, is an important outlet for young children whose home lives are changing without being able to exert control.

Be a Gateway to Educational and Referral Resources for Divorcing Families. The early childhood professional is in a good position to help divorcing families to access educational materials and supportive community resources. As it would be unrealistic for early childhood professionals to be knowledgeable about educational materials and community resources for the wide range of issues affecting young children, parents can be connected with school counselors (if available) who are knowledgeable about relevant resources for divorcing families in their community. Specific suggestions about books and other information sources can be obtained from the Families in Motion Research and Information website at www.uvic.ca/psyc/fmric and other similar informational sites. Perhaps more important than specific suggestions for books or referrals is the attitude toward help seeking modeled by the early childhood professional. The trusted early childhood professional is in a strategic position to share with both divorcing parents the benefits of psychoeducational books and supports. Additionally, the early childhood professional can emphasize to the separated parents that seeking support (such as therapists or counselors) under difficult family circumstances is healthful and usual.

Take Preventative Actions to Avoid Future Academic Problems for Children of Divorce. As summarized above, children with divorced parents are at greater risk for academic underachievement and learning complications than children from intact families. Typically these academic problems are not noticed until well into elementary or secondary school. The early childhood professional who is aware that family disruption and emotional distress can undermine cognitive development and learning potential, is in a position to recognize early signs that the child is not progressing or is even regressing in some areas of learning. The young child in this situation may need additional support to regain lost ground or to help him or her remain focused on learning tasks. In addition to preventing more serious and long-term learning challenges, keeping young children on track in their learning is likely to give them a sense of mastery and competence that will, in turn, enhance their sense of being able to cope with a difficult home situation.

The early childhood professional is also in a position to communicate to both parents the types of learning supports that are needed at home. Especially in the context of constructive and family-inclusive relationships with the early childhood professional, the parents are likely to accept clear instructions about home-based learning supports that need to be in place in both homes. On the other hand, instructions provided to only one parent, and left to be translated by that parent to the other parent, are more likely to be lost in the strained communications between the divorcing parents.

Be Aware of School- and Community-Based Programs for Children in Divorcing Families.   An extensive review of support programs for young children in divorcing families are beyond the scope of this chapter. However, early childhood professionals should be aware that psychoeducational groups for preschool and early school-aged children experiencing parental divorce have been shown to be generally effective, particularly in reducing anxiety and classroom adjustment problems (Burdick & Rossiter, 1988; Kalter & Schreier, 1993; Pedro-Carroll, Sutton, & Wyman, 1999). Typically these groups allow children facing similar family situations to talk about commonly occurring stressors, to normalize children's reactions, to acknowledge and articulate painful feelings, to offer coping strategies, and to foster social competence. Early grade school teachers may join with school counselors to explore the possibility of offering a group program at school or to refer to an appropriate group program in the community. The suggestions of a trusted early childhood professional who maintains positive relationships with both parents post-separation could be all that is needed to help a vulnerable pre- or primary school student to access a helpful children's support program. Of note, children's groups are most effective when both parents participate in the recommended parent activities to support their child's developing coping skills. This information may be included in the early childcare educator's recommendation for a children's support group.

Recognize and Take Action in the Face of Extreme Reactions and Markedly Concerning Behavior in Young Children with Divorcing Parents.   While a certain amount of upheaval and disruption is expected in young children adapting to changes in their families, pervasive and lingering sadness, extremely aggressive or regressive behavior, inconsolable anxiety and fear of a parent, concerning disclosures, and sexually inappropriate behavior can be signs of more serious problems within the family system. Similarly, early childhood professionals may notice that a parent's mental health is deteriorating to an extent that they are unable to manage the care of their young children. Early childhood professionals may need to develop an action plan, in consultation with administrators and supporting professionals, to ensure that any potential risk to a child in this situation be reported in an objective and balanced manner to the proper authorities.

CONCLUDING COMMENTS

Considered within the psychosocial model of the divorce process (Guttman, 1993), early childhood professionals can play key roles in helping young children to adjust to their parents' separation and to subsequent family changes. During stressful family transitions, early educators have the potential to observe, support, communicate, and advocate for young children's needs. They can provide a stable, predictable, nurturing, inclusive and child-oriented care/educational setting, as well as facilitate cooperation between divorcing parents by being consistently nonjudgmental, impartial, constructive and, if necessary, limit-setting in their child-focused informational exchanges with both parents. They can also help children to feel competent in their learning process and social exchanges during this difficult time, and they can advise divorcing parents about accessing psychoeducational materials and support services. Although these roles may require specific knowledge and effort on the part of the early childhood professional, they can make a real difference to young children (and their parents) facing family transitions. It is not surprising that young adults looking back at childhood experiences of parental divorce, often mention the importance of a caregiver or teacher who took an interest and supported them during times of family upheaval.

NOTES

1. Preparation of this chapter was in part funded by a Standard Research Grant awarded to the first author by the Social Sciences and Humanities Research Council of Canada (SSHRC), which is gratefully acknowledged.

2. In most instances, the early childhood professional will be involved with one or both of the child's parents, but the suggestions offered similarly apply to diverse situations where other parental figures (e.g., grandparents) are legal guardians of or otherwise very involved with the child.

REFERENCES

Amato, P.R. (1994). Life-span adjustment of children to their parents' divorce. *Children and Divorce*, 4(1), 143–164.

Amato, P.R. (2001). The children of divorce in the 1990s: An update of the Amato and Keith (1991) Meta-analysis. *Journal of Family Psychology, 15*(3), 355–370.

Amato, P.R., & Gilbreth, J.G. (1999). Nonresident fathers and their children's well-being: A meta-analysis. *Journal of Marriage & the Family, 61*(3), 557–573.

Baker, R., & McMurray, A. (1998). Contact fathers' loss of school involvement. *Journal of Family Studies, 4*(2), 201–214.

Booth, A., & Amato, P.R. (2001). Parental predivorce relations and offspring post-divorce well-being. *Journal of Marriage and the Family, 63*, 197–212.

Burdick Rossiter, A. (1988). A model for group intervention with preschool children experiencing separation and divorce. *American Journal of Orthopsychiatry, 58*(3), 387–396.

Castro-Martin, T., & Bumpass, L. (1989). Recent trends and differentials in marital disruption. *Demography, 26*, 37–51.

Clarke-Stewart, A., Vandell, D.L., McCartney, K., Owen, M.T., & Booth, C. (2000). Effects of parental separation and divorce on very young children. *Journal of Family Psychology, 14*(2), 304–326.

Cummings, E.M., & Davies, P.T. (1994). *Children and marital conflict: The impact of family dispute and resolution.* New York: Guilford Press.

Ehrenberg, M.F., Stewart, L., Roche, D., Carter, A., & Pringle, J. (2002, June). *Teens in divorcing families: Adolescents' perceptions of what helps and hinders.* Paper presented at the Canadian Psychological Association's Annual Convention: Vancouver, B.C.

Emery, R.E. (1994). *Renegotiating family relationships: Divorce, child custody, and mediation.* New York: Guilford Press.

Frieman, B. (1998). What early childhood professionals need to know about divorced fathers. *Early Childhood Education Journal, 25*(4), 239–241.

Galambos, N., & Ehrenberg, M. (1997). The family as health risk and opportunity: A focus on divorce and working families. In J. Schulenberg, J.L. Maggs, & K. Hurrelmann (Eds.), *Health risks and developmental transitions during adolescence* (pp.139–160). New York: Cambridge University Press.

Gould, J. (1998). *Conducting scientifically crafted child custody evaluations.* Thousand Oaks, CA: Sage Publications.

Guidubaldi, J., & Perry, J.D. (1984). Divorce, socioeconomic status, and children's cognitive-social competence at school entry. *American Journal of Orthopsychiatry, 54*(3), 459–468.

Guttman, J. (1993). *Divorce in psychosocial perspective: Theory and research.* Hillsdale, NJ: Lawrence Erlbaum Associates.

Hetherington, E.M. (1989). Coping with family transitions: Winners, losers, and survivors. *Child Development, 60*, 1–14.

Hetherington, M.E., Bridges, M. & Insabella, G.M. (1998). What matters? What does not? Five perspectives on the association between marital transitions and children's adjustment. *American Psychologist, 53*(2), 167–184.

Hetherington, E.M., Cox, M., & Cox, R. (1982). Effects of divorce on parents and children. In M. Lamb (Ed.), *Nontraditional families* (pp. 233–288). Hillsdale, NJ: Erlbaum.

Hoyt, L.A., Cowan, E.L., Pedro-Carroll, J.L., & Alpert-Gillis, L.G. (1990). Anxiety and depression in young children of divorce. *Journal of Clinical Child Psychology, 19*(1), 26–32.

Human Resources Development Canada. (1999). Does parental separation affect children's behaviour? *Applied Research Bulletin* [Special Edition]. Retrieved November 27, 2002, from: http://www.hrdc-drhc.gc.ca/sp-ps/arb-dgra/publications/bulletin/child_dev_02e.shtml

Jeynes, W.H. (1999). Effects of remarriage following divorce on the academic achievement of children. *Journal of Youth and Adolescence, 28*(3), 385–393.

Johnston, J., Kline, M., & Tschann, J. (1989). Ongoing postdivorce conflict: Effects on children of joint custody and frequent access. *American Journal of Orthopsychiatry, 59*(4), 576–592.

Kalter, N., & Schreier, S. (1993). School-based support groups for children of divorce. *Special Services in the Schools, 8*(1), 39–66.

Karr, S.K., & Johnson, P.L. (1991). School stress reported by children in grades 4, 5, and 6. *Psychological Reports, 68*, 427–431.

Kelly, J.B. (2000). Children's adjustment in conflicted marriage and divorce: A decade review of research. *Journal of the American Academy of Child and Adolescent Psychiatry, 39*(8), 963–973.

Kinard, E.M., & Reinherz, H. (1986). Effects of marital disruption on children's school aptitude and achievement. *Journal of Marriage and the Family, 48*, 285–293.

Martinez, C.R., & Forgatch, M.S. (2002). Adjusting to change: Linking family structure transitions with parenting and boys' adjustment. *Journal of Family Psychology, 16*(2), 107–117.

Morrison, D.R., & Cherlin, A.J. (1995). The divorce process and young children's well-being: A prospective analysis. *Journal of Marriage and the Family, 57*, 800–812.

O'Connor, T., & Jenkins, J. (2001). Family settings and children's adjustment: Differential adjustment within and across families. *British Journal of Psychiatry, 179*, 110–115.

Pagani, L., Boulerice, B., Tremblay, R.E., & Vitaro, F. (1997). Behavioural development in children of divorce and remarriage. *Journal of Child Psychology & Psychiatry & Allied Disciplines, 38*, 769–781.

Pedro-Carroll, J., Sutton, S., & Wyman, P. (1999). A two-year follow-up evaluation of a preventive intervention for young children of divorce. *School Psychology, 28*(3), 467–476.

Sammons, W., & Lewis, J. (2000). What schools are doing to help the children of divorce. *Young Children, 55*(5), 64–65.

Schwartz, L.L. (1992). Children's perceptions of divorce. *American Journal of Family Therapy, 20*(4), 324–332.

Shaw, D.B., Winslow, E.B., & Flanagan, C. (1999). A prospective study of the effects of marital status and family relations on young children's adjustment among African American and European American families. *Child Development, 70*(3), 742–755.

Spelman, C. (1998). *Mama and daddy bear's divorce.* Albert Whi.

Statistics Canada. (2000). *Divorces.* Retrieved November 27, 2002, from: http://www.statcan.ca/Daily/English/000928/d000928b.htm

Statistics Canada. (2002). *Divorces* (CANSIM II, table 053-0002). Retrieved November 27, 2002, from: http://www.statcan.ca/english/Pgdb/famil02.htm

Svanum, S., Bringle, R.G., & McLaughlin, J.E. (1982). Father absence and cognitive performance in a large sample of six- to eleven-year old children. *Child Development, 53,* 136–143.

U.S. Census Bureau. (1992). *Marriage, divorce, and remarriage in the 1990s* (P23-180). Retrieved November 27, 2002, from: http://www.census.gov/population/socdemo/marr-div/p23-180.html

U.S. Census Bureau. (2002). *Household relationship and living arrangements of children under 18years, by age, sex, race, Hispanic origin, and metropolitan residence.* Retrieved November 27, 2002, www.census.gov/population/-socdemo/hh-fam/p20–537/2000/tabC2.pdf

Wadsby, M., & Syedin, C.G. (1996). Academic achievement in children of divorce. *Journal of School Psychology, 34*(4), 325–336.

Watts, D.S., & Watts, K.M. (1991). The impact of female-headed single parent families on academic achievement. *Journal of Divorce & Remarriage, 17*(1–2), 97–114.

Whiteside, M.F., & Becker, B.J. (2000). Parental factors and the young child's post-divorce adjustment: A meta-analysis with implications for parenting arrangements. *Journal of Family Psychology, 14*(1), 5–26.

Wilcoxon, S., & Magnuson, S. (1999). Considerations for school counselors serving noncustodial parents: Premises and suggestions. *Professional School Counseling, 2*(4), 275–279.

CHAPTER 4

FAMILY CONTEXT AND PSYCHOLOGICAL DEVELOPMENT IN EARLY CHILDHOOD

Educational Implications

Enrique B. Arranz Freijo

THEORETICAL FRAMEWORK

An analysis of the influence of family context on the psychological development process should begin with a number of basic considerations from the perspective of anthropology. As evolutionary anthropologists have pointed out, the existence of a pressure-free context as regards survival needs such as the search for food, territorial defense and the search for mating partners are one of the key factors in the evolution of the human species. The pressure-free context allows humans to develop an attentional structure which enables them to imitate and learn from their surrounding environment. Another important factor is the multiple demands for adaptation to which the species has had to respond throughout its evolutionary history.

Contemporary Perspectives on Families, Communities, and Schools for Young Children, pages 59–82
Copyright © 2005 by Information Age Publishing

These demands have stimulated humans to develop a wide range of adaptive strategies, an ability facilitated by their high level of biological plasticity, which enables constant learning throughout the entire lifecycle, and in particular during childhood.

Within the field of psychology, it could be said that classic unidirectional approaches, which identify operant conditioning, observational learning and emotional identification as the key aspects of parents' influence over psychological development, have been replaced by a model which sees this influence as a process of internalization of continuous interactions (contextual continuity) that are significant to the subject (emotional-personal significance) and which occur throughout each person's intrafamily interactive life.

Intrafamily interaction is not only constructed by parents with their values, beliefs and attitudes. Rather, it is constructed by both parents and children, who between them generate particular interactions that are influenced by the individual qualities such as personality and temperament, that each party brings to the relationship. These *microsystemic* interactions (at home with parents and siblings, at school with teachers and peers) are equally influenced by *macrosystemic* variables (cultural and social values, political system, economic system, religious beliefs and ideologies), *exosystemic* variables (extended family and work, local and institutional environments) and *mesosystemic* variables (relations between microsystems, e.g., family and peers); together, all these variables make up the ecology of human development (Bronfrenbrenner & Morris, 1998).

The internalization of the continuous and significant interactions that make up an individual's intrafamily interactive life history constitutes the key to understanding the influence of family context on psychological development, and the individual differences resulting from the interactive family microenvironments that are specific to each member of the family group. These microenvironments have been described as *nonshared environments* by researchers working in the field of *behavioral genetics*. According to this approach, studies of family interactions should take into account the genetic and interactive aspects of the environment that are shared by all members of the family group, as well as the genetic and interactive aspects that are not shared and are specific to each member. It is these latter, nonshared aspects that serve to explain the differences found between siblings from the same family (Hetherrington, Reiss, & Plomin, 1994).

The theoretical framework that enables the integration of the aforementioned concepts is known as the *General Systems Theory* applied to the family system (Broderick, 1993). According to this theory, the family is a system, made up of subsystems (parental and fraternal), which in turn relate to other cultural, economic and social systems. The relationships within each subsystem (*intra-subsystem*), between different subsystems (*inter-*

subsystem) and between the family system and other systems (*inter-system*) are bidirectional and are governed by the principle of *self-regulation in accordance with the exchange of information.*

The proposed *Ecological theory, Nonshared and Shared environments* and the *Systems theory* can all be integrated into the idea of a *multi-influenced interactive space,* which could be used to describe the family interactions that influence psychological development. The interactions that occur within this space constitute a continuous and significant context for the subject and are influenced by genetic, social and ecological factors. This approach does not affirm that parents influence their children unidirectionally, and that the best way of measuring this influence is to see whether children reproduce their parents' traits, ideas, skills and attitudes. Instead, it enables a better understanding of how children can develop values, personality traits or attitudes which are influenced by their family interaction, and yet are the direct opposites of those developed by their parents.

FAMILY CONTEXT AND COGNITIVE DEVELOPMENT

Inter-Subsystemic Interactions: Parent–Child Relations

Researchers analyzing the impact of these interactions on cognitive development have tended to adopt two different perspectives, the first of which can be described as *ecological-interactive* and the second as *microsystemic-interactive.* The first takes global measurements of the family context, including ecological variables such as socioeconomic status; while the second focuses more on the analysis of variables related exclusively to the interaction between parents and children within the family microsystem. According to Bronfrenbrenner and Morris (1998), the ecological perspective should be placed inside the *macrosytem* and *exosystem,* while the interactive perspective should be placed inside the *mycrosystem.*

Within the first perspective, a significant amount of research has been carried out in connection with the HOME (*Home Observation for Measurement of the Environment*) scale developed by Caldwell and Bradley (1984). The HOME scale is applied through an interview with the parents in the presence of the child and through direct observation of the physical environment of both the neighborhood and the home; the scale itself incorporates a proposal regarding the quality of family context and is a diagnostic assessment instrument which constitutes the basis for the development of family education policy criteria and programs.

The quality criteria for family context assessed by the scale are as follows: Physical environment: safety of the neighborhood and house/apartment, useful spaces for play and schoolwork; Learning materials: presence of books and instruments for carrying out school activities at home; Academic stimulation: degree of interest shown by parents and motivation provided by them as regards academic achievement; Linguistic stimulation: quantity and quality of the stimulation provided, linguistic interactions and parents' grammatical level; Diversity of experiences: variety of stimuli received by the child within and outside the home, trips, cultural visits; Modeling and stimulation of social maturity: organization of everyday life, use of TV, expression of opinions and emotions; Acceptance: absence of physical punishment, absence of blame: Pride, Affection, Kindness: physical and verbal displays of affection and praise.

The association between high scores on the HOME scale and cognitive development is extremely significant, and has been confirmed by diverse studies. High scores on the HOME scale are associated with high levels of cognitive, linguistic, social and motor development in children aged between 3 and 6; this association was observed by a study carried out by Espy, Molfese, and DiLalla (2001), who assessed children's cognitive development using the Stanford Binet scale, and by the data published by the National Institute of Child Health and Human Development (NICHD, 2002), which assessed a population of 3-year-old children using the Bailey scale.

Researchers have also found a significant association between high scores on the *HOME* scale and high socioeconomic status and between low scores on the HOME scale and low socioeconomic status. This association shows the sensitivity of the family system to variables linked to the *macrosystem*. Although this relationship is by no means true in all cases, it is nevertheless logical that a greater abundance of economic and social resources will increase the family's ability to choose between different educational resources without imposed limitations. The association between socioeconomic status and high levels of childhood development is extensively described in scientific literature (Bradley & Corwyn, 2002).

According to the *microsytemic-interactive* approach, one of the basic references for the quality of parent–child interaction is the concept of *scaffolding*. The scaffolding process comprises all those activities that parents carry out in order to facilitate the process of their child's development in a number of different fields: repetition, presentation of attainable models, immediate correction, reasonable demands, setting of obtainable goals and simplification. As Palacios and González (1998) point out, the process of scaffolding is as important as that of de-scaffolding, which is governed by the *contingency rule* which supposes a balance between children's skill and parents' support. *Sensitive* parents increase their support in areas where their child is less competent, and decrease it as he or she becomes more efficient and independent.

The concept of *scaffolding* lends weight to the Vigotskyan proposal regarding the *zone of proximal development*, which is the area located between *effective development* (that which the child can do independently) and *potential development* (that which the child is able to do with the help of an adult or a more advanced peer). The review carried out by Meadows (1996) documents the relationship between the quality of the *scaffolding* provided by parents and diverse areas of cognitive development, such as the capacity for resolving spatial problems and arithmetical learning in children of different ages.

One of the interactive strategies that forms part of parental *scaffolding* within the *zone of proximal development* and which has been shown to have a significant influence on cognitive development is the use of *decontextualization*, which consists of helping the child move beyond the immediate stimulatory and space–time context during the performance of a task.

The quality of diverse spontaneous interactions with the mother has also been identified as an accelerating factor in cognitive development; this is shown in a study by Bornstein, Haynes, Watson O'Reilly, and Painter (1996), who identify symbolic play with the mother as a predictor of representational skills in 20-month-old children. For their part, Feldman and Greenbaum (1997) identify the quality and synchrony of mother–child interactions at the age of 3 and 9 months as a predictor of symbolic abilities at the age of 2. Similarly, maternal strategies for maintaining interest in a task and participation in the child's activities also appear to be associated with childhood autonomy in the cognitive and social fields in children between the ages of 2 and 4 (Landry, Smith, Swank, & Miller-Loncar, 2000).

The development of theory of mind, defined as the ability to represent another's mind as different from one's own and to use this understanding in everyday situations, is another of the cognitive abilities influenced by family context variables. Among these is that found by Arranz, Artamendi, Olabarrieta, and Martín (2002), which points to the association between secure attachment and ability in false belief tasks in 3 and 4-year-olds. Theory of mind development also appears to be associated with fraternal conversations on emotions, the mother's educational level (Cutting & Dunn, 1999) and the use of a democratic parenting style (Vinden 1997). These data are extremely relevant, since they show the close relationship between emotional and cognitive factors in children's psychological development.

Children's linguistic development is also influenced by family context variables. The complexity and structuring of the mother's language and the reading of stories to children are associated with more advanced development as regards both vocabulary and general language skills. A review by Palacios and González (1998) shows how intrafamily linguistic stimulation influences the acquisition of vocabulary as well as the acquisition of abilities containing simultaneous cognitive and linguistic components. Two of these abilities are the language planning and self-regulating function and the capacity for decontextualization.

The quality of family interaction also influences children's literacy development, something which has a profound effect on their subsequent academic performance (Morrison & Cooney, 2002; Saracho, 2000). According to Morrison and Cooney (2002), parental activities that encourage independence, responsibility, self-regulation and cooperation, such as disciplinary control and displays of affection, also favor early literacy development.

The influence of diverse aspects of family interaction on children's academic performance goes well beyond the mere quality of the learning stimulation provided (Morrison & Cooney, 2002). High scores on the HOME scale (Home Observation and Measurement of the Environment) are associated with high levels of academic performance and a good relationship between parents. A good relationship between parents is also a predictor for academic performance (Grych & Fincham, 2001), as are the democratic parenting style and high parental expectations (Holden, 1997). These results show an interesting associative chain between the quality of parental intra-subsystemic relations (level of marital conflict) and both the quality of the inter-subsystemic interactions (parent–child relations) and the quality of the inter-microsystemic or mesosystemic interactions (relations between the family microsystem and performance in the school microsystem).

Intra-Subsystemic Interactions: Sibling Relations

The resource dilution theory continues to guide a number of research projects; this theory is based on the idea that parents' material, educational and interactive resources are limited and that their progressive dilution among siblings in the same family produces an impoverishment of the rearing context of siblings occupying a lower position in the family group. Younger siblings, therefore, have less advanced cognitive development than only children or firstborn children. Currently, there is evidence both for (Downey, 2001) and against this theory (Arranz, Yenes, Olabarrieta, & Martín, 2001).

The resource dilution theory has recently been the object of severe methodological criticism. Some critics affirm that the effects of birth order are spurious and the product of a failure to take into account associations such as that which occurs between low socioeconomic status and large family size. The effects of resource dilution can be counteracted by a significant age gap between siblings, and are more evident in low socioeconomic classes where resources are more limited. Furthermore, Michalski and Shackelford (2001) point out that differences in intelligence levels are only found when research designs that compare members of different families (interfamily designs) are used, and are not confirmed when the intelligence levels of members of the same family (intrafamily designs) are employed.

Another group of researchers have studied the effect of sibling interaction on cognitive and linguistic development. One of the cognitive abilities researched in relation to sibling interactions is perspective taking, or the ability to understand somebody else's point of view; a pioneering study by Stewart and Marvin (1984) showed how 4-year-olds who acted as subsidiary attachment figures were also more capable of making non-egocentric judgments. Similarly, Howe and Ross (1990) found that 3 and 5-year-olds made verbal references to the feelings and abilities of their younger siblings and performed better during laboratory tasks involving perspective taking. In a longitudinal study, Dunn, Brown, and Beardsall (1991) found an association between everyday conflicts in the home and the development of an understanding of the emotions and intentions of other members of the family, in a sample of 2-year-olds; they also found an association between family conversations about emotions with 3-year-olds and their subsequent performance in emotional perspective taking at the age of 6.

Within the field of research into theory of mind, the next step on the road to perspective taking abilities is the performance of false belief tasks. A study by Youngblade and Dunn (1995) showed that children who engaged in more symbolic play with their siblings at 33 months performed better at false belief and perspective taking tasks at 40 months. The association between sibling interactions and theory of mind development, assessed on the basis of performance at false belief tasks, is confirmed in the studies carried out by Perner, Ruffman, and Leekan (1994) and Ruffman, Perner, Naito, and Clements (1998). The first of these studies found that in a sample of 3 and 4-year-olds, children belonging to larger families performed better at a false belief task. The second study further refined the results by indicating that it is the fact of having older, not younger siblings, that facilitates greater theory of mind development. However, this association has not been confirmed by later studies such as those carried out by Arranz et al. (2002) and Cutting and Dunn (1999). Although the existence of an association between sibling interaction and theory of mind development can be deduced, this area needs to be researched in greater depth.

As regards linguistic development, one of the traditional findings identifies firstborn children as the most verbally skilled, due to the quality of the language scaffolding they receive and their role as intermediary between parents and other siblings (Meismer & Lee, 1980). Currently, researchers are analyzing the quantitative differences between dyadic (mother-firstborn child) and triadic (mother-firstborn child-second born child) interactions. One of the results of this research is the observation of a tendency for second born children to develop deitic personal pronouns (Oshima, Goodz, & Deverensky, 1996).

FAMILY CONTEXT AND SOCIOEMOTIONAL DEVELOPMENT

Inter-Subsystemic Interactions: Parent–Child Relations

As with cognitive development, when analyzing the influence of family interaction on socioemotional development, the research data can be divided into two main groups: ecological-interactive and microsystemic-interactive.

Within the ecological-interactive field, the influences of macrosystemic variables on the rearing process are particularly important. Harkness and Super (1995) confirm the influence of the socioeconomic system on parenting practices by affirming that socialization which encourages submission is typical of economically poor groups, in which there is a significant degree of uncertainty regarding the family's ability to accumulate the necessary resources. In economically privileged groups, on the other hand, greater emphasis is placed on the development of independence and risk-taking.

Within the ecological-interactive framework, the optimum parenting proposal developed by Pettit, Bates, and Dodge (1997) lies somewhere between the macrosystem and the exosystem. The study provides a mainly ecological and diachronic assessment of the quality of the family context in which development takes place during early childhood. After interviewing the family in their own home, the interviewer categorizes them in accordance with a series of quality criteria. Similarly to the HOME scale, the criteria used contain a proposal for an optimum parenting style, assessment and educational intervention.

The quality criteria for family *context* used in the Development History (Pettit et al., 1997) are as follows: General: good income level, absence of stressors such as death or illness in the family, low conflict rate both within and outside the family; Impact of the child on the family: positive adjustment to the reorganization of family life after the birth; Quality and consistence of non-parental care; Quality and consistence of the child's peer relationships; Parents' expressed interest in their child's social development; Infrequent use of punitive discipline: absence of physical punishment and severe disciplinary methods; Absence of physical harm; Low rate of conflict between partners; Low rate of in-home and external conflict; High level of support provided by the social and family network; Absence of stressors; Parents' sense of control over the family situation. According to these authors, supportive parenting, rather than harsh parenting, facilitates psychological development, prevents the appearance of behavioral problems and encourages better adjustment to the school environment during early childhood.

Within the microsystemic-interactive approach, special emphasis should be placed on all the research that has been carried out into parenting styles. From the pioneering studies by Baumrind (1971), right up to the present day, researchers have confirmed the positive effect of a democratic parenting style on children's psychological development. As opposed to authoritarian, permissive and uninvolved parenting styles, the democratic style is characterized by the use of persuasion or *induction* as the fundamental disciplinary technique.

Children reared in this environment demonstrate a stable and contented emotional state, high self-esteem, good self-control and less traditional gender role behavior during childhood; they are also better at understanding other people's points of view. Similarly, children reared using the democratic style are more likely to be accepted by their peers than children reared using the authoritarian style. These positive effects continue throughout adolescence, during which children show high self-esteem, social and moral maturity and greater academic achievements, as well as being less likely to engage in antisocial behavior or to consume drugs (Holden, 1997).

A key component of these parenting styles is the way in which parents deal with conflicts during the rearing process; in a study by Pridham, Denney, Pascoe, Yiu-Ming Chiu, and Graesey (1995), the authors distinguish between authoritative and authoritarian problem resolution styles. According to Pridham et al. (1995) abusive mothers use far fewer problem resolution strategies than non-abusive mothers. Furthermore, the use by mothers of sophisticated problem resolution strategies is associated with their own level of ability. This is the case with clarification and planning strategies, whose use appears to be associated with high levels of verbal capacity in mothers and their ability to solve practical problems. The use of the authoritative style leads to the development of cooperation and positive social adaptation.

Research into parenting styles falls within the sphere of the unidirectional influence model, which is not currently in vogue among academics working in this field. In accordance with the current interactive and bidirectional approach, it is worth noting that parents do not stick to a single style continuously throughout the entire rearing process and, furthermore, the child's response to the use of a certain parenting style will be conditioned by his/her individual characteristics. In this sense, it has been suggested that certain children (with a calm and receptive temperament) facilitate the use of the democratic style more than others with a more unstable or less receptive temperament.

Another field of research related to interactions within the family microsystem is that of the attachment theory; this theory constitutes a good example of the eclectic model that combines the influence of genetic factors and social interactions when analyzing the reasons underlying psychological development. Genetic factors are evident in the existence of a wide range of innate behaviors oriented toward social contact; while the importance of social interactions is apparent in the variability observed when the attachment bond is consolidated as secure, insecure, ambivalent or disorganized, in accordance with the individual interactive relationship that each baby maintains with its attachment figure. According to Sroufe (2002), different types of attachment are consolidated in accordance with the responsivity of the caregiver to the child, and bear no relation whatsoever to the child's temperament.

According to the attachment theory, the internal working model that each child possesses of this attachment relationship will be transferred to other relationships established outside the family; in this sense, analyses have been carried out of research data which show the benefits of a secure attachment in the child's adaptation to other interactive contexts. Thus another chain of significant associations is revealed between inter-sub-systemic interactions (quality of mother–child attachment) and mesosystemic interactions (between the family, peer and school microsystems).

In general, secure attachment remains stable throughout childhood and is therefore a reliable predictor for children's positive adaptation to the kindergarten, preschool and school environments. Similarly, children classified as secure are more successful in their social relationships; according to a review by Sroufe (2002), such children are more empathetic and are better both at initiating social relationships with others and at responding to such attempts themselves. In general, it could be affirmed that the association between secure attachment and a confident, productive exploration of other interactive environments continues throughout early childhood.

Secure attachment is also associated with the development of higher self-esteem and good levels of personal adjustment and mental health (Sroufe, 2002). A study by Wright, Binney, and Smith (1995) shows the association between insecure attachment and the need for psychological assistance in children aged between 8 and 12. Resistant attachment appears to be related to anxiety problems, avoidance attachment to behavioral problems and disorganized attachment to the appearance of dissociative symptoms, according to the review by Sroufe (2002).

Associations have also been observed between the quality of secure attachment and moral development; during early childhood, Kochanska

(1995) observes an association between children's internalization levels, secure attachment and a relatively non-fearful/anxious temperament. For their part, in a sample of adolescents, Van Ijzendorn and Zwart-Wodstra (1995) identified an association between the representation of secure attachment and type-B moral reasoning—mature, autonomous, post-conventional and relatively unaffected by group pressure.

In addition to the quality of attachment, other indicators of the quality of the family environment are associated with children's adaptation to extrafamily interactive environments. One of these is the father's level of receptiveness to the child's proposals for solving a common task, which has been linked to high sociometric status in preschoolers. Another indicator of the quality of family interaction is emotional expressiveness and conversations about emotions between parents and children; emotional expressiveness and the emotional language used by both mother and child are associated with socioemotional development and high sociometric status in preschool children (Gottman, Fainsiber, & Hooven, 1997). Positive associations have also been found between positive perceptions of family relationships with the mother and siblings and the closeness of children's friendships (Sturgess, Dunn, & Davies, 2001).

Negative peer relations are associated with family interactive patterns characterized by harsh and frequent punishments, the establishment of ineffective and incoherent limits and by family discord, according to several authors focusing on school-aged children; the developmental relevance of peer rejection should be highlighted insofar as it is a reliable predictor of subsequent antisocial behavior (Collins & Laursen, 1999).

Children's moral development is also influenced by another group of variables other than those related to the quality of attachment. These include the use of the *democratic* style, positive reinforcement of pro-social behavior such as caring, helping and sharing and the inhibition and control of selfish behavior (Holden, 1997). The use of power and threat-based techniques are counteractive to the internalization of moral values because they are associated with negative emotions such as rage, anger and hostility.

Another key element when analyzing the influence of family context on socioemotional development, is the presence of and children's exposure to marital conflict. From a general perspective, low exposure to marital conflict is a protective factor for socioemotional development, whereas high exposure constitutes a risk factor (Cummings, Goeke-Morey, & Graham, 2002; Grych & Fincham, 2001). Here, another association between intra-subsystemic (between partners) and inter-subsystemic (between parents and children) interactions is revealed.

The fact that marital conflict itself is influenced by macrosystemic variables reveals the complexity of the ecological and systemic approach; this is evident in the link between the couple's professional and economic instability, the consequent depressive response by one or both partners and the subsequent increase in marital conflict, which results in a drop in the quality of the rearing process. The consequences of this deficient rearing process are associated with the development of insecure attachment, externalizing problems, such as aggression and behavioral problems, internalizing problems, such as anxiety and depression, difficulty with peer group adaptation and low intellectual and academic performance (Cummings et al., 2002).

Intra-subsystemic and Mesosystemic Interactions: Sibling Relations

One of the most important contributions made by sibling-oriented research to our understanding of socioemotional development has been to show that children living in the same family do not necessarily receive the same influences or undergo the same interactive experiences; in fact, despite genetic similarity, siblings from the same family are different because they each internalize different intrafamily interactions. In this sense, a review by Hetherington et al. (1994) observes a mean correlation of 0.40 for cognitive measurements between siblings, 0.20 for personality measurements and a concordance of less than 10% for psychopathological traits.

Research into differences between siblings is based on the classic affirmations made by Adlerian theorists regarding the influence of birth order on the development of personality traits. Current data confirm some of the Adlerian hypotheses, such as the tendency of firstborn children to exert their power and the tendency of younger siblings to rebel (Sulloway, 2001). Nevertheless, a study by Arranz et al. (2001) failed to find personality differences in a sample of 903 children aged between 8 and 11. In any case, this difference between firstborn children and younger siblings is based on a difference in intrafamily interaction, resulting from the fact that parents are more likely to delegate authority to older siblings. Nevertheless, even if this is true in many cases, it is not sufficient to enable predictions to be made regarding personality traits based solely on birth order, especially in light of the systemic and inter-systemic complexity of family interactions.

Sibling interactions have also been studied in relation to their positive effect on psychological development and their influence on peer interactions. From a systemic perspective, an association has been observed between high levels of marital conflict and high levels of sibling conflict during early and middle childhood (Dunn & Davies, 2001). This becomes even more important when the association between conflictive sibling relationships and children's aggression toward their peers is considered, as shown in a study by Stormshak, Bellanti, and Sierman (1996), who found conflictive sibling relationships in aggressive 6 and 8-year-olds.

There are three extremely important topics that have not been dealt with in this review: first, the effects of abuse (conceived as dysfunctional rearing) on child development; second the influence of non-parental care; and third, the influence of single-parent and reconstructed families, or those formed by gay and lesbian couples, adoptive families or couples who have had recourse to assisted reproduction techniques. The criterion used in this review were the identification and description of the macro, exo, meso, and microsystemic variables that facilitate psychological development during early childhood; the presence of these variables also constitutes an assessment criterion for the quality of family interaction in less conventional family environments. As regards the three aforementioned topics, readers may wish to consult the works of Bornstein (2002), Golombock (2000), and Lamb (1999).

DISCUSSION OF THE RESEARCH DATA FROM THE PERSPECTIVE OF EARLY CHILDHOOD EDUCATION

The research data presented support the idea expounded within the theoretical framework of this paper, which affirms that the impact of family context on the psychological development process cannot be conceptualized as a unidirectional influence of the parents' characteristics on their children. Rather, parents contribute to the structuring of an interactive space which can improve, inhibit or hinder the said process. From this perspective, the research data should constitute the basis for the development of parent training and educational intervention programs in the family system, which introduce ecological and interactive changes designed to optimize the process of psychological development. In this sense, such intervention programs may focus on the exo, macro, meso, or mycrosytem, or all of these at the same time, depending on the established objective. The following is a summary of the educational implications derived from the data given.

Anthropological analysis enables the establishment of certain primary references with regard to educational intervention within the human family: the family should respond to the socially-oriented behavior of babies and provide a pressure-free context in which the infant can explore new sensations and ideas and engage in play and imitation. The family should also provide a wide range of adaptive demands through the educational resource of optimum frustration, in which care and attention should coexist alongside adequately timed and rationed frustrations, that while not being traumatic, nevertheless generate a conflict that forces the subject to evolve.

Educational Implications for Cognitive Development

From the so-called ecological perspective, the data arising from research carried out, using the HOME scale, recommended that family interaction take place in a secure environment, where children have access to varied materials for both learning and playing. It is also important for parents to take an active interest in their children's school activities and to maintain permanent contact with the school staff. Parents should also provide a model of language stimulation for their children.

It is equally important for the family life to revolve around a series of everyday routines which are adapted to the children's needs, in order to help them structure their activities and develop a sense of security and predictability. Furthermore, as organizers of the family life, parents should try to offer a wide variety of new situations and stimuli. The emotional climate should be one of acceptance of the individual characteristics of each member of the family, and should facilitate the free expression of opinions and emotions.

The association found between high socioeconomic status and high scores on the HOME scale can be explained by a greater availability of resources in families with a higher socioeconomic status; this should be taken into consideration when designing intervention policies aimed at enabling families from lower social classes to construct a high-quality family environment.

If cognitive development is considered from the interactive microsystemic perspective, the research data demonstrate the educational relevance of scaffolding activities governed by the contingency rule, which is a practical application of the systemic principles, since it consists of bidirectional regulations based on the exchange of information between parents and children during the carrying out of a specific task: parents make a demand of the child and receive feedback regarding how he or she reacts to that demand. In accordance with this reaction, parents then modify the level of their request, demanding more in some areas and allowing a greater level of autonomy in others.

Among the scaffolding activities mentioned above, the importance of the use of decontextualization strategies should be highlighted. This decontextualization from the immediate context is achieved through distancing strategies. According to Palacios and Gonzalez (1998), low distancing consists of activities related to that which can be observed directly, such as describing and naming; middle distancing consists of asking the child to relate what he or she is seeing to something that is not present; and high distancing consists of asking the child to construct hypothetical situations based on what could happen if the current conditions of the specific task or activity were changed.

Another educational implication of the data given is the advantage of play, particularly symbolic play, during family interactions, which favors the development of early cognitive skills such as representational ability and symbolization. Parents should provide the information and resources necessary for engaging in play activities at home. As regards theory of mind development, the consolidation of secure attachment, the use of the democratic parenting style and conversations between parents and siblings regarding the mental and emotional states of other members of the family group are of great educational importance.

Parents should also be aware of the educational importance of the quality of the language interactions that take place within the family context: reading of stories, use of varied vocabulary and simple literacy activities. The language acquisitions to which parents can contribute include the self-regulating function and the capacity for decontextualization. The self-regulating function is stimulated during family interactions when children are given problems which force them to think, to plan their actions in their head before carrying them out and to assess the consequences of an action prior to the event. The capacity for decontextualization is stimulated by parents' use of an elaborate linguistic code that is constructed using references to absent or hypothetical concepts, as opposed to a code restricted to the present tense and the immediate stimulatory context.

Parents should also be aware of how a positive relationship between partners, with the subsequent low exposure of children to conflicts, the use of the *democratic* parenting style and positive parental expectations can have a positive influence on children's subsequent academic performance.

As regards the educational implications of sibling interactions, few conclusions can be drawn from the contradictory data obtained by the resource dilution theory. Nevertheless, families with a low socioeconomic status and a high number of children with small age gaps between them, can be identified as potentially less favorable as regards cognitive development.

The approach based on the study of sibling interactions sheds new light on the resource dilution theory, insofar as it shows that siblings are not mere receivers of educational and interactive resources provided by parents, but rather that interaction between them also constitutes an important stimulus for cognitive development. In this sense, sibling interaction is an educational source of positive conflict, play and imitation, since older siblings can help establish the *zone of proximal development* for their younger brothers and sisters. For a more detailed description of this educational approach, see the study by Arranz (2000).

Educational Implications for Socioemotional Development

From an ecological perspective, the research data obtained by the *Development History* (Pettit et al., 1997) offer a series of educational criteria for the establishment of a family context conducive to psychological development. Parents who have recourse to non-parental care should try to ensure the quality and stability of the care provided. They should also be aware of their child's relationship with his/her peers and show interest in his/her social development. Punitive punishment should be avoided, as should excessive exposure to conflict both within and outside the home. This situation should be complemented by strong support from the extended family and social environment.

As regards the research data relative to parenting styles, the main educational implication is the need for parents to be trained in the use of the democratic style. This style consists of reasoning with the child and explaining the logic (induction) of the rules designed to facilitate harmony within the family; no use is made of punitive discipline, physical punishment or withdrawal of privileges, although parents insist that the rules are obeyed, assessing each situation with flexibility. As regards affection, parents are demonstrative and maintain high levels of communication with their children. As mentioned above, the use of the democratic parenting style is associated with good emotional balance, capacity for self-regulation, good self-esteem, the ability to understand another person's point of view, good acceptance by peers, social and moral maturity and a lesser tendency toward the development of antisocial behavior or drug abuse.

The use of the authoritative as opposed to the authoritarian conflict resolution style is also of great educational importance. The authoritative style is characterized by the joint clarification of the problem, with parents giving reasons for their behavior and explaining to the child what is expected of him/her; parent and child then develop a reasoned plan of action for solving the problem and conclude with a perspective taking exercise which helps the child to see the consequences of his/her behavior and its implications for other people. The *authoritarian* style is characterized by the use of coercive solutions, absence of communication, reinforcement of the logical relationship between the punishment and the punishable act, distrust of the child's ability to respond independently and, in some cases, by threats, blame and the use of physical punishment.

From the findings relating to the attachment theory, the obvious conclusion that can be drawn is the idea that educational and preventive interventions should be aimed at achieving a secure attachment between children and their principal caregivers. Such interventions can be carried out even before birth and can be included in birth preparation programs. In a study by Siddiqui and Hagglof (2000) a significant association is found between mothers' ideas of what their relationship with their child will be like and the subsequent real relationship. Identification and early intervention in the area of maternal expectations and ideas regarding interactions with their children may serve to encourage the development of secure attachment. As stated in the review of the data, the existence of secure attachment facilitates children's adaptation to other interactive environments, increases self-esteem, enhances moral development and prevents the development of psychopathological traits.

Parenting styles that are receptive to children's proposals and ideas and which allow emotional expressively as well as establishing clear and consistent limits also enhance children's adaptation to their peer group and social environment. From a preventive point of view, the family relationships of children with peer adjustment problems need to be analyzed in greater detail in order to design intervention strategies focused on families.

Another development area for which educational implications can be identified is that of moral development. Insofar as positive conflict is a key element for this type of development, the family context, which offers both horizontal conflicts with siblings and vertical conflicts with parents, is an optimum educational environment. According to Holden (1997), moral internalization is achieved if parents succeed in making the child feel a certain degree of emotional discomfort in relation to the offence committed and, afterwards, give him/her the opportunity of engaging in self-regulation, so that compliance is not elicited heteronomously (i.e., due to fear of punishment). The internalization of moral values is further aided if parents make moral behavior a key reference for the conferral of their child's identity.

Low exposure to conflict is another very important educational criterion. However, since conflict between partners is inevitable, educational intervention aimed at teaching parents how to solve conflicts in ways that are not traumatic for other members of the family group is fundamental. Grych and Ficham (2001) identify a series of mediating variables for assessing the impact of marital conflict on socioemotional development; these variables include: type of conflict, expression, intensity, resolution methods, children's level of exposure, children's understanding of the conflict, the emotional reactions displayed and the coping strategies used. All these factors should be taken into consideration when developing educational and preventive intervention programs designed to deal with processes of separation, divorce and marital conflict in general.

As regards the educational implications of sibling interactions for socioemotional development, it should be remembered that siblings often initiate the activities involved in psychological development, such as play, imitation and positive conflict, and their effect on this process and their usefulness as an educational resource is evident. Children themselves perceive their relationships with their siblings as a source of conflict, affection, cooperation, play and imitation, as well as a wide range of other experiences and emotions (Arranz et al. 2001; Ross, Wody, & Smith 2000). From an educational point of view, it should also be stressed that parents should avoid direct comparisons and discriminatory differential treatment, attitudes to which children are especially sensitive. Recognition of each sibling as different from the others and the establishment of a separate identification space for each child is highly recommended educational attitudes.

As an epilogue to the discussion on educational implications, a number of final conclusions can be drawn. Firstly, it is evident that both the ecological and the interactive perspectives provide significant research data as regards the influence of the family context on psychological development, and should therefore be considered as complementary, rather than opposing theories. Furthermore, not all the variables labeled ecological or interactive refer only to one or another of the perspectives, but are often closely related to each other, creating interactive chains such as, for example, that existing between parents' professional and economic instability, children's exposure to conflict and the development of various adaptive or behavioral problems.

In light of this, future research should focus on a comparative analysis of the effect of both the ecological and interactive variables; it would be extremely useful to identify which variables should be focused on more or less, depending on the intervention objectives established. In principle, family interventions carried out by institutions will focus on ecological variables, striving to supply families with the economic and educational resources required for establishing a high-quality family environment; while interventions based on parent training will focus more on teaching parents how to use interactive strategies designed to optimize psychological development.

Finally, it should be highlighted that researchers in the field of psychological development and those working in the area of early education should remain in close contact and work together to develop not only palliative programs aimed at high-risk groups, but preventative and educational programs also, designed to promote a culture of parenting within our society.

FAMILY CONTEXT AND PSYCHOLOGICAL DEVELOPMENT: A PROPOSAL FOR OPTIMUM CHILD REARING

The following tables reflect a synthetic outline of a series of variables and criteria that constitute the optimum child-rearing conditions aimed at facilitating cognitive and socioemotional development, and summarize the data presented in this study. Nevertheless, any educational intervention should be adapted in accordance with a rigorous, in-depth assessment of the quality of family interactions; to this end, readers may wish to consult the large amount of scientific literature currently available on family assessment. A synthesis of this area may also be found in a work by Touliatos (2001).

Table 4.1.   Optimum Child Rearing Conditions to Improve Cognitive Development

Ecological conditions

- Pressure-free environment. Basic needs covered.
- Varied adaptive demands. Exposure to optimum frustration.
- Presence of new stimuli.
- Presence of imitation models. Proximal development zone.
- Safe physical environment in the neighborhood and home for engaging in play and schoolwork. (HOME)
- Learning materials. Presence in the home of books and teaching materials (HOME).
- Stimulation and interest shown by parents regarding academic performance. (HOME)
- Linguistic stimulation. Quantity and quality of intrafamily linguistic interactions (HOME)
- Diversity of experiences. Trips, visits, etc. (HOME)
- Social maturity modeling. Organization of everyday life. (HOME)
- Acceptance. Positive adjustment of the child to the family. (HOME)
- Affection. Positive displays of affection. (HOME)
- Medium and high socioeconomic status.

Interactive conditions

- Quality of the Cognitive and Linguistic Scaffolding. Repetitions, presentation of attainable models, immediate correction, reasonable demands, setting of obtainable goals, simplification.
- Application of the contingency rule. Reduction of the help provided in certain tasks as the child's skill increases.
- Use of distancing strategies.
- Symbolic play.
- Positive synchrony of interactions with the mother.
- Use of strategies aimed at maintaining interest in the task.
- Training in understanding the emotional states, wishes, intentions and emotions of others.
- Presentation of new words.
- Training in the self-regulating language function.
- Use of a linguistic code designed to facilitate decontextualization.

Table 4.1.   Optimum Child Rearing Conditions to Improve Cognitive Development (Cont.)

- Good relationship between partners. Low exposure to conflict.
- Use of the democratic parenting style. Emotional warmth and reasoned disciplinary control: use of induction.
- Positive parental expectations regarding the development of their children.
- Stimulation of cooperative games between siblings.
- Use of an older sibling as zone of proximal development for other sibling.
- Development of experiences in which one sibling acts as a security base for another sibling.
- Encouragement given to each sibling to consider the emotional states, wishes and needs of his/her brothers and sisters.
- Encouragement of linguistic interactions between siblings.
- Use of sibling disputes to teach conflict resolution strategies.

Table 4.2.   Optimum Child Rearing Conditions to Improve Socioemotional Development

Ecological conditions

- Positive general family context. Good income level. Absence of stressors. (Development History).
- Positive impact of the child on the family. Good adjustment after the birth. (Development History)
- High quality and consistency of non-parental care. (Development History)
- Parents' expressed interest regarding their child's social development. (Development History)
- Infrequent use of punitive discipline. (Development History)
- Absence of physical harm. (Development History)
- Low rate of marital conflict. (Development History)
- Low rate of conflict outside the home. (Development History)
- Good support from the family and social network during the rearing process. (Development History)
- Few stressors. (Development History)
- Good control by parents over the family situation. (Development History).

Interactive conditions

- Use of the democratic parenting style. Emotional warmth and reasoned disciplinary control: Use of induction.
- Use of the democratic conflict resolution style. Joint clarification, plan of action and perspective taking.

Table 4.2.   Optimum Child Rearing Conditions to Improve Socioemotional Development (Cont.)

- Consolidation of secure attachment.
- Assessment of the pregnant mother's ideas regarding future interactions with her child.
- Receptiveness to the child's proposals when carrying out joint tasks.
- Existence of emotional expressiveness in the family environment, conversations about emotions and experience with controlling emotions.
- Positive reinforcement of pro-social behavior: caring, helping, sharing.
- Inhibition and control of selfish behavior.
- Make the child feel that his/her moral behavior is a fundamental part of his/her personal identity.
- Avoid exposure to marital conflict.
- Encourage conversations about emotions between siblings.
- Encourage the giving and receiving of affection and mutual support between siblings.
- Stimulate cooperation between siblings when faced with everyday adaptive situations (bathtime, laying the table)
- Strengthen the development of self-esteem by offering each sibling different self-identification spaces.
- Use the technique of increasing self-esteem to prevent conflicts based on jealousy.
- Avoid direct comparisons between siblings.
- Avoid blaming and humiliating one sibling in front of another.
- Avoid playing a Solomonic role as regards quantitative distribution unless absolutely necessary.
- Whenever feasible, it is best not to intervene in sibling conflicts as long as their resolution is supervised.
- Be consistent and unchanging with regard to conflict resolution techniques proposed as models.
- Do not accept solutions based on force without using persuasion, leaving no way out and without offering guidance.
- If the child is cognitively capable of understanding another person's point of view (around four years) propose conflict resolutions that take into account his/her sibling's feelings as well as his/her own
- Do not repress conflicts and encourage the child to take into account his/her sibling's feelings as well as his/her own.

REFERENCES

Arranz, E. (2000). Sibling relationships: An educational resource and a way of evaluating the quality of family relationships. *Early Child Development and Care, 164,* 13–28.

Arranz, E., Artamendi, J., Olabarrieta, F., & Martín, J. (2002). Family context and theory of mind development. *Early Child Development and Care, 172*(1), 9–22.

Arranz, E., Yenes, F., Olabarrieta, F., & Martin, J. (2001). Sibling relationships and psychological development in school children. *Infancia y Aprendizaje, 24*, 81–97.

Baumrind, D. (1971). Current patterns of parental authority. *Developmental Psychology Monographs, 4*, 1–102.

Bornstein, M.H. (2002). *Handbok of parenting* (5 Vols.). Mahwah, NJ: LEA Publishers.

Bornstein, M.H., Haynes, M., Watson O'Reilly, A., & Painter, K. (1996). Solitary and collaborative pretense play in early childhood: sources of individual variation in the development of representational competence. *Child development, 67*, 2910–2929.

Bradley, R.H., & Corwyn, R.F. (2002). Socioeconomic status and child development. *Annual Review of Psychology, 53*, 371–399.

Broderick, C.B. (1993). *Understanding family process.* London: Sage.

Bronfenbrenner, U., & Morris, P.A. (1998). The ecology of developmental processes. In R.M. Lerner (Ed.), *Handbook of child sychology, Vol. 1: Theory* (5th ed., pp. 993–1028). New York: Wiley.

Caldwell, B., & Bradley, R. (1984). *HOME observation for measurement of the environment.* Little Rock, AR: Center of Child Development And Education.

Collins, W., & Laursen, B. (1999). *Relationships as developmental contexts. The Minnesota symposia on child psychology.* Mahwah, NJ: LEA Publishers.

Cummings, E.M., Goeke-Morey, & Graham, M.A. (2002). Interparental relations as a dimension of parenting. In J.G. Borkowski, S. L. Ramey, & M. Bristol-Power (Eds.), *Parenting and the child's world: Influences on academic, intellectual, and socioemotional development* (pp. 251–264). Mahwah, NJ: LEA Publishers.

Cutting, A., & Dunn, J. (1999). Theory of mind, emotion understanding, language, and family background: Individual differences and interrelations. *Child Development, 70*, 4, 853–865.

Downey, D.B. (2001). Number of siblings and intellectual development: The resource dilution explanation. *American Psychologist, 56*(6–7), 497–504.

Dunn, J., & Davies, L. (2001). Sibling relationships and interparental conflict. In J.H. Grych & F.D. Fincham (Eds.), *Interparental conflict and child development.* Cambridge: Cambridge University Press.

Dunn, J., Brown, J., & Beardsall, L. (1991). Family talk about feeling states and children's later understanding of others' emotions. *Developmental Psychology, 27*(3), 448–455.

Espy, K.A., Molfese, V.J., & DiLalla, L.F. (2001). Effects of environmental measures on intelligence in young children: Growth curve modeling of longitudinal data. *Merrill Palmer Quaterly, 47*, 42–73.

Feldman, R., & Greenbaum, Ch. (1997). Affect regulation and synchrony in mother-infant play as precursors to the development of symbolic competence. *Infant Mental Health Journal, 18*, 4–23.

Golombock, S. (2000). *Parenting.* London: Routledge.

Gottman, J., Fainsiber, L. & Hooven, C. (1997). *Meta-emotion: How families communicate emotionally.* Mahwah, NJ: LEA Publishers.

Grych, J.H., & Fincham, F. (2001). *Interparental conflict and child development: Theory, research and application.* Cambridge: Cambridge University Press.

Harkness, S., & Super, C. (1995). Culture and parenting. In M.H. Bornstein (Ed.), *Handbook of parenting* (vol 2., pp 211–234). Mahwah, NJ: LEA Publishers.

Hetherhington, M.E., Reiss, D., & Plomin, R. (1994). *Separate social world of siblings.* Hillsdale, NJ: LEA Publishers.

Holden, G.W. (1997). *Parents and the dynamics of child rearing.* Oxford: Westview Press.

Howe, N., & Ross, H.S. (1990). Socialization, perspective taking and the sibling relationship. *Developmental Psychology, 26,* 160–165.

Kochanska G. (1995). Children's temperament, mother's discipline, and security of attachment: Multiple pathways to emerging internalization. *Children Development, 66,* 597–615.

Lamb, M. (1999). *Parenting and child development in "nontraditional" families.* Mahwah, NJ: LEA Publishers.

Landry, S.H., Smith, K., Swak, P.R., & Miller-Loncar, C. (2000). Early maternal and child influences on later independent cognitive and social functioning. *Child Development, 71,* 358–375.

Meadows, S. (1996). *Parenting behaviour and children's cognitive development.* East Sussex: Psychology Press.

Meisner, J.S., & Lee, V. (1980). Cognitive shifts of young children as a function of peer interaction and sibling status. *Journal of Genetic Psychology, 136,* 247–253.

Michalsky, R.L., & Shackelford, T.K. (2001). Methodology, birth order, intelligence, and personality. *American Psychologist, 56*(67), 520–524.

Morrison, F.J., & Cooney, R.R. (2002). Parenting and academic achievement: Multiple paths to early literacy. In J.G. Borkowsky, Sh. Landesman Ramey, & M. Bristol-Power (Eds.), *Parenting and the child's world. Influences on academic, intellectual, and social-emotional development* (pp. 141–160). Mahwah, NJ: LEA Publishers.

National Institute of Child Health and Human Development, NICHD. (2002). Parenting and family influences when children are in child care: Results from the NICHD study of early child care NICHD early child care research network. In J.G. Borkowsky, Sh. Landesman Ramey, & M. Bristol-Power (Eds.), *Parenting and the child's world. Influences on academic, intellectual, and social-emotional development* (pp.99–123). Mahwah, NJ: LEA Publishers.

Oshima-Takane, Y., Goodz, E., & Deverensky, L. (1996). Birth order effects on early language development: Do second born children learn from overhead speech?. Child Development, 67, 621–634.

Palacios, J., & Gonzalez, M. (1998). La estimación cognitiva en las interacciones padres- hijos. In Rodrigo, M.J., & Palacios, J. (Coords), *Familia y desarrollo humano* (pp.277–295). Madrid: Alianza Psicología. (Cognitive stimulation in parent–child interactions. In *Family and human development*).

Perner, J., Ruffiman, T., & Leekam, S. R. (1994). Theory of mind is contagious: You catch it from your sibs. *Child Development, 65,* 1228–1238.

Pettit, G, Bates, J., & Dodge, K.A. (1997). Supportive parenting, ecological context, and children's adjustment: A seven year longitudinal study. *Child Development, 68*(5), 908–923.

Pridham, K., Denney, N., Pascoe, J., Chiu, Y., & Creasey, D. (1995). Mother's solutions to childbearing problems: Conditions and processes. *Journal of Marriage and the Family, 57*, 785–799.

Ross, H., Woody, E., & Smith, M. (2000). Young children's appraisal of their sibling relationships. *Merrill Palmer Quaterly, 46*, 441–464.

Ruffman, T., Perner, J., Naito, M., Parkin, L., & Clements, W. (1998). Older (but not younger) siblings facilitate false belief understanding. *Developmental Psychology, 34*(1), 161–174.

Saracho, O. (2000). Literacy development in the family context. *Early Child Development and Care, 165*, 107–114.

Siddiqui, A., & Hagglof, B. (2000). Does maternal prenatal attachment predict postnatal mother-infant interaction?. *Early Human Development, 59*, 13–25.

Sroufe, L.A. (2002). From infant attachment to promotion of adolescent autonomy: Prospective, longitudinal data on the role of parents in development. In J.G. Borkowsky, Sh. Landesman Ramey, & M. Bristol-Power (Eds.), *Parenting and the child's world. Influences on academic, intellectual, and social-emotional development* (pp. 187–202). Mahwah, NJ: LEA Publishers.

Stewart, R.B., & Marvin, R.S. (1984). Sibling relations: The role of conceptual perspective taking in the ontogeny of sibling caregiving. *Child Development 55*, 1322–1332.

Stormshak, E., Bellanti, CH., & Sierman, K.L. (1996). The quality of sibling relationships and the development of social competence and behavioral control in aggressive children. *Developmental Psychology, 32*, 79–89.

Sturgess, W., Dunn, J., & Davies, L. (2001). Young children´s perceptions of their relationships with family members: Links with family setting, friendships, and adjustment. *International Journal of Behavioral Development, 25*, 521–529.

Sulloway, F.J. (2001). Birth order, sibling competition, and human behavior. In H.R. Holcomb (Ed.), *Conceptual changes in evolutionary psychology: Innovative research strategies* (pp. 39–83). Dordrecht and Boston: Kluwer Academic Publishers.

Touliatos, J., Perlmutter, B.F., & Strauss, M.A. (2001). *Handbook of family measurement techniques* (3 vols). Thousand Oaks, CA: Sage.

Van Ijzendoorn, M.H., & Zwart-Woudstra, G. (1995). Adolescents' attachment representations and moral reasoning. *The Journal of Genetic Psychology, 156*, 359–372.

Vinden, P.G. (1997). *Parenting and theory of mind.* Paper presented at the biennial meeting of the Society for Research in Child Development. Washington, DC.

Wright, J.C., Binney V., & Smith P.K. (1995). Security of attachment in 8–12- years-olds: A revised version of the separation anxiety test, its psychometric properties and clinical interpretation. *Journal of Child Psychology and Psychiatry, 36*, 757–774.

Youngblade, L.M., & Dunn, J. (1995). Individual differences in young children's pretend play with mother and sibling: Links to relationships and understanding of other people's feelings and beliefs. *Child Development, 66*, 1472–1492.

CHAPTER 5

PARENTING SELF-EFFICACY, COMPETENCE IN PARENTING, AND POSSIBLE LINKS TO YOUNG CHILDREN'S SOCIAL AND ACADEMIC OUTCOMES

Priscilla K. Coleman and Katherine H. Karraker

INTRODUCTION

Conceptualizing or defining competent parenting in a general way is a relatively easy task. Most individuals living in western cultures, where children are revered, would agree that good parenting practices encompass those behaviors that most efficiently foster optimal physical, emotional, social, and cognitive development in children. Ideally, these parenting practices also feel appropriate, comfortable, and satisfying to parents, while fostering their own personal growth in the process of child rearing. However, empirical specification of the precise cognitive, affective, and behavioral components and processes associated with competent parenting is exceed-

Contemporary Perspectives on Families, Communities, and Schools for Young Children, pages 83–105
Copyright © 2005 by Information Age Publishing
83

ingly more complex and challenging than simply recognizing good parenting. Identifying these components and processes can lead to interventions for parents who do not spontaneously provide effective parenting and thereby place their children at risk for less optimal development.

Although an abundance of research has been devoted to identifying parental characteristics likely to optimize children's social and academic development, the focus of this chapter is on one particular aspect of parenting competence, parenting self-efficacy beliefs. These cognitions refer to a parent's perceptions of his or her own ability to fulfill the duties and responsibilities inherent in the parenting role (Teti & Gelfand, 1991). Parenting self-efficacy beliefs are essentially analogous to a parent's perceptions of his or her personal power to influence child behavior and development in positive ways. In order to feel efficacious, a parent must have knowledge of the actions that carry the potential to lead to desired outcomes (Wells-Parker, Miller, & Topping, 1990) as well as confidence in his or her own ability to effectively engage in particular parenting behaviors (Bandura, 1989). The choice of this rather specified focus is based on a rapidly expanding literature suggesting the central role that self-efficacy beliefs are likely to play in both affective and behavioral dimensions of parenting (e.g., Bugental, Blue, & Cruzcosa, 1989; Coleman & Karraker, 1998, 2000; Cutrona & Troutman, 1986; Teti & Gelfand, 1991). Efficacious parents seem to enjoy a sense of personal empowerment in parenting that facilitates the management of the varied tasks involved. An efficacious parental outlook can enhance both an intrinsic interest in parenting and commitment to the actual activities involved (Bandura, 1995). Alternatively, inefficacious parents tend to feel heavily burdened by the responsibilities of child care and they often become immobilized by the emotional and physical demands of parenting. Parents who lack a sense of efficacy in their own ability to parent frequently struggle to put knowledge of parenting into action, become self-absorbed rather than focused on their children, experience high levels of emotional arousal, and show a lack of persistence in their parenting efforts (Grusec, Hastings, & Mammone, 1994). These behaviors can then lead to less-than-optimal outcomes in their children.

Our goal in this chapter is to consider the possible influences of variations in parents' self-efficacy beliefs on parenting competence and children's social and cognitive functioning during early childhood. We also speculate on the possible subsequent effects of parenting self-efficacy during early childhood on later academic success. Based on a selective review of studies pertaining to parenting self-efficacy from infancy through adolescence, only a few of which concentrate specifically on early childhood, we propose that parenting self-efficacy during the early childhood period plays a crucial role in enhancing children's social adjustment and learning skills, and help to guarantee their subsequent school success. We also contend that early childhood educators can help to enhance parenting self-efficacy in their students' parents, and that high levels of parenting self-efficacy during early childhood can facilitate the effectiveness of early education and the success of children's later academic pursuits.

We begin by placing the study of parenting self-efficacy beliefs within the broader context of general self-efficacy and parenting competence. Next, the literature pertaining to the acquisition of parenting self-efficacy beliefs is reviewed. In the third section, we describe research that has identified associations between parenting self-efficacy beliefs and both parenting behavioral competence and child social and cognitive outcomes. Then in the fourth and fifth segments, we explore the processes by which parenting self-efficacy beliefs during early childhood might causally influence parenting behavioral competence and child outcomes, respectively. Finally, we conclude with some practical suggestions regarding the community's and early childhood educators' roles in assisting parents of young children to become more efficacious.

BACKGROUND RELEVANT TO THE STUDY OF PARENTING SELF-EFFICACY BELIEFS

For a period spanning nearly 60 years, developmentalists interested in parenting competence have emphasized overt behavior (Smetana, 1994). Parenting cognitions did not capture a significant amount of research attention until a few decades ago (Smetana, 1994). The initial motivation underlying the inclusion of cognitive elements was to enhance the prediction of child outcomes beyond what was possible with the earlier, narrower behavioral focus (Grusec et al., 1994). However, over the last 20 years, the study of parenting cognitions has matured to the point of representing a vital research area worthy of attention in its own right (Smetana, 1994). Today the study of parenting cognitions represents a broad domain, encompassing parents' values, expectations, knowledge, and desires in addition to self-efficacy beliefs. As noted by Teti, O'Connell, and Reiner (1996, p. 238) in a discussion of the subjective side of parenting, "Cognitions and emotions are now placed at the heart of conceptualizations of parenting, with cognitive-affective organizations that parents bring to the dyadic setting viewed as causal to parenting behaviour."

A second contemporary trend in the study of parenting competence that has played an essential role in highlighting the importance of self-efficacy beliefs is the emphasis on a process-oriented or systems theoretical approach. According to Kindermann and Valsiner (1995), the systems perspective focuses on individual adaptation to changing contexts, environmental modifications in response to changing individuals, and the ability of individuals to shape their own environments. As applied to parenting competence and child outcomes, the systems approach encompasses the assumption that parents and children experience ongoing mutual change over time and that the quality of a child's environment at a later time is a function of earlier interactions. According to this perspective, individuals and contexts are both considered fluid systems capable of reciprocal influence.

Adoption of a systems perspective is basic to understanding the powerful role that parenting self-efficacy beliefs seem to play in the experience of parenting from the perspective of both the parent and the child. This perspective also supports the notion that parenting self-efficacy during early childhood can have ramifications for later child social adjustment and academic performance. Taking a systems perspective requires going beyond simple identification of associations among parenting self-efficacy beliefs, parenting behavior, and child outcomes and leads to questions about the causal, mediating, and moderating relations among these variables as well as between these variables and other environmental variables. For example, Coleman and Karraker (1998, 2000) have noted that the available evidence indicates that parenting self-efficacy beliefs may operate as an instrumental mediator in linking parent, child, and situational factors to the quality of parenting and subsequent child outcomes. Thus, a number of parent, child, and situational factors may influence parenting indirectly, by directly modifying parenting self-efficacy, which then in turn influences parenting behavior and child outcomes. Similarly, in a review of relevant literature, Raver and Leadbeater (1999, p. 325) emphasize that "transient and enduring characteristics of both the child and environment may interact in complex ways to support or undermine women's views of themselves as skilled in the parenting role."

Many child and environmental characteristics that increase the demands of the role and/or reduce the amount of time and energy parents are able to put into the parenting may logically undermine parents' feelings of parenting self-efficacy. Among the possible child and environmental factors found to have a negative influence on parents' self-efficacy beliefs are infant colic, difficult child temperament, behavior difficulties, residing in an unsafe neighborhood, and low social support (Cutrona & Troutman, 1986; Gross, Conrad, Fogg, and Wothke, 1994; Jackson, 2000; Leerkes & Crockenberg, 2002; Raver & Leadbeater, 1999; Stifter & Bono, 1998). Other yet to be researched child and environmental factors include child health problems, child learning and social impairments, stressful work environments, or discord in the home. Self-efficacy beliefs may also be related to the level of synchrony, goodness-of-fit, and/or conflict in parent–child relationships (Coleman & Karraker, 1998; Raver & Leadbeater,

1999). Further, sociodemographic characteristics like poverty, religiosity, and maternal education have been found to influence parent and child outcomes through their influence on parenting self-efficacy (Brody et al., 1994; Brody, Flor, & Gibson, 1999; Brody, Stoneman, & Flor, 1996; Conger et al., 1992; Elder, 1995). High parenting self-efficacy may also serve as a critical buffer or moderator between environmental adversity and negative outcomes. The knowledge and sensitivity characterizing more efficacious parents' behavior apparently enable them to promote positive experiences for their children despite environmentally-based adversity (Bandura, 1997; Donovan & Leavitt, 1989; Elder, Eccles, Ardelt, & Lord, 1995).

The contention that self-efficacy beliefs unify many of the variables related to parenting competence is consistent with Bandura's (1989) general claims regarding the power of self-efficacy beliefs to mediate the effects of other personal and situational determinants of behavior. However, as Bandura (2002, p. 278) recently noted, "personal agency and social structure operate interdependently rather than as disembodied entities," underscoring the fact that self-efficacy beliefs must be studied in context.

THE ACQUISITION OF PARENTING SELF-EFFICACY BELIEFS

Why do some parents develop a strong belief in their own parenting self-efficacy whereas others do not? Bandura's (1989) descriptions of the four primary informational sources that relate to personal efficacy provide some suggestions. First, personal accomplishment history (successes and failures) represents the most direct influence on mastery expectations. Thus, parents who are successful at modifying their children's behavior are likely to develop an enhanced sense of parenting self-efficacy in comparison to parents who are less successful. Second, watching others engage in particular activities can generate vicarious estimations in observers pertaining to their own capacity for mastering a particular task. Parents who have watched other parents deal effectively with child-rearing challenges therefore would be expected to develop a strong concept of their own parenting self-efficacy. Inferences such as these, derived from social comparison, are by nature indirect; therefore, self-efficacy beliefs developed in this manner are theoretically more susceptible to change than are those developed through direct experience. Verbal feedback from others regarding one's potential for accomplishment in a given area represents the third avenue through which self-efficacy beliefs may develop. Parents who are appropriately praised for their parenting are likely to experience increased parenting self-efficacy. Although appraisals by others can result in the formation of efficacy expectancies, they tend to be weaker than those derived directly from one's own achievements. The lack of an authentic experiential base is presumed to be the origin of the differential power of direct experiences versus judgments of others. The fourth mechanism relevant to the emergence of self-efficacy beliefs relates to emotional arousal. Individuals anticipate failure when they experience high levels of aversive physiological arousal; and conversely, lower levels of arousal tend to be associated with success expectancies. Thus, parents who experience high levels of personal stress or anger may also show lowered levels of parenting self-efficacy.

Coleman and Karraker (1998), in an extensive review of the parenting self-efficacy literature, discuss several more specific influences on the development of parenting self-efficacy beliefs. First, parenting self-efficacy beliefs may arise at least in part from parents' own early experiences in their families of origin. The basic idea is that parents carry internal representations of attachment relationship dynamics, which originated in their own childhood experiences with primary caregivers, into their own experience of parenting. These relatively stable thoughts and emotions regarding the self and others are hypothesized to have an impact on parents' feelings of efficacy in the parenting role. Further, as noted by Leerkes and Crockenberg (2002), childhood experiences with models of positive parenting behavior offer opportunities for the emergence of parenting self-efficacy beliefs through vicarious learning processes. Although few studies have examined the association between childhood attachment experiences and parenting self-efficacy, Grusec et al. (1994) provided some preliminary support for continuity between the two constructs. More recently, Leerkes and Crockenberg (2002) found a significant correlation between positive remembered experiences with caregivers and high parenting self-efficacy in first-time mothers of infants.

A second, very different, approach to the question of how parenting self-efficacy beliefs develop described by Coleman and Karraker (1998) focuses on the influences of broad social elements. Cultures and communities provide information pertaining to dominant parenting values as well as expert advice regarding the care and development of children. Parents whose personal beliefs and behavior are congruent with those held by the broader culture are inclined to feel more efficacious. Systematic research has not been conducted to explore this potential source of influence.

The third possible avenue of influence on the emergence of parents' self-efficacy beliefs noted by Coleman and Karraker (1998) are experiences of mothers with children, both their own children and other people's. As pointed out by Coleman and Karraker, the notion of parenting self-efficacy beliefs developing as a result of direct experience is consistent with Bandura's (1989) suggestion that direct experiences with the referent behaviors is the most powerful source of information in the formation of efficacy estimations. Research supports this association as well (Coleman & Karraker, 2000; Gross, Rocissano, & Roncoli, 1989).

The final possible source of parenting self-efficacy beliefs outlined by Coleman and Karraker (1998) is the parent's degree of cognitive/behavioral preparation for parenting. Leen and Karraker (2002) found parenting self-efficacy to be related to several components of cognitive readiness for parenting, including the avoidance of role reversals, strong child centeredness, and positive parenting style preferences. A few studies also have addressed relationships between specific indicators of psychological adjustment to pregnancy and postpartum parenting self-confidence, competency, and/or future child outcomes (Bohlin & Hagekull, 1987: Heinicke, Distin, Ramsey-Klee, & Given, 1983).

In addition to the four influences described by Coleman and Karraker (1998), Teti et al. (1996) have noted that sociomarital support may play an important role in the development and maintenance of parenting self-efficacy beliefs through the mechanisms of social persuasion or feedback and modeling. These authors emphasize how the marital partner is in a strategic position to offer encouragement, emotional support, and respite care to the other parent. In a recently published report, Feinberg (2002) also discussed the decisive role of positive co-parenting experiences in buffering the negative effects of parental depression on parenting self-efficacy beliefs.

PARENTING SELF-EFFICACY BELIEFS, PARENTING COMPETENCE, AND CHILD OUTCOMES

A wide range of adaptive parent characteristics and parenting behaviors have been linked with high parenting self-efficacy beliefs in parents of children of varying ages: warm, responsive, stimulating, and non-punitive caretaking (Teti & Gelfand, 1991; Unger & Waudersman, 1985), active maternal coping orientations (Wells-Parker et al., 1990), few maternally perceived child behavior problems (Johnson & Mash, 1989), and positive mental health (Kwok & Wong, 2000). Conversely, maternal depression (Cutrona & Troutman, 1986; Teti & Gelfand, 1991), maternal perceptions of child difficulty (Coleman & Karraker, 2000), elevated parenting stress (Jackson, 2000; Kwok & Wong, 2000), use of coercive disciplinary techniques (Bondy & Mash, 1997), and a passive coping style in the parental role (Wells-Parker et al., 1990) have been found to be correlated with low parenting self-efficacy. In a recently published study, low parenting self-efficacy beliefs in mothers of toddlers were associated with competence-inhibiting maternal behavior (defined as forceful redirection of the child's attention, ignoring and reinforcing misbehavior, and potentially distracting self-conscious behaviors) during administration of a developmental test (Coleman et al., 2002). Parenting self-efficacy beliefs have also been found to be positively associated with concrete behavioral tendencies, such as parental efforts to educate themselves about parenting (Spoth & Conroy, 1993).

Given the above associations, parenting self-efficacy beliefs are likely to be particularly relevant to the development of young children's competence. Preschoolers typically are very active, are rapidly expanding their language/communication abilities, are eager to learn, enjoy interacting with people outside the family, engage in frequent limit testing, and are driven to seek increasing independence from caregivers. These characteristics along with age-related limitations in self-control, knowledge of the world, attention span, concentration, and emotion regulation abilities render this a highly demanding stage of development for parents. Effective provision of the cognitive stimulation, emotional support, social opportunities, structure, and discipline necessary for preschoolers to develop to their full potential requires many of the behavioral characteristics likely to be associated with high self-efficacy, including warmth, responsiveness, knowledge of child development, commitment to parenting, persistence, and well-developed problem-focused coping skills.

The types of positive parenting behaviors that are related to a strong sense of parenting self-efficacy have also been found to impact the behavioral, emotional, and intellectual growth of children (Strand & Wahler, 1996). Considerable evidence indicates that positive maternal behaviors such as frequent verbal exchanges, use of joint attention, connecting language with experiences, and responsiveness of parents in early childhood enhance children's language and social development (Fey, 1986; Goldfield, 1987; Hart & Risley, 1995; Richards, 1984; Snow, 1984). Interestingly, language support tends to be associated with behavior management as well; parents who provide minimal encouragement and opportunities relative to language acquisition tend to be less responsive and more negative in interactions with their children (Hart & Risley, 1995). Harsh, inconsistent parenting of young children has been found to be associated with early onset of behavior problems (Herrenkohl et al., 1995), and early language deficiencies and behavior problems increase the risk for poor academic performance and peer relationship problems (Hinshaw, 1992; Kaiser, Hancock, Cai, Foster, & Hester, 2000).

As we have seen, parenting self-efficacy beliefs are related to parenting competence and parenting competence is associated with positive outcomes in children. However, only a few studies have examined specific relations between parenting self-efficacy beliefs and child outcomes. These relations have been identified in the domains of socioemotional development (Coleman & Karraker, 2003; Donovan & Leavitt, 1985, 1989; Swick & Hassell, 1990), child behavior (Gross et al., 1999; Jackson, 2000), and achievement (Bandura, Barbaranelli, Caprara, & Pastorelli, 2001; Coleman et al., 2002; Elder et al., 1995). Despite the paucity of direct evidence for parenting self-efficacy effects on children's outcomes, the available research supports the contention that such a relation exists. Further support is provided by consideration of the mechanisms through which parenting self-efficacy might influence parenting competence and child outcomes.

PROCESS MECHANISMS LINKING PARENTING SELF-EFFICACY BELIEFS TO COMPETENCE IN PARENTING

In recent years, researchers have moved toward identifying the precise mechanisms through which self-efficacy beliefs potentially influence parenting quality and child outcomes. Without an understanding of how self-efficacy beliefs operate, the meaningfulness of the relations among parental cognitions, actual parenting behavior, and children's behavior and development identified in the literature remains limited. As Coleman and Karraker (1998) point out, possible means of influence may be identified by drawing on the theoretical and empirical work of Bandura and his predecessors.

Coleman and Karraker (1998) note that belief in one's ability to parent effectively is likely to influence the level of stress and/or depression experienced in demanding parenting situations. Available literature supports the association between feeling a lack of control over stress and elevated subjective distress involving anxiety and negative physiological reactions (Bandura, Taylor, Williams, Mefford, & Barchas, 1985). Parents' self-reported stress and depression have frequently been found to be associated with negative effects on parenting, including child abuse and neglect (Halpern, 1993; Mrazek, 1993).

Differences in parenting competence associated with variant levels of self-efficacy beliefs are perhaps best understood when considered with reference to social learning theory. Bandura (1982) proposed that when confronted with stress, individuals with low self-efficacy tend to give up easily (presumably due to failure expectancies), internalize failure, and become less satisfied with the associated role. Similarly, parents with low self-efficacy seem to have trouble putting knowledge of parenting tasks into action, become self-absorbed, react to parenting challenges in an overly emotional manner, and tend to lack persistence in parenting (Grusec et al., 1994).

A second mechanism discussed by Coleman and Karraker (1998) to explain how self-efficacy beliefs may relate to parenting behavior is through motivational processes. Self-efficacy beliefs have been shown to have a direct effect on the setting of task-related goals (Schunk, 1990). Efficacious individuals tend to establish high and specific performance goals, while those possessing low self-efficacy beliefs are more inclined to shy away from formulating ambitious, highly specified behavioral goals (Coleman & Karraker, 1998). People with low self-efficacy beliefs also tend to give up quickly when problems arise and avoid challenging tasks (Bandura, 1989; Sexton & Tuckman, 1991). For example, a parent with low self-efficacy, lacking well-formulated parenting goals, might not follow through with consequences for child misbehavior when doing so becomes highly stressful in the face of child persistence. Coleman and Karraker (1998) note that parents low in parenting self-efficacy are likely to avoid effortful disciplinary techniques, such as induction, opting instead to control behavior through less personally demanding means such as yelling or spanking. Most of the previous research designed to explore the association between self-efficacy and goal formulation has dealt with domains of functioning other than parenting. However, using a sample of rural single, African American parents, Brody et al. (1999) found a linkage between parenting self-efficacy beliefs and the goals that mothers possessed regarding their children's development. In turn, mothers with higher goals for their children reported more competence-promoting parenting practices.

In addition to the affective, motivational, and cognitive means through which self-efficacy beliefs may potentially impact parenting behavior, parenting self-efficacy beliefs may also directly influence parenting behavior through the predisposition to cope with stressors in particular ways (Coleman & Karraker, 1998). High self-efficacy beliefs have been associated with a preference for problem-focused coping (management of the event) (Leen & Karraker, 2002); whereas low self-efficacy beliefs are usually associated with emotion-focused coping (regulation of emotions associated with the event). In general, problem-focused coping strategies are considered to be more effective and health-promoting than are emotion-focused coping strategies (Aldwin & Reverson, 1987; Penley, Tomaka, & Wiebe, 2002). Parents with compromised self-efficacy may therefore be more prone to experiencing feelings of being overwhelmed by the responsibilities and work associated with parenting. Studies by Benedek (1970) and by Pridham and Chang (1992) suggest that mothers with positive self-evaluations of parenting competence may be freer both cognitively and emotionally to attend to their infants' growth, development, and temperament. In summary, more efficacious parents are likely to have high levels of interest in, commitment to, and persistence in parenting, exhibit tolerance for the challenges that arise, cope effectively with stressors, and set ambitious and highly specified goals relative to parenting. Further, they are likely to be receptive to enhancing their knowledge and skills, are unlikely to engage in frequent self-reproach, and are inclined to feel heightened joy and lowered discomfort associated with parenting. Parents with the above qualities might be expected to possess the capacity to focus effectively on other aspects of their lives as well, enabling them to develop competencies and derive satisfaction outside of their roles as parents.

PROCESS MECHANISMS LINKING PARENTING SELF-EFFICACY BELIEFS TO CHILD OUTCOMES

As described above, few studies have explored direct associations between parents' self-efficacy beliefs and children's social and intellectual development. However, as a clearer picture of highly efficacious parents emerges from the literature, hypotheses regarding direct and indirect means through which these parents act as instrumental agents in optimizing their children's competence with peers and academic success are becoming easier to formulate. In the discussion that follows, we will explore hypotheses regarding how and why efficacious parents are able to impact the quality of their children's lives in the hope of encouraging more systematic, process-oriented research attention as well as interventions to enhance parents' self-efficacy and their children's behavior and development.

In the realm of fostering cognitive competence, parents with high self-efficacy are likely to work diligently to cultivate a home environment that is rich in toys, books, and other intellectually stimulating materials well before the child actually enters a formal school setting. Even without extensive material resources, highly efficacious parents can arrange library trips and other excursions and create toys and activities from household items. Based on what is known about parents with high self-efficacy, one would expect highly efficacious parents to also make a concerted personal effort to actively teach their children about the physical and social world. Dyadic interaction is likely to involve questions designed to help children learn as well as detailed enthusiastic responses to children's questions. Further, parents with high self-efficacy seem inclined to provide their children with ample opportunities to explore both inside and outside the home in their efforts to encourage learning, creativity, and autonomy.

As children grow older, parents with high self-efficacy might be expected to encourage independent thinking, problem solving, the development of goals, and to follow through on plans developed. In addition, highly efficacious parents will in all likelihood express interest in their children's education generally and in relation to their children's day-to-day school experiences. Available research does confirm a correlation between high parenting self-efficacy and high value placed on children's educational attainment (Brody et al., 1999).

Based on what we know about efficacious parents, it seems probable that these parents will encourage a daily routine supportive of success in school: plenty of rest, good nutrition, and completion of homework. There is evidence suggesting that parents of less academically and socially competent children, when compared to parents of children who are more competent, tend to be less interested in getting to know their children's teachers, place less value on education, feel less competent, and experience feelings of helplessness in their efforts to solve problems (for a review, see Webster-Stratton, 1993). Moreover, research suggests that efficacious parents are more likely than less efficacious parents to assist their children in ways that foster success in school such as through helping with homework (Ames, 1993; Balli, Demo, & Wedman, 1998; Cooper, Lindsay, Nye, & Greathouse, 1998; Fromme & Eccles, 1998; Hoover-Dempsey, & Sandler, 1997; Shumow, 1998). A substantial body of evidence indicates that parental involvement is directly related to student achievement across childhood while also being associated with child characteristics known to facilitate academic achievement including self-regulation abilities, perceptions of competence, a sense of mastery, and trust in one's own abilities (e.g., Delgado-Gaitan, 1992; Ginsberg & Bronstein, 1993; Grolnick & Slowiaczek, 1994; Mau, 1997; McBride & Lin, 1996; Muller, 1998; Xu & Corno, 1998). According to Hoover-Dempsey et al. (2001), parental involvement is likely to support children's sense of competence and associated success in the classroom through the expression of high expectations, encouragement, reinforcement, and provision of information regarding probable outcomes associated with effort. The positive effects of parental involvement in academic achievement are consistent across various levels of parent education, socioeconomic backgrounds, and ethnicities (Bogenschneider, 1997; Jeynes, 2003; Shaver & Walls, 1998).

Studies focusing specifically on the effects of parental involvement among parents of young children have revealed that involvement enhances parents' knowledge of appropriate educational practices, improves literacy and other educational outcomes, and fosters parental commitment to education (Bryant, Peisner-Feinberg, & Miller-Johnson, 2000; Cooter et al., 1999; Gelfer, 1991). Encouragement of parental involvement early in the educational lives of children therefore carries the potential to effect immediate and long-term positive consequences.

In the social domain, highly efficacious parents would be expected to consistently and effectively serve as sensitively attuned and responsive social partners for their children, leading to positive social behaviors in their children. In support of this hypothesis, Gondoli and Silverberg (1997) observed that parenting self-efficacy was positively related to responsiveness in mothers of adolescents. Further, parental responsiveness has consistently been found to be strongly associated with psychological adjustment and competence across various domains in childhood and adolescence (Maccoby & Martin, 1983). Highly efficacious parents would also seem inclined to be proactive in fostering positive sibling relationships, which offer a medium for practicing social skills in an accepting social context. Moreover, parents with high self-efficacy could be expected to understand the merits of providing even very young children with frequent opportunities for interaction with peers outside the home. Parents with high self-efficacy are likely to encourage honesty, kindness, reciprocity, and other prosocial behaviors in their children. For example, Brody et al. (1999) found that African American mothers with high self-efficacy tended to adopt the following parenting goals for their children: to be respectful, to get along with others, and to be well behaved. Such coaching should render the children of efficacious parents appealing social partners. Some evidence for this notion was provided by the results of a study conducted by Gross et al. (1999). Specifically, parents of preschoolers with behavior problems in an urban day care center were found to have low parenting self-efficacy. A similar association was detected by Jackson (2000) in a study of poor single mothers of preschoolers residing in a rural setting.

With warm, nurturing parent–child relationships tending to be more common among dyads with an efficacious parent (Bugental et al., 1989), children of parents with high self-efficacy, compared to children of parents with low self-efficacy, will probably feel more comfortable sharing social difficulties with their parents for the purpose of identifying useful solutions. These children will in all likelihood therefore be privy to helpful advice and reassurance. Although very few available studies have examined links between parenting self-efficacy and children's competence with peers, Melon, Ladd, and Hsu (1993) examined a related construct, perceptions of parenting difficulty among mothers of preschoolers. In this study, extensive maternal social networks predicted lower perceptions of parenting difficulty and greater levels of peer acceptance in children. Research has also revealed that among families experiencing high levels of distress, parents are inclined to develop beliefs about their inefficacy as parents, which then cause negative emotions to escalate and negative communication behaviors to ensue (Bugental & Shennum, 1984).

Parenting self-efficacy may also be associated with child outcomes that are indirectly related to social and academic success. For example, because parents with high self-efficacy tend to be emotionally stable, committed, sensitive, and supportive parents, their children are likely to develop healthy attachments, adaptive self-regulation abilities, and high self-efficacy themselves. For example, McFarlane, Bellisssimo, and Norman (1995) found a relationship between adolescents' reports of high social support from family members and high social self-efficacy. Further, research supports positive associations between secure attachment, high self-efficacy, and self-regulation or self-control and both social and academic competence in children (Armsden & Greenberg, 1987; Bandura, Babaranelli,

Caprara, & Pastorelli, 1996; Brody et al., 1999; Cohn, 1990; Steinberg, Elmen, & Mounts, 1989).

Another less direct route between parents' self-efficacy beliefs and adaptive child outcomes relates to parental modeling. Parents possessing high self-efficacy tend to be mentally healthy and optimistic, and are likely to have high general self-efficacy beliefs (Coleman & Karraker, 2000). Therefore, in areas of their lives outside of direct parenting interactions, parents with high self-efficacy beliefs are inclined to provide positive role models for their children. For example, children of highly efficacious parents would be expected to model commitment to their jobs, families, and friends. The extent to which highly efficacious parents demonstrate high levels of competence in other aspects of their lives and thereby provide healthy models for their children have not been systematically examined. However, research by Colletta (1981) suggests that parents with positive social connections experience greater feelings of well-being, general self-efficacy, and positive emotional connections to their children.

This theoretical analysis and associated empirical evidence provide compelling grounds for associations between self-efficacy and various parenting and child outcomes. Nevertheless, as noted by Coleman and Karraker (2003), assumptions about causal relations among these variables may be premature at this stage in the study of parenting self-efficacy. Most of the available studies have incorporated data from only one point of measurement, allowing for the possibility that particular child characteristics or behaviors impact parenting self-efficacy beliefs rather than the reverse. Moreover, it is important to remain cognizant of the possibility that complex, multidirectional relationships between parenting self-efficacy and other variables relevant to parenting are operative in the development of parenting competence and children's development (Coleman & Karraker, 1998).

APPLICATIONS TO EARLY CHILDHOOD EDUCATION

Researchers who study parenting competence from a systems perspective have strongly advocated targeting parenting self-efficacy beliefs along with parenting behaviors in intervention efforts by therapists and parent educators (Brody et al., 1999; Coleman & Karraker, 1998; 2000; Gross et al., 1999; Raver & Leadbeater, 1999). Parent training interventions designed specifically to elevate parents' self-efficacy beliefs carry the potential to positively alter both subjective and behavioral responses to parenting even under the most stressful environmental demands (Elder, 1995; Elder et al., 1995). Efficacious individuals experience trust in their own abilities during difficult situations and are apt to view problems as energizing challenges rather than as reasons to reduce personal efforts (Jerusalem & Mittag, 1995). In particular, parents who are unusually stressed (e.g., if they are young, impaired physically or mentally, have adopted an older child with behavioral/emotional difficulties, have a child with a physical ailment, or are poor, etc.) need to build their sense of personal efficacy in order to be competent parents when facing sometimes unrelenting stressors. Interventions tailored to meeting the multifaceted challenges of parenting by focusing on elevating self-efficacy beliefs have the potential to make a difference between experiencing hope and success rather than discouragement and failure in the most trying of child rearing contexts. Ideally such intervention strategies will be designed and implemented with sensitivity to individual differences in parents' experiential histories, cultural backgrounds, personality characteristics, and current living conditions.

Although parent-focused intervention programs provide a convenient and appropriate setting for efforts to improve parenting self-efficacy, many parents who might benefit from such programs either do not have programs available to them or decline to take advantage of opportunities to participate in such programs. Early childhood education programs, although often primarily child-focused, can implement both formal and informal strategies to help promote the development of high parenting self-efficacy in parents of young children. Our knowledge regarding how parenting self-efficacy beliefs develop and about the characteristics of parents who possess high parenting self-efficacy beliefs can be used to derive a number of suggestions for enhancing parenting self-efficacy in the context of programs for young children.

Highly efficacious parents are likely to welcome and enjoy involvement in their children's classrooms and school. Teachers would be wise to identify the more efficacious parents and tap into their interest and energy in their efforts to build more dynamic classrooms. Further, involving less efficacious parents in the classroom setting may provide unique opportunities for teachers to assist them in becoming more knowledgeable of effective means of aiding their children with academic tasks and social challenges. Teachers are in a strategic position to offer specific feedback regarding parents' efforts to help their children inside and outside the classroom and for modeling appropriate ways to instill excitement for and commitment to learning in children. Low efficacious parents may initially benefit from being assigned tasks with a high probability of success, or even from being paired with children other than their own, who may be more likely to be cooperative and rewarding when interacting with a non-parent adult. Increasing parents' successes in interacting with children should lead to increases in parenting self-efficacy.

As noted earlier, parents of less socially and academically competent children tend not to be interested in getting to know their children's teachers, devalue education, or feel incompetent (for a review see Webster-Stratton, 1993). They also experience feelings of helplessness in their efforts to resolve child-related problems (Webster-Stratton, 1993). Further, parents of children who experience problems in school are likely to have low self-efficacy and as a result refrain from getting involved with their children's education. As noted by Cullingford and Morrison (1999) in a study of home/school liaison workers "what parents need more than anything to be involved are confidence and self-esteem" (p. 258). Therefore teachers of children who experience difficulty socially or academically ought to make a concerted effort to reach out to and approach the parents of these children in a warm, welcoming manner, while offering concrete suggestions regarding specific ways to help their children become more successful. As parents see evidence of their efforts paying off in terms of ameliorating child problems, their feelings of helplessness are likely to wane as their self-perceptions of competence increase.

Research suggests that teacher invitations to parents to become involved in their children's school activities are more effective predictors of actual involvement than demographic characteristics such as socioeconomic status (Daubert & Epstein, 1993). However, the effectiveness of teachers' encouragement is likely to be challenged by the complexity and hectic pace of contemporary life, particularly with a majority of today's parents working full-time outside the home. Teachers can be encouraged to explore various methods of eliciting parenting involvement from parents who suffer from low levels of personal efficacy and are the least inclined to participate in their children's schooling, such as by scheduling parent-involvement activities at times convenient for working parents and by implementing brief parent involvement activities that can be done during drop-off and pick-up time or at home. This is particularly important in light of research suggesting that many early childhood teachers and teachers in training frequently feel ill-prepared for and uncertain about their roles and responsibilities relative to developing relationships with parents (Bernhard et al., 1998; Morrison & Taylor, 1998). Identification of the specific forms of parental involvement that possess the most power to make a difference in children's success at school is essential (Jeynes, 2003). Some work has been done in this area. For example, Hoge, Smit, and Crist (1997) found that high parental expectations for student success superceded parental interest and involvement in the school as a predictor of children's achievement. However, other evidence suggests that high parental expectations in the context of a less supportive or nurturing parenting style can create inordinate pressure and negatively impact children's competence (Zellman & Waterman, 1998).

CONCLUSION

For years researchers and clinicians have diligently explored ways to help build healthy families by finding effective means of supporting parents in their efforts to raise children to become intellectually, emotionally, and socially competent beings. In this lengthy, rather arduous process, it has been unusual for the pieces to fall together as eloquently as they have in the study of parenting self-efficacy beliefs. Although the work on parenting self-efficacy beliefs is just getting off the ground, the existing foundation offers encouraging evidence suggesting that these cognitions hold promise for unifying the complexities inherent in the study of parenting competence. Moreover, targeting these beliefs in a contextually sensitive manner with awareness of the real world challenges confronting contemporary parents in the effort to enhance parenting competence should prove to be quite fruitful in the years ahead.

REFERENCES

Ames, C. (1993). How school-to-home communications influence parent beliefs and perceptions. *Equity and Choice, 9,* 44–49.

Armsden, G.C., & Greenberg, M.T. (1987). The Inventory of Parent and Peer Attachment: Individual differences and their relationships to psychological well-being in adolescence. *Journal of Youth and Adolescence, 16,* 427–454.

Aldwin, C.M., & Revenson, T.A. (1987). Does coping help? A reexamination of the relation between coping and mental health. *Journal of Personality and Social Psychology, 53,* 337–348.

Ballli, S.J., Demo, D.H., & Wedman, J.F. (1998). Family involvement with children's homework: An intervention in the middle grades. *Family Relations, 47,* 142–146.

Bandura, A. (1982). Self-efficacy in human agency. *American Psychologist, 37,* 122–147.

Bandura, A. (1989). Regulation of cognitive processes through perceived self-efficacy. *Developmental Psychology, 25,* 729–735.

Bandura, A. (1995). Exercise of personal and collective efficacy in changing societies. In A. Bandura (Ed.), *Self-efficacy in changing societies,* (pp. 1–45). New York: Cambridge University Press.

Bandura, A. (1997). *Self-efficacy: The exercise of control.* New York: W. H. Freeman.

Bandura, A. (2002). Social cognitive theory in cultural context. *Applied Psychology: An International Review, 51,* 269–290.

Bandura, A., Babaranelli, C., Caprara, G. V., & Pastorelli, C. (1996). Multifaceted impact of self-efficacy on academic functioning. *Child Development, 67,* 1206–1222.

Bandura, A., Babaranelli, C., Caprara, G. V., & Pastorelli, C. (2001). Self- efficacy beliefs as shapers of children's aspirations and career trajectories. *Child Development, 72,* 187–206.

Bandura, A., Taylor, C, B., Williams, S.L., Mefford, I.N., & Barchas, J.D. (1985). Catecholamine secretion as a function of perceived coping self-efficacy. *Journal of Consulting and Clinical Psychology, 53,* 406–414.

Benedek, T. (1970). Parenthood during the life cycle. In E.J. Anthony & T. Benedek (Eds.), *Parenthood: Its psychology and psychopathology* (pp. 185–206). Boston: Little, Brown.

Bernhard, J.K., Lefebvre, M.L., Kilbride, K.M., Chud, G., & Lange, R. (1998). Troubled relationships in early childhood education: Parent-teacher interactions in ethnoculturally diverse child care settings. *Early Education & Development, 9,* 5–28.

Bogenschneider, K. (1997). Parental involvement in adolescent schooling: A proximal process with transcontextual validity. *Journal of Marriage and the Family, 59,* 718–733.

Bohlin, G., & Hagekull, B. (1987). Good mothering: Maternal attitudes and mother-infant interaction. *Infant Mental Health Journal, 8,* 352–363.

Bondy, E.M., & Mash, E.J. (1999). Parenting efficacy, perceived control over caregiving failure, and mothers' reactions to preschool children's misbehavior. *Child Study Journal, 29,* 157–173.

Brody, G.H., Flor, D.L., & Gibson, N.M. (1999). Linking maternal efficacy beliefs, developmental goals, parenting practices, and child competence in rural single-parent African American Families. *Child Development, 70,* 1197–1208.

Brody, G.H., Stoneman, Z., & Flor, D. (1996). Parental religiosity, family processes, and youth competence in rural, two-parent African American families. *Developmental Psychology, 32,* 696–706.

Brody, G.H., Stoneman, Z., Flor, D., & McCrary, C., Hastings, L., & Conyers, O. (1994). Financial resources, parent functioning, parent co-caregiving, and early adolescent competence in rural two-parent African American families, *Child Development, 65,* 590–605.

Bryant, D., Peisner-Feinberg, E., & Miller-Johnson, S. (2000, April). Head Start parents' roles in the educational lives of their children. Paper presented at the Annual Conference of the American Educational Research Association, New Orleans, LA.

Bugental, D.B., Blue, J., & Cruzcosa, M. (1989). Perceived control over caregiving outcomes: Implications for child abuse. *Developmental Psychology, 25,* 532–539.

Bugental, D.B., & Shennum, W.A. (1984). "Difficult " children as elicitors and targets of adult communication patterns: An attributional-behavioral transactional analysis. *Monographs of the Society for Research in Child Development, 49,* (1. Serial No. 205).

Cohn, D.A. (1990). Child-mother attachment at six years and social competence at school. *Child Development, 61,* 152–162.

Coleman, P.K., Bryan, S., King, B., Nazir, M., Rogers, N., & Trent, A. (2002). Parenting behavior, maternal self-efficacy beliefs, and toddler performance on the Bayley Scales of Infant Development. *Early Child Development and Care, 172,* 123–140.

Coleman, P.K., & Karraker, K.H. (2003). Maternal self-efficacy beliefs, competence in parenting, and toddlers' behavior and developmental status. *Infant Mental Health Journal, 24,* 126–148.

Coleman, P.K., & Karraker, K.H. (2000). Parenting self-efficacy among mothers of school-age children: Conceptualization, measurement, and predictors. *Family Relations 49*, 13–24.

Coleman, P.K., & Karraker, K.H. (1998). Self-efficacy and parenting quality: Findings and future applications. *Developmental Review, 18*, 47–85.

Colletta, N.D. (1981). Social support and the risk of maternal rejection by adolescent mothers. *Journal of Psychology, 109*, 191–197.

Conger, R.D., Conger, K.J., Elder, G.H., Lorenz, F.O., Simons, R.L., & Whitbeck, L.B. (1992). A family process model of economic hardship and adjustment of early adolescent boys. *Child Development 63*, 526–541.

Cooper, H., Lindsay, J.J., Nye, B., & Greenhouse, S. (1998). Relationships among attitudes about homework, amount of homework assigned and completed, and student achievement. *Journal of Educational Psychology, 90*, 70–83.

Cooter, R.B. Jr., Mills-House, E., Marrin, P., Mathews, B.A., Campbell, S., & Baker, T. (1999). Family and community involvement: The bedrock of reading success. *Reading Teacher, 52*, 891–896.

Cullingford, C., & Morrison, M. (1999). Relationships between parents and schools: A case study. *Educational Review, 51*, 253–262.

Cutrona, C., & Troutman, B. (1986). Social support, infant temperament, and parenting self-efficacy: A mediational model of postpartum depression. *Child Development, 57*, 1507–1518.

Dauber, S.L., & Epstein, J.L. (1993). Parents' attitudes and practices of involvement in inner city elementary and middle schools. In N.F. Chavkin (Ed.), *Families and schools in a pluralistic society* (pp. 53–71). Albany: State University of New York Press.

Delgado-Gaitan, C. (1992). School matters in the Mexican-American home: Socializing children to education. *American Educational Research Journal, Personality 29*, 495–513.

Donovan, W.L., & Leavitt, L.A. (1985). Simulating conditions of learned helplessness: Effects of interventions and attributions. *Child Development, 56*, 594–603.

Donovan, W.L., & Leavitt, L.A. (1989). Maternal self-efficacy and infant attachment: Integrating physiology, perceptions, and behavior. *Child Development, 60*, 460–472.

Eccles, J.S., Lord, S., Buchanan, C.M. (1996). School transitions in early adolescence: What are we doing to our young people? In J.A. Graber, J. Brooks-Gunn, & A. Petersen (Eds.), *Transitions through adolescence* (pp. 251–284). Mahwah, NJ: Lawrence Erlbaum.

Elder, G.H. (1995). Life trajectories in changing societies. In A. Bandura (Ed.), *Self-efficacy in changing societies*, (pp. 46–68). New York: Cambridge University Press.

Elder, G.H., Eccles, J.S., Ardelt, M., & Lord, S. (1995). Inner city parents under economic pressure: Perspectives on the strategies of parenting. *Journal of Marriage and the Family, 57*, 771–784.

Feinberg, M.E. (2002). Coparenting and the transition you parenthood: A framework for prevention. *Clinical Child and Family Psychology Review, 5*, 173–195.

Fey, M. E. (1986). *Language intervention with young children*. Boston: Allyn & Bacon.

Frome, P. M., & Eccles, J. S. (1998). Parents' influence on children's achievement-related perceptions. *Journal of Personality and Social Psychology, 74*, 435–452.

Gelfer, J. I. (1991). Teacher-parent partnerships: Enhancing communications. *Childhood Education, 67,* 164–169.

Ginsburg, G. S., & Bronstein, P. (1993). Family factors related to children's intrinsic/extrinsic motivational orientation and academic performance, *Child Development, 64,* 1461–1474.

Goldfield, B. (1987). The contributions of child and caregiver to referential and expressive language. *Applied Psycholinguistics, 8,* 267–280.

Gondoli, D. M., & Silverberg, S. B. (1997). Maternal emotional distress and diminished responsiveness: The mediational role of parenting efficacy and parental perspective taking, *Developmental Psychology, 33,* 861–868.

Grolnick, W.S., & Slowiaczek, M.L. (1994). Parents' involvement in children's schooling: A multidimensional conceptualization and motivational model. *Child Development, 65,* 237–252.

Gross, D., Conrad, B., Fogg, L., & Wothke, W. (1994). A longitudinal model of maternal self-efficacy, depression, and difficult temperament in toddlerhood. *Research in Nursing & Health, 17,* 207–215.

Gross, D., Rocissano, L., & Roncoli, M. (1989). Maternal confidence during toddlerhood: Comparison of preterm and fullterm groups. *Research in Nursing & Health, 12,* 1–9.

Gross, D., Sambrook, A., & Fogg, L. (1999). Behavior problems among young children in low-income urban day care centers. *Research in Nursing & Health, 22,* 15–25.

Grusec, J.E., Hastings, P., & Mammone, N. (1994). Parenting cognitions and relationship schemas. In J.G. Smetana (Ed.), *Beliefs about parenting: Origins and developmental implications* (pp. 5–19). San Francisco: Jossey-Bass.

Halpern, R. (1993). Poverty and infant development. In C.H. Zeanah (Ed.), *Handbook of infant mental health* (pp. 73–86). New York, Guilford Press.

Hart, B., & Risley, T.R. (1995). *Meaningful differences in the everyday experience of young American children.* Baltimore: Brooks.

Heinicke, C.M., Distin, S.D., Ramsey-Klee, D.M., & Given, K. (1983). Pre-birth parent characteristics and family development in the first year of life. *Child Development, 54,* 194–208.

Herrenkohl, E.C., Herrenkohl, R.C., Rupert, L.J., Egolf, B.P., & Lutz, J.G. (1995). Risk factors for behavioral dysfunction: The relative impact of maltreatment, SES, physical health problems, cognitive ability, and quality of parent–child interaction, *Child Abuse & Neglect, 19,* 191–203.

Hinshaw, S.P. (1992). Externalizing behavior problems and academic underachievement in childhood and adolescence: Causal relationships and underlying mechanisms. *Psychological Bulletin, 111,* 127–135.

Hoge, D.R., Smit, E., & Crist, J.T. (1997). Four family process factors predicting academic achievement for sixth and seventh grade. *Educational Research Quarterly, 21,* 27–42.

Hoover-Dempsey, K.V., & Sandler, H.M. (1997). Why do parents become involved in their children's education? *Review of Educational Research, 67,* 3–42.

Hoover-Dempsey, K.V., Battiato, A.C., Walker, J.M.T., Reed, R.P., DeJong, J.M., & Jones, K.P. (2001). Parental involvement in homework, *Educational Psychologist, 26,* 195–209.

Jackson, A.P. (2000). Maternal self-efficacy and children's influence on stress and parenting among single black mothers in poverty. *Journal of Family Issues, 21,* 3–16.

Jerusalem, M., & Mittag, W. (1995). Self-efficacy in stressful life transitions. In Bandura (Ed.), *Self-efficacy in changing societies,* (pp. 177–201). New York: Cambridge University Press.

Jeynes, W.H. (2003). A meta-analysis: The effects of parental involvement on minority children's academic achievement. *Education and Urban Society, 35,* 202–218.

Johnson, C., & Mash, E.J. (1989). A measure of parenting satisfaction and efficacy. *Journal of Clinical and Child Psychiatry, 18,* 167–175.

Kaiser, A.P., Hancock, T.B., Cai, X., Foster, E.M., & Hester, P.P. (2000). Parent-reported behavior problems and language delays in boys and girls enrolled in Head Start classrooms. *Behavioral Disorders, 26,* 26–41.

Kindermann, T.A., & Valsiner, J. (1995). Directions for the study of developing person-context relations. In T.A. Kindermann & J. Valsiner (Eds.), *Development of person-context relations* (pp. 227–240). Hillsdale, NJ: Lawrence Erlbaum.

Kwok, S., & Wong, D. (2000). Mental health of parents with young children in Hong Kong: The roles of parenting stress and parenting self-efficacy. *Child and Family Social Work, 5,* 57–65.

Leen, E., & Karraker, K. (April 2002). An examination of the role of cognitive readiness and self-efficacy in parenting stress and coping. Poster presented at the *International Conference on Infant Studies,* Toronto, Canada.

Leerkes, E.M., & Crockenberg, S.C. (2002). The development of maternal self-efficacy and its impact on maternal behavior. *Infancy, 3,* 227–247.

Maccoby, E.E., & Martin, J.A. (1983). Socialization in the context of the family. In E.M. Hetherington (Ed.), *Handbook of child psychology: Vol. 4. Socialization, personality, and social development.* (pp. 1–101). New York: Wiley.

Mau, W. (1997). Parental influences on the high school student's academic achievement: A comparison of Asian Immigrants, Asian Americans, and White Americans. *Psychology in the Schools, 34,* 267–277.

McBride, B.A., & Lin, H. (1996). Parental involvement in prekindergarten at-risk programs: Multiple perspectives. *Journal of Education for Students Placed at Risk, 1,* 349–372.

McFarlane, A.H., Bellissimo, A., & Norman, G.R. (1995). The role of family and peers in social self-efficacy: Links to depression in adolescence. *American Journal of Orthopsychiatry, 65,* 402–410.

Melon, G.F., Ladd, G.W., & Hsu, H. (1993). Maternal support networks, maternal cognitions, and young children's social and cognitive development, *Child Development, 64,* 1401–1417.

Mrazek, P. (1993). Maltreatment and infant development. In C.H. Zeanah (Ed.), *Handbook of infant mental health,* (pp. 159–170). New York, Guilford Press.

Muller, C. (1998). Gender differences in parental involvement and adolescents' Mathematical achievement. *Sociology of Education, 71,* 336–356.

Penley, J.A., Tomaka, J., & Wiebe, J.S. (2002). The association of coping to physical and psychological health outcomes: A meta-analytic review. *Journal of Behavioral Medicine, 25,* 551–603.

Pridham, K.F., & Chang, A.S. (1992). Transition to being the mother of a new infant in the first 3 months: Maternal problem solving and self-appraisals. *Journal of Advanced Nursing, 17,* 204–216.

Raver, C.C., & Leadbeater, B.J. (1999). Mothering under pressure: Environment, child, and dyadic correlates of maternal self-efficacy among low-income women. *Journal of Family Psychology, 13,* 523–534.

Richards, B.J. (1984). Child-directed speech and influences on language acquisition: Methodology and interpretation. In C. Galloway & B.J. Richards (Eds.), *Input and interaction in language acquisition* (pp. 74–106). Cambridge: Cambridge University Press.

Schunk, D.H. (1990). Goal setting and self-efficacy during self-regulated learning. *Educational Psychologist, 25,* 71–86.

Sexton, T.L., & Tuckman, B.W. (1991). Self-beliefs and behavior: The role of self-efficacy and outcome expectation over time. *Personality and Individual Differences, 12,* 725–736.

Shaver, A.V., & Walls, R.T. (1998). Effect if Title 1 parent involvement on student reading and mathematics achievement. *Journal of Research and Development in Education, 31,* 90–97.

Shumow, L. (1998). Promoting parental attunement to children's mathematical reasoning though parent education. *Journal of Applied Developmental Psychology, 19,* 109–127.

Smetana, J.G. (1994). Editor's notes. In J.G. Smetana (Ed.), Beliefs about parenting: Origins and developmental implications (pp.1–4). San Francisco: Jossey-Bass.

Snow, C.E. (1984). Parent–child interaction and the development of communicative ability. In R.L. Schiefelbusch & J. Pickar (Eds.), *The acquisition of communicative competence* (pp. 69–108).
Baltimore: University Park Press.

Spoth, R., & Conroy, S. (1993). Survey of prevention-relevant beliefs and efforts to enhance parenting skills among rural parents. *The Journal of Rural Health, 9,* 227–239.

Steinberg, L., Elmen, J.D., & Mounts, N.S. (1989). Authoritative parenting, psychosocial maturity, and academic success among adolescents. *Child Development, 60,* 1424–1436.

Stifter, C.A., & Bono, M.A. (1998). The effect of infant colic on maternal self-perceptions and mother-infant attachment. *Child: Care, Health, and Development, 24,* 339–351.

Strand, P.S., & Wahler, R.G. (1996). Predicting maladaptive parenting: Role of maternal object relations, *Journal of Clinical Child Psychology, 25,* 43–51.

Swick, K.J., & Hassell, T. (1990). Parental efficacy and the development of social competence in young children. *Journal of Instructional Psychology, 17,* 24–32.

Teti, D.M., & Gelfand, D.M. (1991). Behavioral competence among mothers of infants in the first year: The mediational role of maternal self-efficacy. *Child Development, 62,* 918–929.

Teti, D.M., O'Connell, M.A., & Reiner, C.D. (1996). Parenting sensitivity, Parental depression and child health: The mediational role of parenting self-efficacy. *Early Development and Parenting, 5,* 237–250.

Unger, D.G., & Waudersman, L.P. (1985). Social support and adolescent mothers: Action research contributions to theory and application. *Journal of Social Issues, 41,* 29–45.

Webster-Stratton, C. (1993). Strategies for helping early school-aged children with oppositional defiant and conduct disorders: The importance of home-school partnerships. *School Psychology Review, 22,* 437–457.

Wells-Parker, E., Miller, D.I., & Topping, S. (1990). Development of control of outcome scales and self-efficacy scales for women in four life roles. *Journal of Personality Assessment, 54,* 564–575.

Xu, J., & Corno, L. (1998). Case studies of families doing third grade homework. *Teacher's College Record, 100,* 402–236.

Zellman, G.L., & Waterman, J.M. (1998). Understanding the impact of parent school involvement on children's educational outcomes. *Journal of Educational Research, 91,* 370–380.

CHAPTER 6

EMOTION REGULATION

Implications for Children's School Readiness and Achievement

Julia M. Braungart-Rieker and Ashley L. Hill

INTRODUCTION

I first noticed David during circle-time one day, while observing a kindergarten classroom of 26 children. This classroom was filled with bright, energetic, and enthusiastic learners for the most part—children who were eager to share information with each other and with the teacher. David, however was spinning on his knees, howling, and veering away from the group. After being asked to rejoin the circle and even physically encouraged by an assistant teacher to sit with the other children, David's emotions quickly flipped to extreme anger; he began yelling and waving his arms, eventually running away from the teacher. The other children began to quiet—some even looked uncomfortable—while watching David lose control. Eventually, David had to leave the classroom with the assistance of a teacher. Circle-time resumed, but the tone had clearly changed. Some children looked concerned; others were getting antsy; the remaining teachers looked flustered. For David, this was not a particularly unusual event, although, at times, he was able to be calm. On many other occasions, however, David was observed

Contemporary Perspectives on Families, Communities, and Schools for Young Children, pages 107–129
Copyright © 2005 by Information Age Publishing

to paint on other children's paper, push others, and show heightened resistance to teachers' directions. During a field trip to a natural history museum one day, David became very fearful of a mask that he saw—sobbing that he "hated this place" and that he wanted to leave.

Why do some children like David have such a difficult time in the classroom? In David's particular case, his trouble with handling and controlling his emotions seemed most noticeable. Although David was capable of learning, his heightened arousal and inappropriate responses to emotionally-laden situations often prevented him from achieving the social and cognitive goals of a kindergarten classroom.

The goal of this chapter is to discuss the development of emotion regulation and examine its possible links with school-related behaviors and skills. Given the processes involved in the development of emotional control and regulation, the conceptual issues and empirical findings discussed in this chapter focus on children—from early infancy to early childhood. As can be seen in Figure 6.1, we present a model in which emotion regulation is central to the associations among child, family, and school. This chapter focuses on the theoretical support and empirical evidence underlying these pathways. The chapter is divided into several sections. First, we review the major theoretical issues surrounding emotion regulation, including its definition and course of development from infancy to childhood. Next, we discuss predictors and correlates of emotion regulation in terms of examining individual differences. That is, why do some children have a harder time than others when dealing with negative emotions and what are some factors that may explain some of these differences? Such factors include children's temperament, parenting skills and the parent–child

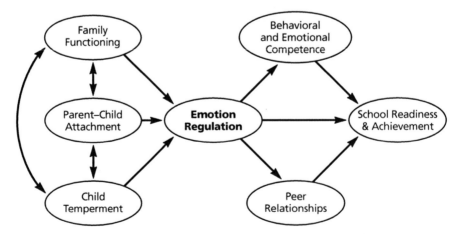

Figure 6.1.   Emotion regulation: A mediator linking family and school.

attachment relationship, as well as overall family functioning. Third, we discuss how emotion regulation relates to various factors that might affect children's school readiness. Topics include behavioral and emotional competence in the classroom and peer relationships. We conclude by revisiting the emotion regulation model and propose ways for studying the potential pathways that link child, family, and school outcomes.

WHAT IS EMOTION REGULATION?

Definitional Issues

As Thompson (1994) pointed out in a monograph devoted to the topic of emotion regulation, there is surprising diversity in the ways in which different researchers conceptualize emotion regulation. Despite such diversity, most definitions of emotion regulation include aspects surrounding a person's ability to modulate, control, or reduce the intensive and temporal features of an emotion (Thompson, 1994). In addition, regulation can occur at the neurophysiological, hormonal, attentional, and behavioral levels (Calkins, 1994; Fox, 1994; Rothbart & Derryberry, 1981; Stansbury & Gunnar, 1994; Thompson, 1994). Much of the empirical work, however, has tended to focus on behavioral expressions of regulation, probably because they are more convenient to observe and measure.

In infancy, caregivers obviously play a large role in helping infants manage their emotions. However, infants also have the capability of regulating their affect. Behavioral displays of regulation include attention, avoidance, self-comforting, and signaling to caregivers for assistance, which can be observed during contexts in which an infant is likely to get upset. Such behaviors have been shown to reduce the intensity of distress (Buss & Goldsmith, 1998; Rothbart, Ziaie, & O'Boyle, 1992; Stifter & Braungart, 1995). As children develop, additional resources involving more cognitively oriented skills emerge (Saarni, 1997). We describe these various behavioral and cognitive strategies in more detail below.

The Developmental Course of Emotion Regulation

According to Kopp (1989), caregivers play a crucial role in serving as an external support system for regulating emotions. Infants also, however, have internal capabilities which enable them to make attempts to self regulate. Kopp (1989) points out that initially, the emotional regulating system consists of reflexive adaptations and simple behaviors. For example, rooting and sucking reflexes are examples of rudimentary behaviors that may facilitate an infant's ability to regulate distress (Kessen & Leutzendorff, 1963). Simple repetitive behaviors, described by Piaget (e.g., 1954) as "primary circular reactions" may provide the infant with a means for making early associations between motoric responses (bringing hand to mouth) and regulation of distress.

By about the third month, infants begin to gain more voluntary control of gross motor actions. For example, infants will have more success with hand-to-mouth movement, which provides them with a more efficient means of self-comforting. In addition, skills such as head rotation enables infants to control the focus of their visual field. Behaviors such as gaze aversion (turning attention away from a source of arousal) and attending toward objects has been shown to reduce distress (Rothbart et al., 1992; Stifter & Braungart, 1995).

Between 3 and approximately 7 to 9 months, cognitive growth seems to play a role in major changes in emotional reactions and regulation (Kopp, 1989). During this period, infants become better able to anticipate events, show intentionality in behavior, increased planfulness, and improved memory (Gesell & Amatruda, 1941; Piaget, 1954). Such changes in the cognitive system have implications for infants' social and emotional savviness. For example, studies involving the Still-Face Paradigm (Tronick et al., 1978)—a situation in which a parent, typically the mother, ceases interaction with the infant but remains in full frontal view—have shown that infants not only exhibit frustration upon their caregivers' lack of responsiveness (Fogel, 1982; Stoller & Field, 1982; Toda & Fogel, 1993; Weinberg & Tronick, 1994), but show increased levels of gaze aversion as well (Field, 1994). Results from studies involving the still-face reveal that infants have developed expectations about maternal responsiveness; when mothers violate such expectations, infants become upset but also attempt to regulate their distress. Furthermore, some infants will make positive bids toward their mother as a way to re-engage her (e.g., Cohn, Campbell, & Ross, 1992). Thus, even within the 3–8 month period, infants are showing fairly sophisticated means of self-regulating as well as attempting to regulate the mother-infant interaction.

By the end of the first year, dramatic changes have occurred in infants' motoric, cognitive, and social skills (Gesell & Amatruda, 1941; Piaget, 1954). Such advances have implications for changes in emotional regulatory abilities as well. The ability to communicate with gestures and early language allows infants to more clearly express their needs. With increasing locomotor and fine-motor skills, they are better able to physically control their environment. For example, they can seek proximity to a caregiver when they are upset (Ainsworth et al., 1978; Bowlby, 1969; Campos et al., 1983); they can also use toys or objects as a way to distract themselves (Braungart & Stifter, 1991; Gibson & Radner, 1979; Kopp, 1989).

During the second year of life, toddlers are developing a more sophisticated sense of the self as well as the ability to understand causes of distress (Kopp, 1989). Such changes suggest that toddlers become aware of their own distress and begin to realize that their own behavior can help alleviate negative feelings. In a study involving several emotionally laden situations, Grolnick, Bridges, and Connell (1996) found that 2-year-olds most frequently dealt with their distress by using active engagement with substitute objects, irrespective of the context of the situation (delay of gratification task versus maternal separation). In addition, toddlers who used more active engagement were less distressed than those who used other types of strategies (e.g., focusing on the forbidden toy). Furthermore, classic studies by Mischel (e.g., 1974) have demonstrated that children who orient their attention away from a forbidden object are better able to delay their gratification. Thus, focusing attention away from sources of arousal appears to facilitate behavioral control as well as emotion regulation.

As children develop, and as alternative methods such as interviewing children can be used to study regulation, more cognitively-oriented skills are apparent. For example, Saarni (1997) interviewed school-aged children about the types of strategies that they would use during various stressful situations. The strategies that emerged, with the most adaptive strategy listed first and the least adaptive listed last were: Problem solving (attempting to change the situation), support seeking from caregivers or peers, distancing-avoidance, internalizing, and antisocial behaviors. Similarly, when children were asked to describe what they did when attempting to feel better, Rossman (1992) found the following factors to be most effective: use of caregivers, solitary distraction-avoidance, seeking out peers, and self-calming behaviors (e.g., taking lots of deep breaths).

Kopp (1989) has proposed that emotion regulation becomes more "planful" as children's cognitive abilities increase. For example, children who were able to discriminate on spatially incompatible and compatible tasks were also more likely to be rated by parents as better able to shift and focus attention (Gerardi-Caulton, 2000). Children who performed well on the spatial conflict tasks also performed better on delay of gratification tasks. Thus, such skills may contribute to school readiness by the employment of cognitive abilities that allow a child to voluntarily regulate their emotions and pursue specific goals within the context of school.

It becomes clear that a tremendous amount of change in regulating emotions occurs during the first several years of life. Motoric and cognitive changes seem to explain such major shifts in children's abilities to regulate or attempt to regulate their emotions (Kopp, 1982, 1989). However, it also becomes apparent that there is wide variation in children's abilities to regulate—even within a given age. Thus, a challenge to researchers is to explain such individual variation. Why do some children show better regulation than others? And what are the implications of such individual differences?

PREDICTORS AND CORRELATES OF EMOTION REGULATION: THE RELEVANCE OF INFANCY

Explaining individual differences in emotion regulation is an important challenge. Older children who appear to have difficulties in managing emotions (e.g., anger) are at risk for developing behavioral disorders (Cole, Michel, & Teti, 1994; Dodge & Garber, 1991). Although psychopathological outcomes may represent extreme deficits in emotion regulation, less than optimal outcomes may also occur for children who struggle with regulating their emotions. For example, Calkins (1994) has speculated that children who have trouble managing anger may have difficulties in establishing positive peer relationships. Thus, understanding individual differences in emotion regulation—even during infancy seems crucial. Given that the development of emotion regulation is complex, it is probably not surprising that multiple factors should be considered in explaining individual differences in emotion regulation. More specifically, factors considered to be more endogenous to the child (e.g., temperament) as well as parenting and family characteristics are likely related to the developing emotion regulation system.

Temperament

Several theorists have proposed that temperament and emotion regulation are related. How they are related, however, is not always agreed upon. For example, Rothbart and Derryberry (1981) proposed that emotion regulation is a component of temperament. Children who can efficiently modulate their arousal may appear to be less emotional. Rothbart and Derryberry (1981) also mention, however, that emotionality (reactivity) and regulation are not merely opposite ends of one continuum. For example, some children may have a high tendency to react quickly and intensely to emotionally-laden situations yet are able to recover quickly. Other children, however, will have more trouble at modulating or reducing heightened negativity. Thus, just because a child appears highly emotional, it doesn't necessarily follow that their regulation is low.

Parenting and the Parent–Child Attachment Relationship

Some theorists have argued that attachment security directly impacts the development of emotion regulation. Attachment refers to the affective bond between the infant and caregiver that develops over time (Bowlby, 1969). Not all children, however, are securely attached to their parents. Ainsworth (1973) has theorized that maternal sensitivity and responsiveness to the infant's affective signals affect the way in which the infant organizes emotional experience and regulates "felt security" (Sroufe & Waters, 1977). In other words, if the attachment figure is available and responsive to the infant's distress signals, negative affect can be regulated with strategies that involve seeking of comfort and support from the attachment figure. It is argued that infants develop an internal working model of the expectations regarding the mothers' emotional availability and responsiveness. If the parent is emotionally unavailable or rejecting of the infant, the infant may not learn to rely on others (Main, Kaplan, & Cassidy, 1985). Indeed a meta-analysis involving data from numerous studies found that infants whose mothers are more sensitive are more likely to be secure rather than insecure in their attachment relationship (De Wolff & van Ijzendoorn, 1997).

According to Cassidy (1994), infants who are secure in their attachment seem to show appropriate levels of emotion and recovery from distress during situations designed to activate the attachment system (e.g., parent–child separations and reunions), whereas insecure infants may either over-regulate (avoidant infants) or under-regulate (resistant infants) their emotions. Main (1990) has suggested that infants become avoidant or resistant as a way to adapt to a caregiving environment that is not meeting his/her emotional needs. For example, infants classified as insecure avoidant develop an avoidant strategy as a way to override or suppress attachment-related emotions. Insecure-resistant infants, on the other hand, may have heightened emotionality and dysregulation toward caregivers as a strategy for eliciting greater attention from their less responsive caregiver.

Such arguments suggest that security status must be established before such patterns in emotion regulation emerge. In other words, once infants have formed a stable internal working model of the parent-infant relationship—somewhere after seven months of age (Ainsworth et al., 1978; Bowlby, 1969)—their expectations about how the parent will respond to their emotional needs will be established. Thus, these stable expectations, whether positive or negative, may then influence the extent to which infants regulate their own emotions.

Another explanation, however, is that early appearing temperamental differences, coupled with parents' abilities to respond to their infants in sensitive and non-rejecting ways, lead to individual variation in regulation and attachment. Belsky and Rovine (1987) found that mothers rated infants later classified as Avoidant (A) or secure (subtypes B1 and B2) as less fussy in temperament at 3-months, whereas infants later classified as secure (subtypes B3 and B4) or Resistant (C) were prone to be more fussy. But what seems to distinguish less fussy As from B1-B2s as well as more fussy Cs from B3-B4s is the level of parental sensitivity (e.g., de Wolff & van Ijzendoorn, 1997). Thus, infants who tend to be less fussy in temperament but whose parents are rejecting or low in sensitivity may be at risk for developing an avoidant style of attachment. In contrast, similarly low-fussy infants whose mothers are more sensitive may be more likely to develop a B1-B2 attachment style. For those infants found to be higher in temperamental fussiness, if their parents are sensitive, they may develop a B3-B4 style, whereas fussy infants whose parents don't meet their emotional needs may be at risk for a resistant attachment status.

Thus, attachment classification and *how* an infant regulates his/her emotions (e.g., over-regulate or under-regulate) may be a function of temperamental style and the quality of the caregiving environment. Furthermore, early signs of such differences are apparent prior to a fully-developed attachment relationship. For example, Cohn et al. (1992) found that infants' positive affect during the still-face at 6-months was related to secure attachment at 12 months. In terms of regulatory behaviors, Braungart-Rieker, Garwood, Powers, and Notaro (1998) found that 4-month-old infants whose mothers and fathers were more sensitive during a face-to-face interaction showed more parent-focused orientation during a still-face episode. Given that parent sensitivity has been shown to predict the quality of the infant-parent attachment relationship later, an infant showing more parent-focused regulation during the still-face may be showing signs of a positive developing internal working model of the infant-parent relationship. In a follow-up to this study, Braungart-Rieker, Garwood, Powers, and Wang (2001) found that affective and regulatory behaviors at the 4-month still-face distinguished infant-mother attachment groups at 12-months. More specifically, infants whose mothers were more sensitive and who showed higher levels of regulation during the still-face at 4-months (self-comforting and focused attention away from the source of their arousal—the mother) were more likely to develop a secure infant-mother attachment relationship by 12 months. Interestingly, for a subgroup of infants later classified as secure (B3-B4s) overall negative affect was high during the still-face but attempts to regulate was also higher, compared to infants who were later classified as insecure resistant. Thus, sensitive parenting may foster young infants' abilities to regulate their emotions, which in turn promotes a more secure attachment relationship. Such linkages with attachment are important to understand because studies examining the sequelae of attachment have found that security is related to greater compliance to maternal requests (Londerville & Main, 1981), reduced risk for behavioral problems (Tizard & Hodges, 1978), and increased popularity with peers (Sroufe, Fox, & Pancake, 1983)—outcomes important for success in the classroom setting.

Family Functioning

The quality of the spousal relationship also appears to affect children's emotional well being (e.g., Cummings & Davies, 1996; Emery, 1982). Cummings and Davies (1996) have suggested several possible ways in which exposure to marital conflict affects children's emotional security. In brief, effects may be indirect in that parents' whose marriage is highly conflicted may interact with their children in less than optimal ways. Effects may also be direct, however, if children observe unresolved tensions in their parents. Young children may perceive open hostility as a threat to their own safety— even if these perceptions are fairly unsophisticated (as with infants). Empirical studies involving parents of infants have found that the infant-father relationship may be especially vulnerable to negative marital relations; fathers showed less quantity and quality of interactions with their infants when they rated their marital relationship as poor. Mothers, on the other hand, seemed to play a compensatory role when the marriage was conflicted (Belsky, Youngblade, Rovine, & Volling, 1991). Owen and Cox (1997), however, found that infants exposed to hostile marital relationships suffered negative consequences with both the mother and the father. Such infants were likely to show disorganized behaviors during the Strange Situation, indicating that the ability to regulate their emotional behaviors with attachment figures was affected by negative spousal interactions.

Numerous studies of children beyond infancy also show the negative emotional effects of family conflict. When observing parents in conflict, distress responses shown by children include motor inhibition and freezing; self-reported anger, distress, concern, self-blame, and fear; behavioral responses of anger, distress, and hostile aggression; physiological indications of stress reactions (e.g., blood pressure, heart rate elevation, galvanic skin response); and children's concerned mediation in the parents' disputes (e.g., Davies & Cummings, 1998; Grych, 1998; Shamir, DuRocher-Schudlich, & Cummings, 2002). Davies and Cummings (1998) argue that children's emotional security is compromised when they are repeatedly exposed to marital conflict which may impact how they deal with emotionally laden situations even outside of the home. Thus, the quality of the marriage and overall family functioning appears to be an important contributor in the development of emotion regulation.

In the remaining sections of this chapter we will explore how emotion regulation as a characteristic of the child affects school readiness and achievement. We will also explore ideas for future research that may inform intervention strategies for this important early transition period to the context of school.

Emotion Regulation as a Child Characteristic of School Readiness

Several researchers have recently argued that emotional development matters for school readiness (Blair, 2002; Raver, 2002). For example, Blair argues for a neurobiological model that integrates cognition and emotion and states, "...self-regulatory skills underlie many of the behaviors and attributes that are associated with successful school adjustment" (p. 112). In fact, prediction of GPA in middle school indicates that social-emotional factors, such as emotion regulation, are important for children's school performance (Gumora & Arsenio, 2002). In a study involving middle school students, emotional disposition, negative academic affect, and emotion regulation were unique predictors of students' GPA over and above cognitive factors such as academic achievement and efficacy. Specifically, students who reported more emotions that were negative during routine school tasks performed worse academically, even after controlling for cognitive differences. In addition, in a study involving 7th graders, self-regulation, along with self-efficacy and test anxiety, emerged as one of the best predictors of performance (Pintrich & de Groot, 1990).

The integration of cognition and emotion has been a long debated topic within developmental psychology, but recent work has shown that regulatory skills involve *effortful cognitive* factors, such as attention and working memory which monitor the internal goal-state of the individual and the external demands of the environment (Derryberry & Reed, 1996; Posner & DiGirolamo, 1998). These regulatory abilities are important early on in a child's academic career. Indeed, the external demands of the kindergarten environment have led researchers to label this period as a 'transition period' or a 'sensitive period' of development that provides new influences to the developing child and thus, may have long-term implications for school achievement (Pianta & Walsh, 1996; Rimm-Kaufman & Pianta, 2000). These new demands emphasize social and emotional factors, such as socializing with peers, understanding and following routines, establishing independence from adults, and being alert for longer periods of time. These social and emotional demands can challenge the 5-year-old child. It has also been found that adjustment during the first years of school predicts later school success (Pianta & Walsh, 1996). Furthermore, individual differences in school performance remain stable after the first few years of school (e.g., Alexander & Entwistle, 1988).

Emotion Regulation and Behavioral and Emotional Competence within the Context of School

There are several ways emotion regulation could be linked with school achievement; however, there is little evidence in the literature of a direct relationship (Blair, 2002). Instead, examining the processes affected by emotion regulation, such as socialization, may provide the link between emotion regulation and school success. Most theorists agree that regulation helps to achieve behavioral and social appropriateness or to adjust emotional responses in order to meet social rules (Kopp, 1989). In fact, a certain process of emotion regulation is important for socialization: the ability to inhibit a prevailing behavior or emotion, to modulate a response, or to have the flexibility to adjust a response in order to meet external demands or internal goals. Although the ability to inhibit or change responses have been extensively studied over the years, it is only recently that researchers have conceptualized this aspect of emotion regulation as "effortful control" (Murray & Kochanska, 2002). Ahadi and Rothbart (1994) define effortful control as "individual differences in the ability to voluntarily sustain focus on a task, to voluntarily shift emotion from one task to another, to voluntarily initiate action, and to voluntarily inhibit action" (p.196). Thus, effortful control allows for flexible responding, so that a child with this ability can resolve internal demands, such as planning and restraining behavior, but also can dynamically respond to contextual situations and be spontaneous and enthusiastic when it is appropriate. In this sense, optimal effortful control is similar to Block and Block's (1980) definition of ego-resiliency. In Block and Block's (1980) longitudinal study, teachers characterized ego-resilient children as more empathetic, bright, self-accepting, able to cope with stress, novelty seeking, fluent, appropriate in their expression of emotion, self-reliant, creative and competent than ego-brittle children. Such skills are needed to adjust to the novel demands of kindergarten and thus are important for school readiness.

In fact, effortful control skills are highlighted in what kindergarten teachers think are the most important characteristics of children who are school ready according to data from the National Center for Educational Statistics survey on kindergarten readiness (Lewitt & Baker, 1995). Teachers' main concerns were regulatory aspects of the children's behavior. Specifically, 84% of teachers reported that children needed to be able to communicate thoughts, needs, and wants verbally, 76% reported that children needed to be curious and enthusiastic, and 60% stated that children needed to be able to follow directions, not be disruptive, and be sensitive to other children's feelings. On the other hand, only 21% reported that children needed to be able to use pencils and paintbrushes, 10% knowing the alphabet and 7% being able to count to 20. In a similar survey, a national sample of kindergarten teachers reported comparable regulatory skills that are needed in kindergarten; they also reported, however, that generally about half of the class had specific problems (Rimm-Kaufman, Pianta, & Cox, 2000). Furthermore, one of the largest problems reported by kindergarten teachers was difficulty following directions; specifically 46.16% of the teachers cited this as the largest problem in their classrooms. Thus, kindergarten teachers think that an important aspect of school readiness is the ability to understand and follow social rules, and socioemotional researchers have found that effortful control is a necessary ability to achieve socialization. For example, preschool children who could regulate attention were better liked by peers, viewed by adults as more socially appropriate, and more resilient to stress (Eisenberg et al., 1997). Thus, socialization includes accepting adults' expectations of academic achievement and in order to do this, effortful regulation must be employed to allow children to be goal-directed and able to follow directions, understand roles and rules within the school context.

Research supports the idea that a child's socialization in the classroom is predictive of a child's success in school. For example, school liking is predicted by participation in the classroom and classroom participation leads to higher levels of achievement (Ladd, Buhs, & Seid, 2000). Specifically, cooperative participation mediated the relationship between school liking and school achievement. In other words, children who were willing to follow classroom rules, to fill role expectations and were cooperative in response to the teacher and the demands of the classroom liked school more and had higher levels of achievement than children less able to socialize to the classroom context.

Children's reported liking of school is related to factors that are representative of effortful control. For example, the idea of cooperative participation is valued in Western culture and is thought to be related to the concept of social responsibility (Wentzel, 1991). Furthermore, Ladd and colleagues describe the value of cooperative participation as ". . . children who feel positively about school may be more disposed to 'identify' with this context and, therefore, adapt to teacher's requests and adhere to classroom rules" (p. 273). These ideas relate to effortful control in that emotion regulation, adaptability to a new set of rules, and flexibility in responding are necessary to meet the new behavioral, emotional, and social demands of in early education contexts. Thus, there may be a certain socialization process unique to the context of school.

Emotion Regulation and Social Relationships as a Link to School Readiness

Researchers have suggested that positive peer relationships are one important factor for adjustment to preschool (Sroufe & Rutter, 1984). Furthermore, early behavior problems and lack of positive peer relationships in the 1st grade, among other factors, are predictive of risks associated with high-school dropout (Jimerson, Egeland, Sroufe, & Carlson, 2000; Parker & Asher, 1987). Thus, early peer relationships may have long-term implications for school success and have been cited as an important goal of early childhood education (Guralnick, 1993). Teachers in early childhood education also report that they consider factors contributing to positive peer relationships as important for school functioning (Rimm-Kaufman et al., 2000).

Vygotsky (1978) postulated that the zone of proximal development allows for peers and adults to facilitate a child's learning. A child's ability to regulate emotions may permit more and higher quality opportunities for educational exchanges within the child's zone of proximal development with both peers and teachers. Emotion regulation also provides a child with the skills needed to be prosocial and socially competent (Fabes et al., 1999; Kochanska, Murray, & Harlan, 2000). Thus, peer relationships may provide contexts for learning and growth, and positive interactions may lead to school liking which has been related to other forms of school achievement and readiness (Ladd et al., 2000). Related to the idea of the zone of proximal development, researchers believe that emotion regulation itself develops within the context of peer relationships, in addition to relationships with adults (von Salisch, 2001). Thus, not only is emotion regulation important for social functioning, but experiences with peers facilitate further development of emotion regulation. However, social competence with peers may not be the only form of social skills a child needs; high-quality relationships with teachers are important as well. For example, Pianta and Nimetz (1991) have shown that teacher–child relationships in kindergarten are predictive of future school achievement.

Research on emotion regulation and peers has shown that emotion regulation is an important factor in children's abilities to have positive peer relationships. Specifically, preschoolers who expressed positive emotions during play and who were rated as low in emotional intensity, were more likely to be observed by raters as prosocial (Garner & Estep, 2001). In addition, expressing positive emotions during play was negatively related to nonconstructive anger reactions during peer interactions. Furthermore, preschool boys who were unable to mask expressions of anger and disappointment in the presence of adults were more likely to be rated as displaying disruptive behaviors (Cole, Zahn-Waxler, & Smith, 1994). These results suggest that children who are better able to modulate their emotional reactions, but also express positive emotions in a proper social context are using emotion regulation to engage in prosocial behavior. This highlights the idea that emotion regulation is utilized not only to inhibit negative emotions, but also to enhance positive emotions when appropriate (Malatesta & Haviland, 1985; Walden & Smith, 1997).

As a particular process of emotion regulation, effortful control may be important for social competence. Eisenberg and colleagues describe the combination of behavioral and attentional control as effortful control. Attentional control has been linked to social competence in several studies. For example, Raver, Blackburn, Bancroft, and Torp (1999) found that attention regulation during a delay task predicted both teacher and peer ratings of social competence. In addition, attention regulation, an aspect of effortful control, is tied to social competence in several studies, through empathetic/sympathetic responding. For example, children who were sympathetic were also rated as socially competent (Eisenberg & Fabes, 1995; Eisenberg et al., 1996).

In one study, a link between attentional regulation and empathy was explored (Trommsdorf & Friedlmeier, 1999). Children who witnessed a peer in a distressing situation were more likely to help if they experienced empathy, rather than distress. Interestingly, when presented with a motivational conflict to finish a cognitive task in a limited amount of time, the experience of empathy was correlated with distress. In this distraction situation, a lack of volitional will to shift and focus attention may have caused a child that normally would be able to emphasize and help her peer, to feel distress because her motivations were in conflict. She could either follow the instructions of the authority figure researcher, or help the peer in distress.

Other studies illustrate the relationship between empathy/sympathy, emotion regulation, emotionality, and social competence. In a study with 6 to 8-year-olds, children rated by teachers as low in emotion regulation were also low in sympathy (Eisenberg et al., 1996). In contrast, children with moderate to high ratings of regulation were rated as sympathetic as the level of their general emotionality increased. Thus, children who experience higher levels of positive and negative emotions are more likely to feel sympathy, if they also are able to regulate their emotions. As several researchers have argued, emotion regulation allows an individual to reduce personal distress in response to another's distress, which makes room for sympathy (Eisenberg, et al., 1998; Trommsdorf & Friedlmeier, 1999).

Individual Differences in Emotion Regulation: Implications for School Success

Thus far, we have explored how positive peer relationships may contribute to school functioning and have also discussed how a lack of adequate regulation could result in children being characterized as disruptive and less socially competent. The development of effortful control is thought to occur between the ages of 3 and 5 (Kochanska et al., 2000). However, within this developmental trajectory there are individual differences in a child's ability to regulate emotions. Therefore, although social competence has been found to be an important outcome of effortful control, it is possible that differences in the development of self-control could lead to problems in social outcomes. These problems may occur when responses are not adaptive to situations or internal goals, or when control is characterized by over-control or under-control. In a longitudinal study, teachers identified characteristics of under-control and over-control behaviors in children (Block & Block, 1980). Compared to children with over-control problems, children with under-control problems were characterized as more assertive, aggressive, active, outgoing, competitive, attention seeking, overactive to frustration, less complaint, unable to delay gratification, jealous and exploitative and less compliant, orderly, shy, yielding, reflective, helpful, private, or considerate.

In a study concerning how teacher–child relationships are important in the process of school adjustment, indices of under- and over-control were important factors in the teacher's decision to hold back a student in kindergarten (Pianta & Steinberg, 1992). For example, children who exhibited more conflict with teachers and showed more anger were more likely to be retained in kindergarten, to exhibit conduct problems within the classroom, and to be rated by parents as having acting-out problems at home. Children who were rated as low on open communication with teachers were also reported to be anxious by parents. On the other hand, children who were rated as competent by parents had warm and open relationships with their teachers and exhibited social skills within the classroom.

These patterns of control that correlate with kindergarten retention are synonymous with ideas of effortful control, under-control, and over-control. For example, children with conduct problems, conflict with teachers, and acting out behavior problems likely have an under-control of emotions and behaviors. Children who have a less open relationship with teachers and who are anxious are representative of children with over-control of emotions and behaviors. Both of these patterns do not allow for a flexibility of responding that are important for functioning in the context of school. For example, those children who had open and warm relationships with teachers, were competent and exhibited social skills in the classroom were able to utilize regulation to allow for flexible responding, which led to positive relationships with the teacher and peers. In fact, the few children who were predicted to be retained in kindergarten because of scores on an intelligence test but were promoted, had a positive relationship with their teacher.

Under- and over-control problems may be an indication of behavior problems such as externalizing and internalizing disorders. In fact, lower and higher effortful control scores have been significantly and nonlinearly related to mother report of behavior problems (Murray & Kochanska, 2002), such that higher and lower effortful control scores relate to total behavior problems (both externalizing and internalizing behavior problems). This study is the first to examine a possible continuum of control, from under-control to over-control. The nonlinear function of effortful control suggests that over- and under-control can indeed be indices of behavior problems.

In another study, it is illustrated how teacher-reported externalizing and internalizing patterns may affect school functioning. Specifically, externalizing behavior in children was predicted by observed inappropriate behavior and by the lack of goal-directed activity in the classroom. Internalizing behavior was also negatively related to goal-directed activity in the classroom as well as a low proportion of time spent interacting with peers (Winsler & Wallace, 2002). Thus, emotion regulation, specifically effortful control, which is a process that allows for goal-directed behavior through attention shifting and focusing, is an important factor for success in school.

We have discussed that kindergarten presents several social and emotional demands (Rimm-Kaufman & Pianta, 2000) and that individual differences may result in problems functioning in early schooling. Central to this issue is that effortful control characterized by flexible responding may increase a child's resiliency to stress in this new challenging environment. There is further physiological evidence that supports the view that lack of regulation is related to high levels of stress. In one study, there was evidence that negative affect and extroversion, aspects related to under-control, were related to higher levels of cortisol (Davis, Donzella, Krueger, & Gunnar, 1999). Furthermore, higher levels of cortisol are thought to represent a lack of coping (Levine & Wiener, 1988). Thus, children who were more likely to display negative emotions and who were more impulsive, were more likely to exhibit physiological reactions to stress in the first week of elementary school. It is interesting to note that these children may be more likely to have problems adapting and may be more reactive to the context of school, the new roles and rules, than a child that does not have these tendencies of under-control.

In addition, young children who exhibit poor self-control and aggression are more likely to show an increase in cortisol over the day in a day care setting (Dettling, Gunnar, & Donzella, 1999). Thus, it is clear that children with behavior problems in school contexts are having a difficult time engaging in regulation skills necessary for this kind of social context.

CONCLUSIONS AND DIRECTIONS FOR FUTURE RESEARCH

In this chapter, we reviewed conceptual issues and empirical studies relevant to the development of emotion regulation and its potential links with school-readiness and performance. Beginning in infancy, children are able to make attempts to regulate their emotions, not only by signaling to caregivers to receive external support, but also by engaging in self-regulating behaviors such as comforting (e.g., thumb sucking) and focusing their attention away from sources of arousal. As children develop, more cognitively oriented skills come into use such as making attempts to change the situation, or engaging in thoughts to help feel better when the situation cannot be changed.

However, it is also important to understand individual differences in children's abilities to regulate their emotions. Research has shown that factors such as temperament (Braungart-Rieker et al., 1998; Rothbart & Derryberry, 1981), the quality of the parent–child attachment relationship (Braungart-Rieker et al., 2001; Cassidy, 1994), and overall family functioning such as the quality of the spousal relationship are related to children's feelings of security (Cummings & Davies, 1996) as well as their abilities to successfully modulate their arousal. With the entry into school, it becomes apparent that when children are having problems regulating their emotions, children also struggle with controlling their behavior (Winsler & Wallace, 2002), have more negative peer interactions (Fabes et al., 1999), and have difficulties in managing the social and cognitive challenges in the classroom setting.

We see that the processes involved in linking child, family, and school are quite complex. Our model presented at the beginning of this chapter (Figure 6.1) depicts some of the processes and pathways highlighted in this chapter. At the core of these associations lies emotion regulation. That is, emotion regulation serves to mediate the associations between child and family factors along with behavioral and academic performance in the school context. To the extent that a child is struggling in school—much like the example of David presented at the beginning of this chapter—interventionists might focus on issues related to emotion regulation. In addition, more longitudinal research is needed to examine how these various factors and processes promote school success. It should also be noted that our model is by no means a comprehensive one; additional factors such as children's cognitive and learning abilities, socioeconomic factors, quality of the school, and even cultural factors (to name a few) should also be considered, particularly if one is using these studies to inform practitioners or teachers about potential prevention or intervention strategies. Nonetheless, it becomes apparent that the processes involved in the development of emotional regulatory skills are important to study when trying to understand children's behavior and success in the classroom setting.

REFERENCES

Ahadi, S.A., & Rothbart, M.K. (1994). Temperament, development, and the big five. In C. Halverson, Jr., G. Kohnstamm, & R.Martin (Eds.), *The developing structure of temperament and personality from infancy to adulthood* (pp. 189–207). Hillsdale, NJ: Erlbaum.

Ainsworth, M.D.S. (1973). The development of infant-mother attachment. In B.M.Caldwell & J.N. Ricciuti (Eds.), *Review of child development research* (Vol. 3). Chicago: University of Chicago Press.

Ainsworth, M.D.S., Blehar, M., Waters, E., & Wall, S. (1978). *Patterns of attachment.* Hillsdale, MJ: Erlbaum.

Alexander, K., & Entwistle, D. (1988). Achievement in the first two years of school: Patterns and processes. *Monographs of the Society for Research in Child Development, 53*, (2, Serial No. 218).

Belsky, J., & Rovine, M. (1987). Temperament and attachment security in the strange situation: An empirical rapprochement. *Child Development, 58*, 787–795.

Belsky, J., Youngblade, L., Rovine, M., & Volling, B. (1991). Patterns of marital change and parent–child interaction. *Journal of Marriage and the Family, 53*, 487–498.

Bowlby, J. (1969). *Attachment: Vol. 1. Attachment and loss.* New York: Basic Books.

Blair, C. (2002). School Readiness. *American Psychologist, 57*, 111–127.

Block, J., & Block, J. H. (1980). *The California Child Q Set.* Palo Alto, CA: Consulting Press.

Braungart, J.M., & Stifter, C.A. (1991). Regulation of negative reactivity during the Strange Sitation: Temperament and attachment in 12-month-old infants. *Infant Behavior and Development, 14*, 349–364.

Braungart-Rieker, J.M., Garwood, M.M., Powers, B.P., & Notaro, P.C. (1998). Infant affect and affect regulation during the still-face paradigm with mothers and fathers: the role of infant characteristics and parent sensitivity. *Developmental Psychology, 34*, 1428–1437.

Braungart-Rieker, J.M., Garwood, M.M., Powers, B.P., & Wang, X. (2001). Maternal sensitivity, infant affect, and affect regulation during the still-face paradigm. *Child Development, 72*, 252–270.

Buss, K.A., & Goldsmith, H.H. (1998). Fear and anger regulation in infancy: Effects on the temporal dynamics of affective expression. *Child Development, 69*, 359–374.

Calkins, S.D. (1994). Origins and outcomes of individual differences in emotion regulation. *Monographs of the Society for Research in Child Development, 59* (1–2, Serial No. 240).

Campos, J.J., Barrett, K.C., Lamb, M.E., Goldsmith, H.H., & Stenberg, C. (1983). Socioemotional development. In P.H. Mussen (Series Ed.) M.M. Haith & J.J Campos (Vol. Eds.), *Handbook of child psychology: Vol. 2. Infancy and developmental psychobiology* (4th ed., pp. 783–916). New York: Wiley.

Cassidy, J. (1994). Emotion regulation: Influences of attachment relationships. *Monographs for the Society of Research in Child Development, 59* (1–2, Serial No. 240).

Cohn, J.F., Campbell, S.B., & Ross, S. (1992). Infant responses in the still-face paradigm at 6-months predicts avoidant and secure attachment at 12 months. *Development and Psychopathology, 3,* 367–376.

Cole, P.M., Michel, M.K., & Teti, L.O. (1994). The development of emotion regulation and dysregulation: A clinical perspective. *Monographs of the Society for Research in Child Development, 59* (1–2, Serial No. 240).

Cole, P.M., Zahn-Waxler, C., & Smith, K.D. (1994). Expressive control during disappointment: Variations related to preschoolers' behavior problems. *Developmental Psychology, 30,* 835–846.

Cummings, E.M., & Davies, P. (1996). Emotional security as a regulatory process in normal development and the development of psychopathology. *Development and Psychopathology, 8,* 123–139.

Davies, P.T., & Cummings, E.M. (1998). Exploring children's emotional security as a mediator of the link between marital relaions and child adjustment. *Child Development, 69,* 124–139.

Davis, E.P., Donzella, B., Krueger, W.K., & Gunnar, M.R. (1999). The start of a new school year: Individual differences in salivary cortisol response in relation to child temperament. *Developmental Psychobiology, 35,* 188–196.

Derryberry, D., & Reed, M.A. (1996). Regulatory processes and the development of cognitive representations. *Development and Psychopathology, 8,* 215–234.

Dettling, A.C., Gunnar, M.R., & Donzella, B. (1999). Cortisol levels of young children in full-day childcare centers: Relations with age and temperament. *Psychoneuroendocrinology, 24,* 519–536.

DeWolff, M.S., & van Ijzendoorn, M.H. (1997). Sensitivity and attachment: A meta-analysis on parental antecedents of infant attachment. *Child Development, 68,* 571–591.

Dodge, K.A., & Garber, J. (1991). Domains of emotion regulation. In J. Garber & K.A. Dodge (Eds.), *The development of emotion regulation and dysregulation.* Cambridge: Cambridge University Press.

Eisenberg, N., & Fabes, R. (1995). The relation of young children's vicarious emotional responding to social competence, regulation, and emotionality. *Cognition and Emotion, 9,* 203–229.

Eisenberg, N., Fabes, R., Murphy, B. Karbon, M., Smith, M., & Maszk, P. (1996). The relations of children's dispositional empathy-related responding to their emotionality and regulation , and social functioning. *Developmental Psychology, 32,* 195–209.

Eisenberg, N., Fabes, R., Shepard,S.A., Murpy, B.C., Jones, S., & Guthrie, I.K. (1998). Contemporaneous and longitudinal prediction of children's sympathy from dispositional regulation and emotionality. *Developmental Psychology, 34,* 910–924.

Eisenberg, N., Guthrie, I.K., Fabes, R.A., Reiser, M., Murphy, B.C., Holgren, R., & Losoya, S. (1997). The relations of regulation and emotionality to resiliency and competent social functioning in elementary school children. *Child Development, 68,* 295–311.

Emery, R.E. (1982). Interparental conflict and the children of discord and divorce. *Psychological Bulletin, 92,* 310–330.

Fabes, R.A., Eisenberg, N., Jones, S., Smith, M., Guthrie, I., Poulin, R., Shepard, S., & Friedman, J. (1999). Regulation, emotionality, and preschoolers' socially competent peer interactions. *Child Development, 70,* 432–442.

Field, T. (1994). The effects of mothers' physical and emotional unavailability on emotion regulation. *Monographs of the Society for Research in Child Development, 59* (1–2, Serial No. 240).

Fogel, A. (1982). Affect dynamics in early infancy: Affective tolerance. In T. Field & A. Fogel (Eds.), *Emotion and early interaction* (pp. 25–56). Hillsdale, NJ: Erlbaum.

Fox, N.A. (1994). Dynamic cerebral processes underlying emotion regulation. *Monographs for the Society of Research in Child Development, 59* (1–2, Serial No. 240).

Garner, P.W. & Estep, K.M. (2001). Emotional competence, emotion socialization, and young children's peer-related social competence. *Early Education and Development, 12,* 29–48.

Gerardi-Caulton, G. (2000). Sensitivity to spatial conflict and the development of self-regulation in children 24–36 months of age. *Developmental Science, 3,* 397–404.

Gesell, A.L., & Amatruda, G.S. (1941). *Developmental diagnosis: Normal and abnormal child development.* New York: Hoeber.

Gibson, J., & Radner, N. (1979). Attention: The perceiver as performer. In G.A. Hale & M. Lewis (Eds.), *Attention and cognitive development* (pp. 1–22). New York: Plenum.

Grolnick, W.W., Bridges, L.J., & Connell, J.P. (1996). Emotion regulation in two-year-olds: Strategies and emotional expression in four contexts. *Child Development, 67,* 928–941.

Grych, J.H. (1998). Children's appraisals of interparental conflict: Situational and contextual influences. *Journal of Family Psychology, 12,* 437–453.

Gumora, G., & Arsenio, W.F. (2002). Emotionality, emotion regulation, and school performance in middle school children. *Journal of School Psychology, 40,* 395–413.

Guralnick, M.J. (1993). Developmentally appropriate practice in the assessment and intervention of children's peer relations. *Topics in Early Childhood Special Education, 13,* 344–371.

Jimerson, S., Egeland, B., Sroufe, A., & Carlson, B. (2000). A prospective longitudinal study of high school dropouts examining multiple predictors across development. *Journal of School Psychology, 38,* 525–549.

Kessen, W., & Leutzendorff, A.W. (1963). The effect of non-nutritive sucking on movement in the human newborn. *Journal of Comparative and Physiological Psychology, 56,* 69–72.

Kochanska, G., Murray, K., & Harlan, E.T. (2000). Effortful Control in early childhood: Continuity and change, antecedents, and implications for social development. *Developmental Psychology, 36,* 220–232.

Kopp, C.B. (1982). Antecedents of self-regulation: A developmental perspective. *Developmental Psychology, 18,* 199–214.

Kopp, C.B. (1989). Regulation of distress and negative emotions: A developmental view. *Developmental Psychology, 25,* 343–354.

Ladd, G.W. & Buhs, E.S., & Seid, M. (2000). Children's initial sentiments about kindergarten: Is school liking an antecedent of early classroom participation and achievement? *Merrill-Palmer Quarterly, 46,* 255–279.

Levine, S., & Wiener, S-G (1988). Psychoendocrine aspects of mother-infant relationships in nonhuman primates. *Psychoneuroendocrinology, 13,* 143–154.

Lewitt, E.M., & Baker, L.S. (1995). School Readiness. *The Future of Children, 5,* 128–139.

Londerville, S., & Main, M. (1981). Security of attachment, compliance, and maternal training methods n the second year of life. *Developmental Psychology, 17,* 289–299.

Main. M. (1990). Cross-cultural studies of attachment organization: Recent studies, changing methodologies, and the concept of conditional strategies. *Human Development, 33,* 48–61.

Main, M., Kaplan, N., & Cassidy, J. (1985). Security in infancy, childhood, and adulthood: A move to the level of representation. In I. Bretherton & E. Waters (Eds.), *Growing points in attachment theory and research, Monographs of the Society for Research in Child Development,* pp. 66–106. Vol. 50, Nos. 1–2.

Malatesta, C.Z., & Haviland, J.M. (1985). Signals, symbols, and socialization: The modification of emotional expressiong in human development. In M. Lewis & C. Saarni (Eds.), *The socialization of emotions* (pp. 89–116). New York: Plenum Press.

Mischel, W. (1974). Processes in delay of gratification. In L. Berkowitz (Ed.), *Progress in experimental personality research* (Vol. 3, pp. 249–292). New York: Academic.

Murray, K.T., & Kochanska, G. (2002). Effortful control: Factor structure and relation to externalizing and internalizing behaviors. *Journal of Abnormal Child Psychology, 30,* 503–514.

Owen, M.T., & Cox, M.J. (1997). Marital conflict and the development of infant-parent attachment relationships. *Journal of Family Psychology, 11,* 152–164.

Parker, J.G., & Asher, S.R. (1987). Peer relations and later personal adjustment: Are low accepted children at risk? *Psychological Bulletin, 102,* 357–389.

Piaget, J. (1954). *The construction of reality in the child.* New York: Basic Books.

Pianta, R.C., & Nimetz, S.L. (1991). Relationships between children and teachers: Associations with home and classroom behavior. *Journal of Applied Developmental Psychology, 12,* 379–393.

Pianta, R.C., & Steinberg, M. (1992). Teacher–child relationships and the process of adjusting to school. *New Directions for Child Development, 57,* 61–80.

Pianta, R.C., & Walsh, D.J. (1996). *High-risk children in schools: Constructing sustaining relationships.* New York: Routledge.

Pintrich, P.R., & de Groot, E.V. (1990). Motivational and self-regulated learning components of classroom academic performance. *Journal of Educational Psychology, 82,* 33–40.

Posner, M.I., & DiGirolamo, G.J. (1998). Conflict, target detection and cognitive control. In R. Parasuraman (Ed.), *The attentive brain* (pp. 401–423). Cambridge, MA: MIT Press.

Raver, C.C. (2002). Emotions Matter: Making the case for the role of young children's Emotional development for early school readiness. *Social Policy Report, 16*(3).

Raver, C.C., Blackburn, E.K., Bancroft, M., & Torp, N. (1999). Relations betweeneffective emotional self-regulation, attentional control, and low-income preschoolers' social competence with peers. *Early Education and Development, 10,* 333–350.

Rimm-Kaufman, S.E., & Pianta, R.C. (2000). An ecological perspective on the transition to kindergarten: A theoretical framework to guide empirical research. *Journal of Applied Developmental Psychology, 21,* 491–511.

Rimm-Kaufman, S.E., Pianta, R.C., & Cox, M.J. (2000). Teachers' judgments of problems in the transition to kindergarten. *Early Childhood Research Quaterly,15,* 147–166.

Rossman, B.B.R. (1992). School-age children's perceptions of coping with distress: Strategies for emotion regulation and the moderation of adjustment. *Journal of Child Psychology and Psychiatry, 33,* 1373 – 1397.

Rothbart, M.K., & Derryberry, D. (1981). Development of individual differences in temperament. In M.E. Lamb & A.L. Brown (Eds.), *Advances in developmental psychology, vol. 1,* pp. 37–86. Hillsdale, NJ: Lawrence Erlbaum Associates.

Rothbart, M.K., Ziaie, J., & O'Boyle, C.G. (1992). Self-regulation and emotion in infancy. *New Directions for Child Development, 55,* 7–24.

Saarni, C. (1997). Coping with aversive feelings. *Motivation and Emotion, 21,* 45–63.

Shamir, H., Du Rocher-Schudlich, T., & Cummings, E.M. (2002). Marital conflict, parenting styles, and children's representations of family relationships. *Parenting: Science and Practice, 1–2,* 123–151.

Sroufe, L.A., Fox, N.E., & Pancake, V.R. (1983). Attachment and dependency in developmental perspective. *Child Development, 54,* 1615–1627.

Sroufe, L.A., & Rutter, M. (1984). The domain of developmental psychopathology. *Child Development, 55,* 17–25.

Sroufe, L.A., & Waters, E. (1977). Attachment as an organizational construct. *Child Development, 48,* 1187–1199.

Stansbury, K., & Gunnar, M.R. (1994). Adrenocortical activity and emotion regulation. *Monographs for the Society of Research in Child Development, 59*(1–2, Serial No. 240).

Stifter, C.A. & Braungart, J.M. (1995). The regulation of negative reactivity in infancy: Function and development. *Developmental Psychology, 31,* 448–455.

Stoller, S.A., & Field, T. (1982). Alteration of mother and infant behavior and heart rate during a still-face perturbation of face-to-face interaction. In T. Field & A. Fogel (Eds), *Emotion and early interaction* (pp. 57–82). Hillsdale, NJ: Erlbaum.

Thompson, R.A. (1994). Emotion regulation: A theme in search of definition. *Monographs for the Society of Research in Child Development, 59* (1–2, Serial No. 240).

Tizard, B., & Hodges, J. (1978). The effect of early institutional rearing on the development of eight-year-old children. *Journal of Child Psychology and Psychiatry, 19*, 99–118.

Toda, S., & Fogel, A. (1993). Infant response to the still-face situation at 3 and 6 months. *Developmental Psychology, 29*, 532–538.

Tronick, E.Z., Als, H., Adamson, L., Wise, S., & Brazelton, T.B. (1978). The infant's response to entrapment between contradictory messages in face-to-face interaction. *American Academy of child Psychiatry, 17*, 1–13.

Trommsdorff, G., & Friedlmeier, W. (1999). Motivational conflict and prosocial behavior in kindergarten children. *International Journal of Behavioral Development, 23*, 413–429.

von Salisch, M. (2001). Children's emotional development: Challenges in their relationships to parents, peers, and friends. *International Journal of Behavioral Development, 25*, 310–319.

Vygotsky, L. (1978). *Mind in society.* Cambridge, MA: Harvard University Press.

Walden, T.A., & Smith, M.C. (1997). Emotion regulation. *Motivation and Emotion, 21*, 7–25.

Weinberg, M.K., & Tronick, E.Z. (1994). Beyond the face: An empirical study of infant affective configurations of facial, vocal, gestural, and regulatory behaviors. *Child Development, 65*, 1503–1515.

Wentzel, K.R. (1991). Social competence at school: Relation between social responsibility and academic achievement. *Review of Educational Research, 61*, 1–24.

Winsler, A., & Wallace, G.L. (2002). Behavior problems and social skills in preschool children: Parent-teacher agreement and relations with classroom observations. *Early Education and Development, 13*, 41–58.

CHAPTER 7

YOUNG CHILDREN'S ACHIEVEMENT

Does Neighborhood Residence Matter?

**Rebecca C. Fauth, Tama Leventhal,
and Jeanne Brooks-Gunn**

INTRODUCTION

In the last 30 years, the United States has witnessed marked decreases in the economic well-being of children. In the late 1990s, 18% of all children under the age of 6 were poor; this figure is nearly double when limiting the scope to Black and Hispanic children (30% and 27%, respectively; Jargowsky, 1997; U.S. Department of Health and Human Services, 1999). Poor children and their families are more likely to grow up in areas of concentrated poverty than their non-poor counterparts. In fact, more than half of all poor children are raised in neighborhoods, primarily in urban areas, with an average poverty rate of 20%; more than 17% are reared in very poor neighborhoods with poverty rates in excess of 40% (Jargowsky, 1997; U.S. Department of Health and Human Services, 1999). Growing up in poverty, both at the family and neighborhood levels, has detrimental

Contemporary Perspectives on Families, Communities, and Schools for Young Children, pages 131–161
131

impacts on young children's well-being across multiple domains including children's school readiness and educational outcomes (see Brooks-Gunn & Duncan, 1997; Leventhal & Brooks-Gunn, 2000).

Partially as a result of these trends, neighborhoods came to the forefront of the child development research agenda. The rising number of young children growing up in poor neighborhoods was largely due to demographic shifts, beginning in the 1970s, in family composition, labor force participation, residential patterns, and industrialization as well as an influx of government funds to build public housing primarily in socially isolated areas (Hernandez, 1993; Massey & Denton, 1993; Wilson, 1987, 1997). Coinciding with these demographic changes was the resurgence of social disorganization theory (Shaw & McKay, 1942), as a way of understanding the staggering incidences of crime and delinquency experienced by poor children and families residing in urban neighborhoods. The theory purports that the constellation of certain structural factors in neighborhoods—poverty, residential immobility, and ethnic heterogeneity—impede the formation of neighborhood institutions necessary to monitor residents' behavior and promote optimal child well-being (Bursik, 1988; Kornhauser, 1978; Sampson, 1992; Sampson & Groves, 1989; Sampson & Morenoff, 1997). Finally, the developmental-ecological approach, most notably proffered by Bronfenbrenner (1979, 1989), came into vogue among researchers interested in better understanding contextual influences on children's development. These historical and theoretical occurrences were the impetus for the landmark literature reviews on neighborhood effects on children's outcomes by Jencks and Mayer (1990) and, later, by Leventhal and Brooks-Gunn (2000).

In line with these contributions, the goal of this chapter is to provide a closer examination of the methodological, empirical, and theoretical advances in examining neighborhoods and their potential impact on young children's (birth to 8-years of age) school readiness and educational outcomes, in particular children's IQ, verbal ability, and achievement test scores as well as their school performance and grade repetition. The years between birth and age 8 are an important time for children's development (see Shonkoff & Phillips, 2000, for a review); it is during this epoch that children develop the tools—including cognitive competencies—necessary for a seamless transition into school as well early academic success. Understanding how neighborhood residence may facilitate children's educational well-being through the use of empirical research may help to inform social policies targeted at young children and their primary caregivers.

The first section of the chapter highlights important methodological issues to consider when investigating neighborhoods, such as measuring neighborhood effects and appropriate study designs. Current research findings concerning neighborhood structural effects (income/SES and racial/ethnic diversity) on young children's achievement will be summarized in the second section. The following section outlines three potential pathways—institutional resources (quality and quantity of community resources), relationships and ties (parenting, home environment, and support networks), and norms and collective efficacy (community social institutions, peers, drugs, and violence)—through which neighborhood effects may operate on young children's school readiness and educational outcomes and summarizes the existing research focusing on these links. The final section will synthesize the research findings and suggest future directions for research on neighborhood contexts and young children's achievement. Although the chapter will highlight research based on studies of young children, in some circumstances, research with older children and adolescents will be drawn upon because of limited research on young children and neighborhood contexts.

METHODOLOGICAL ISSUES IN STUDYING NEIGHBORHOODS

This section highlights keys methodological issues to consider when studying neighborhood effects on young children's school readiness and educational outcomes including definitions of neighborhoods, identification and measurement of neighborhood dimensions, study designs, and sample selection problems.

Defining Neighborhoods

The geographic boundaries of a neighborhood are commonly based on data from an administrative agency such as the Census Bureau. A neighborhood is generally defined according to census tracts, areas populated by approximately 3,000 to 8,000 individuals that reflect prominent physical features frequently associated with a particular neighborhood (e.g., major streets, railroads, ethnic divisions, etc.). Other administrative data sources from, for example, schools or police districts are sometimes used (usually in concert with census data) in order to provide a more nuanced description of neighborhoods. Occasionally, researchers classify larger census units such as entire zip codes as the boundary for different neighborhoods. On a smaller scale, researchers may combine two or three adjacent and relatively homogenous tracts into "neighborhood clusters" (e.g., Brody et al., 2001; Sampson, Raudenbush, & Earls, 1997). Some researchers prefer to downsize the geography of the neighborhood and utilize census blocks or block groups (census tracts contain 1 to 4 block groups) as the boundaries between nearby neighborhoods. When neighborhood boundaries are not specifically identified in studies, residents' conceptions of neighborhood boundaries seem to approximate census tracts (Coulton, Korbin, Chan, & Su, 2001; Sampson, 1997). The identification of neighborhood boundaries when studying young children should consider the fact that smaller units such as blocks, block groups, or census tracts may more adequately capture the restricted geography of young children than larger units such as zip codes.

Neighborhood Dimensions

Distinction must be made between neighborhood structure and neighborhood processes when defining neighborhood dimensions. Neighborhood structure is captured by sociodemographic attributes including median income, employment rate, and racial/ethnic composition. Conversely, neighborhood processes include the social organizational aspects of neighborhoods such as informal social control and institutional resources. Census-based measures of neighborhood structural characteristics, most notably neighborhood income or socioeconomic status (SES), are frequently utilized in studies of neighborhood effects. It is recognized that high SES/affluence (e.g., income, percent professionals, and percent college-educated) and low SES/poverty (e.g., percent poor, percent female-headed households, percent on public assistance, and percent unemployment) may affect children differently (both compared with middle-income neighborhoods), thus warranting separate examinations of each on young children's outcomes (Brooks-Gunn, Duncan, Klebanov, & Sealand, 1993; Jencks & Mayer, 1990). Racial/ethnic diversity (e.g., percent Black, percent Latino, and percent foreign-born) and residential instability are two alternate neighborhood structural characteristics frequently considered in studies (e.g., Brooks-Gunn, Duncan, & Aber, 1997).

Unlike the neighborhood structural dimensions discussed, defining neighborhoods in terms of social organizational features allows researchers to hypothesize about the processes or pathways through which neighborhoods affect young children. Examples of social organizational characteristics include the degree of physical (e.g., abandoned housing or graffiti) and social (e.g., public drinking or prostitution) disorder within the neighborhood; informal social control which describes the degree to which residents monitor the behavior of others to ensure they act in accordance with socially accepted practices; and social cohesion which considers the quality and quantity of social connections present in neighborhoods. These types of neighborhood dimensions are not available from the Census Bureau and, as such, are typically captured via parent- or child-report. Use of the same informant for both neighborhood characteristics as well as for the individual-level measures of interest is problematic because of the confounding of reporters (i.e., a parent who is suffering from depression may rate her neighborhood more negatively than a non-depressed parent and may also rate her child as having more behavior problems than a non-depressed parent). As described elsewhere, alternative methodologies are recommended such as neighborhood observations (e.g., systematic coding of social and physical characteristics; Sampson & Raudenbush, 1999), survey of community residents (non-study participants interviewed about social organization; Sampson et al., 1997), and administrative records from state and city agencies (e.g., school quality measures from education department; Leventhal & Brooks-Gunn, 2000).

Study Designs

To study neighborhood effects on young children's achievement, four research designs have been utilized: (1) national or multisite studies, (2) city or regional studies, (3) neighborhood-based designs, and (4) experimental or quasi-experimental designs.

National or multisite studies. These studies typically include a large range of neighborhood types, which allows for variation on measures of neighborhood dimensions (Duncan, Connell, & Klebanov, 1997; Duncan & Raudenbush, 1999). Neighborhood effects are then estimated based on a few children or families from each neighborhood. Although these studies were not specifically designed to study neighborhood effects, much of the extant neighborhood research on young children has used national data sets including the National Longitudinal Survey of Youth-Child Supplement (NLSY-CS; Baker & Mott, 1989) and the Infant Health and Development Program (IHDP; Gross, Spiker, & Haynes, 1997).

City or regional studies. These studies investigate neighborhood effects within a city or metropolitan area. While the quantity and quality of neighborhoods sampled for these studies varies, the focus is frequently on poor, urban neighborhoods. The number of children per neighborhood included in regional studies is not uniform, thus potentially violating the assumption of independent observations necessary for standard analytic approaches such as Ordinary Least Squares regression (i.e., children living in the same neighborhoods are more likely to be similar on an outcome than children residing in different neighborhoods). Similarly, the variation in the number of children per neighborhood sampled as well in the range of neighborhoods included makes the use of more sophisticated techniques including hierarchical or multilevel modeling problematic (Byrk & Raudenbush, 1992). The Beginning School Study in Baltimore is an example of a regional study which examined children from young childhood through young adulthood (Entwisle, Alexander, & Olson, 1994).

Neighborhood-based studies. These studies are designed to target certain types of neighborhoods and include a representative range of neighborhood types from the population of neighborhoods examined. Furthermore, a certain number of individuals per neighborhood are sampled to ensure appropriate sample sizes for multilevel analyses (Duncan & Raudenbush, 1999). An example of a neighborhood-based study is the Project on Human Development in Chicago Neighborhoods (PHDCN) in which approximately 6,000 children and youth were sampled from 80 neighborhoods that varied by SES (3 levels) and racial/ethnic composition (7 levels; Sampson et al., 1997). Researchers using this type of study design have found, with both child and adolescent samples, large variability within neighborhoods, possibly even larger than variation found across different neighborhoods (Cook, Shagle, & Degirmencioglu, 1997; Coulton, Korbin, & Su, 1999; Elliott et al., 1996; Furstenberg, Cook, Eccles, Elder, & Sameroff, 1999).

Experimental or quasi-experimental designs. Studies of this type randomly assign families to relocate to particular types of neighborhoods. Nearly all of these studies have used housing mobility programs wherein low-income families residing in high-poverty neighborhoods were offered the opportunity to move to low-poverty neighborhoods. Assignment of families to move is usually randomized (e.g., lottery-based) or quasi-randomized (e.g., based on housing availability), which minimizes selection bias. Examples include the Gautreaux Program in Chicago based on court-ordered housing desegregation and the Moving to Opportunity for Fair Housing Demonstration (MTO) in five U.S. cities, a U.S. Department of Housing and Urban Development funded research demonstration.

Selection Bias

The most common criticism of the first three study designs summarized is that they may suffer from selection bias. Taking economic circumstances into account, families still have some degree of choice regarding the neighborhoods in which they live; residence in a highly disadvantaged neighborhood may be seen as a choice dependent upon constructs not captured by the variables in the model such as parental depression or motivation. Child (e.g., sex, age) and family (e.g., income, parents education, family structure) demographic characteristics are frequently included in analytic models as an attempt to account for problems relating to selection bias. While this approach is preferable to the alternative option of only including neighborhood-level characteristics in models, it does not completely alleviate problems due to selection because neighborhood dimensions are defined, in part, by family composition. Variables suspected of influencing neighborhood choice such as parent mental health are likely to be unmeasured in studies and, therefore, excluded from models (Duncan et al., 1997; Tienda, 1991). Omission of these variables could lead to under- or overestimation of neighborhood effects. Although the use of sibling or cousin models, which hold family characteristics constant, instrumental variable analysis, which minimizes unmeasured correlations between neighborhood characteristics and children's outcomes, and behavior genetic models, which differentiate between genetic and environmental influences, have been used by researchers to address selection issues (Aaronson, 1997; Caspi, Taylor, Moffitt, & Plomin, 2000; Foster & McLanahan, 1996), experimental designs are the preferred method of tackling selection bias as residents are randomly assigned to neighborhoods. Not surprisingly, experimental studies of this sort are rare.

NEIGHBORHOODS AND YOUNG CHILDREN'S SCHOOL READINESS AND EDUCATIONAL OUTCOMES

The literature review presented below follows from a previous survey of neighborhood research from 1990 to 1998 (Leventhal & Brooks-Gunn, 2000) by integrating the latest work that has been completed examining the effects of neighborhoods on young children's school readiness and educational outcomes. For very young children (birth to 4-years of age), IQ and verbal ability scores are the primary outcomes considered. Reading and math achievement as well as school performance (e.g., grades) and grade repetition also are examined for school aged children (5- to 8-years). The studies reviewed focus on the direct impacts of two census-based neighborhood structural dimensions, namely, income/SES (affluence and poverty) and racial/ethnic diversity, on children's outcomes as well as experimental evidence linking moves from high- to low-poverty neighborhoods on children's achievement. Due to potential selection biases as described above, each of the studies mentioned in this section statistically controlled for individual and family sociodemographic characteristics such as child sex and age; family income, composition, and race/ethnicity; and maternal education and age. Indirect (mediated) neighborhood effects will be considered in the subsequent section.

Income/SES

Neighborhood-level income or SES is most consistently associated with children's school readiness and educational outcomes (after accounting for child and family characteristics). Furthermore, it is generally the case that high-SES or affluence has stronger impacts on children's school readiness and educational outcomes than does low-SES or poverty, especially for White children. Most of the studies are based on large, multisite samples including the IHDP and the NLSY-CS with some additional experimental evidence from studies where low-income children were relocated from poor to less poor neighborhoods. See Table 7.1 for a summary of the empirical evidence presented.

Using large national datasets, Brooks-Gunn and colleagues found that residing in an affluent neighborhood (proportion of residents with incomes greater than $30,000) compared with a middle-income neighborhood (proportion of residents with incomes between $10,000 and $30,000) was positively associated with 3-year-olds', but not 1- or 2-year-olds', IQ scores (Klebanov, Brooks-Gunn, McCarton, & McCormick, 1998) and that these effects may be stronger for White than Black children (Brooks-Gunn et al., 1993; Chase-Lansdale, Gordon, Brooks-Gunn, & Klebanov, 1997). The positive association between residence in a high-SES neighborhood and children's IQ scores remains when children enter school at 5- to 6-years of age (Duncan, Brooks-Gunn, & Klebanov, 1994). Similar positive effects of neighborhood affluence are found on these early school-aged children's reading and verbal ability (Chase-Lansdale & Gordon, 1996; Chase-Lansdale et al., 1997), although the strength of these effects may depend on the children's sex (male) and race/ethnicity (White). A recent Canadian study corroborated these findings; neighborhood affluence was positively associated with 4- to 5-year olds' verbal ability scores (Kohen, Brooks-Gunn, Leventhal, & Hertzman, 2002).

Several studies have found effects of neighborhood low-SES/poverty on children's outcomes. In one U.S. national sample, a negative association was found between neighborhood poverty and girls' math achievement (Chase-Lansdale et al., 1997). Two non-U.S. studies in Britain and Canada have also found negative associations between neighborhood deprivation/poverty and 4- to 5-year-old children's verbal ability scores (Kohen et al., 2002; McCulloch & Joshi, 2001). Additional studies using related indicators of neighborhood low-SES report a similar pattern of results. For example, among fifth grade children from working- to lower-class neighborhoods in Milwaukee, an association was found between neighborhood SES risk (e.g., large proportion of female-headed households, low mean income, and low adult education attainment) and children's poor performance in school which included scores on standardized reading and math

Table 7.1. Summary of Studies Used to Examine Neighborhood Effects on Young Children's School Readiness and Educational Outcomes

Study	Design	Sample	Neighborhood Data	Findings from Studies
Children of National Longitudinal Survey of Youth (NLSY-CS)	Children born to women in nationally representative study assessed biennially since 1986	(1) 673 children aged 5–6 years (approx. 40% Black) (2) 882 3–4-year olds and 697 5–6-year olds (approx. 40% Black)	1980 Census tract data; 70% only study child in tract	(1) *Chase-Lansdale & Gordon* (1996): SES positive association with 5–6-year olds' PPVT-R and reading achievement; racial similarity positive association with 5–6-year olds' PPVT-R. (2) *Chase-Lansdale, Gordon, Brooks-Gunn, & Klebanov* (1997): High SES positive association with 5–6-year olds' PPVT-R (boys only) and reading achievement (Whites only); low SES negative association with girls' math achievement; male joblessness negative association with boys' reading achievement and positive association with girls' reading and math achievement; ethnic diversity negative association with Whites' PPVT-R
Infant Health & Development Program (IHDP)	Early intervention for LBW premature infants at 8 sites across country	(1) 894 3-year olds (over 50% Black) (2) 793 3–5-year olds (approx. 60% Black) (3) 895 5-year olds (approx. 55% Black) (4) 347 1- to 3-year olds	1980 Census tract data; average 1.1 cases per tract	(1) *Brooks-Gunn, Duncan, Klebanov & Sealand* (1993): Affluence positive association with 3-year olds' IQ (2) *Chase-Lansdale, Gordon, Brooks-Gunn, & Klebanov* (1997): High SES positive association with White 3-year olds' IQ (boys only) and boys' PPVT-R and 5-year olds' PPVT-R (boys only) and verbal IQ; ethnic diversity negative association with White 5-year olds' verbal IQ and PPVT-R (3) *Duncan, Brooks-Gunn, & Klebanov* (1994): Affluence positive association with 5-year olds' IQ (4) *Klebanov, Brooks-Gunn, McCarton, & McCormick* (1998): Affluence & low-income no association with 1–2-year olds' IQ; affluence positive association with 3-year olds' IQ

table continues

139

Table 7.1. Summary of Studies Used to Examine Neighborhood Effects on Young Children's School Readiness and Educational Outcomes (Cont.)

Study	Design	Sample	Neighborhood Data	Findings from Studies
Canadian National Longitudinal Survey of Children and Youth (NLSCY)	Clustered probability sample of Canadian residential households with children 0–11-years old	3,350 children aged 4–5-years	1991 Census tract data; average 1.3 cases per tract	*Kohen, Brooks-Gunn, Leventhal, & Hertzman* (2002): Affluence positive association with 4–5-year olds' PPVT-R; poverty negative association with 4–5-year olds' PPVT-R
British National Child Development Study (NCDS)	Sample of all 17,000 people born in Britain during a week in 1958 and their children	2290 4–18-year olds from 1532 families	1991 Census tract data	*McCulloch & Joshi* (2001): Negative association between neighborhood deprivation score and 4–5-year olds' PPVT (only significant difference between most and least deprived)
Longitudinal study of children's development	Students drawn from Milwaukee public schools	168 5th graders (approx. 50% Black)	1990 Census tract data; police department records of crime; child and parent perceptions of neighborhood danger	*Shumow, Vandell, & Posner* (1999): High SES/low crime positive association with 5th graders' school performance
Upstate New York Sample	Students drawn from urban school district	1,040 8–11-year-olds (approx. 75% Black)	1980 Census tract data	*Halpern-Felsher et al.* (1997): Low SES positive association with 8–11-year-old Black males' educational risk
Gautreaux Study	Quasi-experimental design	342 Black and Latino families	N/A	*Rosenbaum, Kulieke, & Rubinowitz* (1988): Moves to more affluent suburbs positive association with 6–18-year olds' placement in special education programs compared with children who remained in high-poverty urban neighborhoods
Moving to Opportunity (Baltimore site evaluation)	Randomized design in 5 cities	1384 mostly Black & Latino 5–18-year olds	1990 Census data	*Ludwig, Ladd, & Duncan* (2001): Moving to low poverty neighborhoods positive association with 5–12-year olds' reading and math achievement compared with children who remained in high-poverty neighborhoods
Moving to Opportunity (New York City site evaluation)	Randomized design in 5 cities	588 Black & Latino 6–18-year olds	1990 Census data	*Leventhal & Brooks-Gunn* (2004): Moving to low-poverty neighborhoods positive association with 6–10-year old boys' grade repetition compared with children who remained in high-poverty neighborhoods

Note: PPVT-R = Peabody Picture Vocabulary Test-Revised

tests as well as children's school grades (Shumow, Vandell, & Posner, 1999). Another study which examined a large sample of urban children aged 8- to 11-years from New York state found that the rate of male joblessness in a neighborhood was positively associated with Black boys' educational risk (Halpern-Felsher et al., 1997).

Recent evidence using experimental data from children who participated in the MTO demonstration provides mixed results. Five- to 12-year-old children who moved to low-poverty neighborhoods in Baltimore scored 7% higher on standardized reading and math tests than children who remained in high-poverty neighborhoods (Ludwig, Ladd, & Duncan, 2001). Evidence from the New York City MTO found that male children 6- to 10-years of age who moved from high- to low-poverty neighborhoods were marginally more likely to repeat a grade than their peers who remained in high-poverty neighborhoods 2.5 years following relocation (Leventhal & Brooks-Gunn, 2004). Early results from the Gautreaux Program in Chicago found both positive and negative impacts of moving from high-poverty, urban neighborhoods into low-poverty, suburban neighborhoods (Rosenbaum, Kulieke, & Rubinowitz, 1988). Educational standards were considerably higher in the suburban schools compared with inner-city schools, yet children in the suburban schools did not fare worse academically. Moreover, the children expressed more positive attitudes about their new, suburban schools compared with their old, urban schools. On the down side, however, children who moved to the suburbs were more likely to be placed in special education classrooms than they were in the inner-city.

Ethnic Heterogeneity

Only a few studies have documented significant negative associations between neighborhood racial/ethnic heterogeneity or diversity (presence of ethnic minorities and foreign-born residents) and children's achievement (controlling for family characteristics including SES). Specifically, residence in an ethnically diverse neighborhood was negatively associated with 5- and 6-year-old children's verbal ability scores in two large studies of young children (Chase-Lansdale & Gordon, 1996; Chase-Lansdale et al., 1997). This association was stronger for White than Black children.

PATHWAYS OF NEIGHBORHOOD EFFECTS
ON YOUNG CHILDREN'S SCHOOL READINESS
AND EDUCATIONAL OUTCOMES

The research presented in the previous section highlights direct associations between the type of neighborhood children reside in and their school readiness and educational outcomes. While informative, these studies do not illustrate the potential pathways through which these neighborhood effects are transmitted to young children. Although not yet widely tested empirically, many experts believe neighborhoods influence children indirectly, operating through (or mediated by) a variety of mechanisms including community social organization, families, schools, and peers (see Jencks & Mayer, 1990; Leventhal & Brooks-Gunn, 2000, for reviews). The effects of neighborhoods on children's achievement may also depend upon (or interact with) the presence of other influences such as the family environment. Empirical investigations of these hypotheses have been thwarted primarily due to the lack of a coherent theoretical framework delineating the pathway between neighborhoods and particular outcomes for children of a certain age as well as by methodological limitations, namely, appropriate study designs (e.g., neighborhood-based designs) and neighborhood measures.

Building on previous theoretical developments (Conger, Ge, Elder, Lorenz, & Simons, 1994; Jencks & Mayer, 1990; McLoyd, 1990; Sampson et al., 1997; Shaw & McKay, 1942), a recent review of the current neighborhood research highlighted three potential explanatory models for neighborhood effects on children's outcomes, each concentrating on a different pathway of influence (Leventhal & Brooks-Gunn, 2000). The first model, institutional resources, hypothesizes that the availability, accessibility, affordability, and quality of community resources transmit neighborhood effects to young children's outcomes. Relationships and ties, the second model, posits that parental characteristics, behavior, support networks, and the home environment mediate the influence of neighborhoods on children's outcomes. Finally, the norms and collective efficacy model focuses on the role of community formal and informal institutions in place to monitor residents' behavior, most notably peer group behavior, and physical risk to residents as potential mediators.

The theoretical frames are intended to complement, rather than conflict, with each other. That is, institutional resources (e.g., child care centers) or relationships and ties (e.g., home environment) may better account for the association between residence in a high-SES neighborhood and school readiness than would the norms/collective efficacy model. Furthermore, the salience of one model may depend upon the age of the child. For example, the norms/collective efficacy may be most influential for school-age children as younger children, under 4 years of age, may have limited access to peer groups. While both the relationships and ties and the institutional resources pathways will be pertinent for all young children (birth to 8-years of age), the specific aspect of each pathway that most strongly influences children may differ depending on children's age. The three theoretical models are presented in more depth with a focus on aspects of each model that are most relevant for young children's achievement.

Institutional Resources

The quality, quantity, and accessibility (both economic and physical) of learning, recreational, and medical facilities as well as child care and schools are relevant to young children's educational and school readiness outcomes. Community-level analyses exploring the role of neighborhood resources on children's outcomes are rare; thus, the relevant data on each community resource is extrapolated to inform how these resources may mediate neighborhood effects on children's achievement.

The presence of learning activities and centers within the community such as libraries, family resource centers, literacy programs, and museums families can utilize to stimulate their children's learning may facilitate their educational and school readiness outcomes. Although one study of very young children found that learning experiences outside of the home did not mediate neighborhood structural effects on 3-year-old children's IQ scores (Klebanov et al., 1998). Additional research with school-age children is warranted because as children age they likely have greater access to these resources than their younger counterparts. The presence of organized social and recreational activities including sports programs, art and theater programs, and community centers may also foster children's well-being. Contrary to expectations, one study found that family participation in recreation or sports programs was associated with neighborhood poverty in a nonlinear fashion; participation was lowest for residents in moderately poor neighborhoods and highest for families residing in high-poverty neighborhoods (Rankin & Quane, 2000). Although access to these supplementary programs may be limited in moderately low-income neighborhoods, research suggests that when neighborhoods have few learning, recreational, or social activities readily available, parents will utilize alternate strategies to obtain these resources for their children such as reaching out extralocally to nearby communities (Elder, Eccles, Ardelt, & Lord, 1995; Jarrett, 1997; Parke & O'Neil, 1999).

For preschool children, the availability, accessibility, and quality of child care available within the community are important institutional resources through which neighborhood effects may be transmitted to children's school readiness. A large body of research exists highlighting the benefits of high quality child care and early intervention programs for children's cognitive, socioemotional, and physical development as well as on parenting outcomes (Andrews et al., 1982; Benasich, Brooks-Gunn, & Clewell, 1992; Brooks-Gunn, Berlin, & Fuligni, 2000; Brooks-Gunn et al., 1994; Campbell et al., 2001; Campbell & Ramey, 1994; Erickson, Korfmacher, & Egeland, 1992; Johnson & Walker, 1991; Liaw & Brooks-Gunn, 1994; Love et al., 2002; McKey et al., 1985; Olds et al., 1997). Low-income parents who do not receive government subsidies or vouchers for child care may face extreme difficulties accessing affordable, high quality child care for their children. In fact, one study found that the quantity and quality of child care in poor neighborhoods were low, which indicates that child care may be a resource for which residents in these neighborhoods compete (Fuller, Coonerty, Kipnis, & Choong, 1997).

Among school-age children, schools represent a prominent community institutional resource that likely influences their educational outcomes. The social and economic make-up of the neighborhood may shape school characteristics including quality, climate, and demographics, which may then influence children's outcomes (see Jencks & Mayer, 1990). A study utilizing experimental data found that low-income children who moved from high-poverty neighborhoods to low- and moderately low-poverty neighborhoods were more likely to attend schools with higher aggregated pass rates on achievement tests than children who remained in high-poverty neighborhoods. These discrepancies in school environment were primarily attributable to neighborhood structure (Ludwig & Ladd, 1998). School-age children may also benefit from after-school programs. The rewards of these types of programs may be especially pronounced for low-income children residing in high-crime neighborhoods where the alternative to after-school programs may be self-care (see Vandell & Shumow, 1999).

The final community resource that may serve as a mediator of neighborhood effects on young children's outcomes is access to medical services. The quantity of health-related services in a community is generally excluded from studies of child health. Evidence exists that access to certain types of medical facilities (e.g., primary vs. emergency care) may vary depending upon neighborhood SES (Brooks-Gunn, McCormick, Klebanov, & McCarton, 1998).

Relationships and Ties

According to the relationships and ties model, parental relationships, parental mental health, and parenting are the conduits between neighborhood effects and young children's cognitive and educational outcomes. The literature on economic disadvantage and parental unemployment forges a pathway between economic hardship and children's outcomes through parents' mental health and, subsequently, their parenting techniques (Conger et al., 1994; McLoyd, 1990). Within this framework, parents' social supports are believed to moderate/mediate parents' well-being and their behavior. Expansion of this framework to explore the role of neighborhood disadvantage on parenting vis-à-vis parents' psychological well-being may be useful. While scant research exists that examines this expanded framework, studies have examined associations between neighborhoods and various parenting mechanisms and parental mental health. Although many of the studies mentioned in this section examine children's mental health outcomes, a large body of research has established a link between children's mental health and their cognitive and academic outcomes (see Fauth, Brady-Smith, & Brooks-Gunn, 2003; Hinshaw, 1992, for reviews).

More mentally and physically healthy parents are better able to interact and act as a supportive presence for their children, as well as stimulate children's cognitive development (Jackson, Brooks-Gunn, Huang, & Glassman, 2000; Lovejoy, Graczyk, O'Hare, & Neuman, 2000; Zaslow & Eldred, 1998). Neighborhood effects are thought to influence a variety of parental characteristics such as mental and physical health, irritability, coping skills, and efficacy. Ample evidence exists citing the association between neighborhood structural conditions, most notably SES, and adults' mental and physical health (e.g., Cubbin, LeClere, & Smith, 2000; Diez Roux et al., 2001; Goldsmith, Holzer, & Manderscheid, 1998; Kahlmeier, Schindler, Grize, & Braun-Fahrlander, 2001; Malmstrom, Johansson, & Sundquist, 2001; Ross, 2000; Ross & Mirowsky, 2001). Moreover, recent experimental evidence found that low-income parents who moved from high- to low-poverty neighborhoods reported improved mental and physical health compared with parents who remained in high-poverty neighborhoods (Katz, Kling, & Liebman, 2001; Leventhal & Brooks-Gunn, in press).

Parents' access to family members and friends and other social connections within the neighborhood may buffer children from the deleterious effects of neighborhood poverty via improved parental mental health and parenting (Cook et al., 1997; Conger et al., 1994; Elder et al., 1995; McLoyd, 1990; Ross & Jang, 2000; Ross, Reynolds, & Geis, 2000). Another potential benefit of neighborhood social networks for parents of younger children, is that these nearby family and friends can serve as informal child care providers (Logan & Spitze, 1994). Density of support may vary by neighborhood SES and racial/ethnic diversity with the strongest levels of social support found in middle-income (versus with poor and affluent neighborhoods) as well as those with high immigrant, primarily Latino, populations (Klebanov, Brooks-Gunn, & Duncan, 1994; Molnar, Buka, Brennan, & Earls, in press; Rosenbaum, Popkin, Kaufman, & Rusin, 1991).

Social support may do little to bolster positive parenting in the most disadvantaged communities. One study found that as neighborhood quality declines, the positive association between social support and maternal nurturance and the negative association between social support and punishment were attenuated (Ceballo & McLoyd, 2002). Although not a neighborhood effect per se, childhood moves may negatively impact children's educational outcomes due, in part, to subsequent declines in social relationships following residential relocation (Pribesh & Downey, 1999). Finally, a number of studies have found that neighborhoods with high rates of child maltreatment and abuse were generally lacking social resources compared with low-risk neighborhoods, regardless of neighborhood SES (Deccio, Horner, & Wilson, 1994; Garbarino & Kostelny, 1992; Garbarino & Sherman, 1980; Korbin & Coulton, 1997).

Parental behaviors that may be affected by neighborhood conditions, especially poverty and danger, include warmth, harshness, and supervision and monitoring. Residence in poor, dangerous neighborhoods was associated with lower maternal warmth for mothers of 3-year-old children (Klebanov et al., 1994; Pinderhughes, Nix, Foster, & Jones, 2001) and higher rates of hostile control and inconsistent discipline for mothers of kindergarteners (Hill & Herman-Stahl, 2002). Although conducted with adolescent children, Simons and his colleagues (1996) found that the effect of community disadvantage on boys' externalizing and internalizing behavior problems was mediated by quality of parenting (i.e., warmth, harshness, hostility, and communication). Nurturing, supportive parenting may help to buffer children from some of the negative consequences of growing up in a disadvantaged neighborhood including affiliation with deviant peers (Brody et al., 2001) and exposure to violence (O'Donnell, Schwab-Stone, & Muyeed, 2002). Research on family economic hardship reveals that parental stress and anxiety, resulting from residence in poor, dangerous neighborhoods, may lead to increases in harsh parenting (Conger et al., 1994; McLoyd, 1990). One study did, in fact, find that neighborhood danger was positively associated with the use of harsh control and verbal aggression among parents (Earls, McGuire, & Shay, 1994). A recent study using data from a neighborhood-based design found positive associations between neighborhood concentrated disadvantage and crime and parent-to-child physical aggression (Molnar et al., 2003).

High levels of parental supervision and monitoring may be related to neighborhood poverty and danger and could serve to insulate children from harmful community influences, which may then promote school readiness and later school success, a notion supported by qualitative data (Furstenberg, 1993; Jarrett, 1997, 1999). The bulk of empirical studies that have supported the link between neighborhood disadvantage, parental supervision, and positive children's outcomes have been with adolescent samples, given the salience of these parenting dimensions for this age group (Gonzales, Cauce, Friedman, & Mason, 1996; Lamborn, Dornbusch, & Steinberg, 1996; Taylor, 2000).

Several aspects of the home environment may mediate the association between neighborhood effects and children's outcomes, namely the learning and physical environment, the presence of routines and structure, and exposure to violence. The provision of learning experiences within the home includes the presence of reading materials, children's work space, and age-appropriate toys within the home (Bradley, 1995; Caldwell & Bradley, 1984). One study found that the positive association between neighborhood affluence and kindergarten and preschool children's IQ and vocabulary scores were mediated by the home learning environment (Klebanov, Brooks-Gunn, Chase-Lansdale, & Gordon, 1997). Another study revealed that the quality of the home environment accounted for the association between parental report of neighborhood risk and early school-age children's social competence and reading achievement as reported by teachers (Greenberg, Coie, Lengua, & Pinderhughes, 1999).

The physical environment of the home includes such characteristics as safety, cleanliness, space allocation, lighting, and décor (Bradley, 1995; Caldwell & Bradley, 1984). Residence in a neighborhood with a high proportion of poor residents is unfavorably associated with the quality of the physical home environment (Klebanov et al., 1994). Experimental and non-experimental studies have documented associations between neighborhood SES and children's health outcomes (e.g., injuries, asthma), which may be due, in part, to the physical quality of the home and its immediate environs (Durkin, Davidson, Kuhn, & O'Connor, 1994; Katz et al., 2001).

The provision of structure and routines within the home including regular mealtimes, homework, and bedtimes times are thought to be central to children's development and help to promote familial strength and solidarity (Boyce, Jensen, James, & Peacock, 1983; Bradley, 1995). Albeit empirically unsupported, Wilson (1987, 1991) maintains that the lack of organizational capacity in poor neighborhoods makes it difficult for parents to provide regulated structure and routine in children's lives. This link needs to be examined further especially in terms of how structure and routines in the home affect children's school readiness and educational outcomes, although one qualitative study found that parents residing in poor neighborhoods often institute in-home learning routines (Jarrett, 1997).

Finally, children's exposure to violence (via witnessing or victimization) within the home and community is another mechanism through which neighborhood effects may be transmitted to children; although most studies have focused on children's mental health outcomes as opposed to achievement. Research has shown that low-income children growing up in the inner-city are exposed to high levels of violence even in their early years (Buka, Stichick, Birdthistle, & Earls, 2001; Martinez & Richters, 1993; Richters & Martinez, 1993). Children's exposure to violence has been linked to adverse mental health outcomes with potentially long-term effects such as behavior problems, depression, anxiety, oppositional and conduct disorders, and alcohol use, as well as school-related problems (Aneshensel & Sucoff, 1996; Buka et al., 2001; Fitzpatrick, 1993; Gorman-Smith & Tolan, 1998; Margolin & Gordis, 2000; Osofsky, 1999; Schwab-Stone et al., 1995; Schwab-Stone et al., 1999).

Norms and Collective Efficacy

This third model draws from social disorganization theory and related work on community collective efficacy (Sampson, 1992; Sampson et al., 1997; Shaw & McKay, 1942). Social disorganization theory posits that neighborhood disadvantage including high rates of poverty, single-parent families, and high mobility, intrudes upon social organizational processes in neighborhoods resulting in fewer formal and informal regulatory mechanisms that serve as monitors of residents', especially youth's behavior. Collective efficacy comprises the extent of intra-neighborhood social connections and the willingness of neighbors to intervene on behalf of their community, which then facilitates the community's ability to maintain public order (Sampson et al., 1999; Sampson et al., 1997). Neighborhood collective efficacy and norms are disrupted when structural change occurs such as the loss of local employment opportunities or settlement of the area by immigrants (Coulton & Pandey, 1992; Wilson, 1987, 1997). A number of researchers have empirically examined various components of this model. Much of this work, however, has focused on adolescent samples and has examined non-school-related outcomes.

Peers, the central agent through which community-level socialization may affect children, are especially influential when community institutions and norms fail to regulate peer group behavior (Sampson, 1992; Sampson & Groves, 1989; Shaw & McKay, 1942). Research focusing on adolescent outcomes has found that the influence of peers both mediates and moderates neighborhood effects on youth's outcomes (Dubow, Edwards, & Ippolito, 1997; Elliott et al., 1996; Gonzales et al., 1996; Sampson & Groves, 1989; Simons et al., 1996). One study found that contact with well-functioning neighborhood peers was positively associated with youths' academic well-being (Darling & Steinberg, 1997). Although peer influences are strongest during adolescence, younger children may still be affected by fellow children. For instance, a study of preschool children found that most peer interactions and exposure to aggressive peers occurred in neighborhood settings as opposed to other salient early childhood settings including child care, family, and organized play groups. Furthermore, poor children from single-parent homes were most likely to be exposed to these aggressive neighborhood peers (Sinclair, Pettit, Harrist, Dodge, & Bates, 1994). Aggressive play may be most prevalent in unmonitored settings.

The absence of community formal and informal institutions are thought to be associated with pervasiveness of risk to residents (e.g., danger, violence, crime, and access to illegal or harmful substances). In fact, a Canadian study found strong negative associations between neighborhood disorder (e.g., persons arguing, shouting, fighting in a hostile or threatening manner, as observed by interviewers) and preschool aged children's verbal ability after controlling for family and neighborhood structural dimensions as well as maternal mental health (Kohen et al., 2002). Also, neighborhood disorder appeared to mediate the effect of neighborhood affluence on children's verbal scores. Neighborhood characteristics thought to be associated with community social organization such as poverty, residential instability, and child care burden were related to community levels of child maltreatment in a number of studies (Coulton, Korbin, & Su, 1996; Coulton, Korbin, Su, & Chow, 1995; Korbin & Coulton, 1997). Finally, across two housing programs in which poor families moved from high- to low-poverty neighborhoods, parents reported getting away from drugs and gangs as their primary motivation for moving (Briggs, 1997; Goering et al., 1999). Follow-ups of these mobility programs revealed that children who moved to low-poverty neighborhoods were less likely to be exposed to violence than peers who remained in high-poverty neighborhoods (Fauth, Leventhal, & Brooks-Gunn, in press; Katz et al., 2001).

SUMMARY, POLICY IMPLICATIONS, AND FUTURE DIRECTIONS

The importance of the early years on children's brain and cognitive development has been in the forefront of child development research for nearly a decade (Shatz, 1992; Shonkoff & Phillips, 2000; Shore, 1997). Evidence suggests that early childhood may be a critical period of development in which economic disadvantage can have particularly pernicious effects on children's achievement (Klebanov et al., 1998; Smith, Brooks-Gunn, & Klebanov, 1997). Neighborhoods are an important developmental context to consider when explaining the effects of poverty on children, especially since poor families are more likely to reside in areas of concentrated poverty that non-poor families. To this end, this chapter reviewed the existing evidence on neighborhood effects on young children's school readiness and educational outcomes. The empirical evidence was separated into direct neighborhood effects on children's outcomes as well as possible pathways of influences ("indirect" effects). Methodological considerations were also presented.

Residence in structurally advantaged neighborhoods was favorably associated with children's scores on a range of school readiness measures as early as 3-years of age (independent of family SES). These effects persisted well into children's entry into formal schooling. The lack of neighborhood effects on very young children's (birth- to 2-years of age) school readiness outcomes is most likely due to the importance of more proximal familial influences during the early years during the preschool years and beyond, more distal contextual influences, such as neighborhoods, become increasingly important for development. There was also some evidence that boys may benefit more than girls from residence in a high-SES neighborhood, which could be a function of greater parental autonomy granted to boys (compared with girls) or greater sensitivity to social context influences (see, e.g., literature on early maternal employment; Brooks-Gunn, Waldfogel, & Han, 2002; Desai, Chase-Lansdale, & Michael, 1989; Harvey, 1999). Finally, several studies documented unfavorable associations between neighborhood structural disadvantage and children's educational outcomes.

Overall, the magnitude of neighborhood effects reported in these studies was small in comparison to the estimated impacts of family-level variables on outcomes. Nonetheless, neighborhood effects accounted for a small to modest proportion of the variance in the outcomes, above and beyond individual- and family-level characteristics. Evidence from the few experimental studies that have included younger children in their samples corroborates the non-experimental work. Neighborhood effects were generally larger in these studies than in the nonexperimental literature (particularly for mental health outcomes, which were not reviewed here; Katz et al., 2001; Leventhal & Brooks-Gunn, 2003).

The mechanisms behind neighborhood effects on children are likely to be varied and intricate. As such, a large portion of this chapter was dedicated to explaining three possible pathways connecting neighborhoods to young children's school readiness and educational outcomes. Although three theoretical frames were presented, it is likely that the first two, institutional resources and relationships and ties, exert a greater influence on younger children than the norms and collective efficacy model, which may play a greater part in the development of adolescent children. That is, young children's restricted exposure to their neighborhoods may reduce the salience of neighborhood-level processes, such as peer groups, during their development. In addition, norms and collective mechanisms may be less operative for children's educational outcomes than their behavior problems and mental health. The limited research testing indirect pathways attests to the intricacy of explaining neighborhood effects on children's outcomes.

Future research will need to build on the existing neighborhood research base by conducting more conceptually driven work as well as designing studies that overcome some of the methodological hurdles that have impeded this field of study. Such a charge will entail studies designed to test for neighborhood effects by permitting examination of within- and between-neighborhood variation in children's educational outcomes. In addition, many important neighborhood process measures, such as social networks and social control as well as individual- and family-level mechanisms (e.g., home learning environment) must be assessed in conjunction with high-quality data on children's achievement. The use of community surveys (independent samples from study participants), systematic observations of neighborhoods, and available administrative databases (e.g., school quality data from education departments) are recommended for tapping neighborhood processes. Experimental studies as well as quasi and natural experiments where residents from one type of neighborhood (e.g., poor) relocate to new neighborhoods (e.g., nonpoor) are another preferred method of assessing neighborhood effects, as these studies help to alleviate analytical difficulties stemming from selection bias. More research focusing on neighborhood effects on young children's (0- to 8-years of age) outcomes is needed to fill in the gaps in existing research, as well as to clarify how neighborhood influences may differentially affect younger and older children. Along the same lines, longitudinal studies examining the timing, duration, and persistence of neighborhood income (both affluence and poverty) on children's development are needed. These subtleties have been examined at the family level and do seem to affect the impact of family income on children's outcomes (Duncan & Brooks-Gunn, 1997).

Together, the empirical research reviewed on neighborhood effects (direct and indirect) on children's educational outcomes reveals that even in young childhood, social contexts beyond the family have important developmental consequences. Greater understanding of the dynamics and pathways of neighborhood influences on children's achievement will help to better inform the kinds of policies that should be implemented including the targets of interventions, timing of interventions, and potential consequences of interventions. The positive associations between neighborhood affluence and children's school readiness and educational outcomes imply that relocating poor families to high-SES, resource rich neighborhoods may be a sound policy strategy, yet more research is needed to better understand why these types of interventions work (e.g., improved school quality, more employment opportunities for parents, fewer deviant peers, etc.), at what stage in children's development they are best implemented, and potential risks of residential mobility on low-SES children's outcomes.

Researchers and policymakers also need to consider how poor neighborhoods can be improved as residential mobility may not be an appealing option for all families. The existing neighborhood research on young children's achievement provides a foundation for future studies aimed at designing policies to address neighborhood inequities in child outcomes.

ACKNOWLEDGMENTS

The authors would like to thank the National Science Foundation, the National Institute of Child Health and Human Development, and the Spencer Foundation. Additional support was provided by the MacArthur Foundation. Correspondence regarding this paper should be addressed to: Rebecca C. Fauth, National Center for Children and Families, Box 39, 525 West 120th Street, New York, NY 10027; Tel: (212) 678-3904; Fax: (212) 678-3676; and email: RCF25@columbia.edu.

REFERENCES

Aaronson, D. (1997). Sibling estimates of neighborhood effects. In J. Brooks-Gunn, G.J. Duncan & J.L. Aber (Eds.), *Neighborhood poverty: Vol. 2. Policy implications in studying neighborhoods* (pp. 80–93). New York: Russell Sage Foundation.

Andrews, S.R., Blumenthal, J.B., Johnson, D.L., Kahn, A.J., Ferguson, C.J., Lasater, T.M., et al. (1982). The skills of mothering: A study of Parent Child Development Centers (New Orleans, Birmingham, Houston). *Monographs of the Society for Research in Child Development, 47*(6, Serial No. 198).

Aneshensel, C.S., & Sucoff, C.A. (1996). The neighborhood context of adolescent mental health. *Journal of Health and Social Behavior, 37*, 293–310.

Baker, P.C., & Mott, F.L. (1989). *NLSY child handbook 1989: A guide and resource document for the National Longitudinal Survey of Youth 1986 Child Data.* Columbus: Center for Human Resources Research, Ohio State University.

Benasich, A.A., Brooks-Gunn, J., & Clewell, B.C. (1992). How do mothers benefit from early intervention programs? *Journal of Applied Developmental Psychology, 13*, 311–362.

Boyce, W.T., Jensen, E.W., James, S.A., & Peacock, J.L. (1983). The Family Routines Inventory: Theoretical origins. *Social Science and Medicine, 17*, 193–200.

Bradley, R.H. (1995). Environment and parenting. In M.H. Bornstein (Ed.), *Handbook of parenting, Vol. 2: Biology and ecology of parenting* (pp. 235–261). Mahwah, NJ: Lawrence Erlbaum Associates.

Briggs, X. d.S. (1997). *Yonkers revisited: The early impacts of scattered-site public housing on families and neighborhoods.* New York: Teachers College, Columbia University.

Brody, G.H., Ge, X., Conger, R., Gibbons, F.X., Murry, V.M., Gerrad, M., et al. (2001). The influence of neighborhood disadvantage, collective socialization, and parenting on African American children's affiliation with deviant peers. *Child Development, 72*, 1231–1246.

Bronfenbrenner, U. (1979). *The ecology of human development*. Cambridge, MA: Harvard University Press.

Bronfenbrenner, U. (1989). Ecological systems theory. In R. Vasta (Ed.), *Annals of child development—Six theories of child development: Revised formulations and current issues* (pp. 187–250). Greenwich, CT: JAI Press.

Brooks-Gunn, J., Berlin, L.J., & Fuligni, A.S. (2000). Early childhood intervention programs: What about the family? In J.P. Shonkoff & S.J. Meisels (Eds.), *Handbook of early childhood intervention* (2nd ed., pp. 549–588). New York: Cambridge University Press.

Brooks-Gunn, J., & Duncan, G.J. (1997). The effects of poverty on children. *Future of Children, 7*, 55–71.

Brooks-Gunn, J., Duncan, G.J., & Aber, J.L. (Eds.). (1997). *Neighborhood poverty: Vol. 1. Context and consequences for children*. New York: Russell Sage Foundation.

Brooks-Gunn, J., Duncan, G.J., Klebanov, P.K., & Sealand, N. (1993). Do neighborhoods influence child and adolescent development? *American Journal of Sociology, 99*, 353–395.

Brooks-Gunn, J., McCormick, M., Shapiro, S., Benasich, A.A., & Black, G. (1994). The effects of early education intervention on maternal employment, public assistance, and health insurance: The Infant Health and Development Program. *American Journal of Public Health, 84*, 924–931.

Brooks-Gunn, J., McCormick, M.C., Klebanov, P.K., & McCarton, C. (1998). Health care use of 3 year-old low birthweight premature children: Effects of family and neighborhood poverty. *The Journal of Pediatrics, 132*, 971–975.

Brooks-Gunn, J., Waldfogel, J., & Han, W.J. (2002). The effects of early maternal employment on child cognitive development. *Child Development, 73*(4), 1052–1072.

Buka, S.L., Stichick, T.L., Birdthistle, I., & Earls, F.J. (2001). Youth exposure to violence: Prevalence, risks, and consequences. *American Journal of Orthopsychiatry, 71*(3), 298–310.

Bursik, R.J. (1988). Social disorganization and theories of crime and delinquency: Problems and prospects. *Criminology, 26*, 515–552.

Byrk, A.S., & Raudenbush, S.W. (1992). *Hierarchical linear models: Applications and data analysis methods*. Newbury Park, CA: Sage.

Caldwell, B.M., & Bradley, R.H. (1984). *Home observation for measurement of the environment*. Little Rock: University of Arkansas.

Campbell, F.A., Pungello, E.P., Miller-Johnson, S., Burchinal, M., & Ramey, C.T. (2001). The development of cognitive and academic abilities: Growth curves from an early childhood educational experiment. *Developmental Psychology, 37*, 231–242.

Campbell, F.A., & Ramey, C.T. (1994). Effects of early intervention on intellectual and academic achievement: A follow-up study from low-income families. *Child Development, 65*, 684–698.

Caspi, A., Taylor, A., Moffitt, T.E., & Plomin, R. (2000). Neighborhood deprivation affects children's mental health: Environmental risk identified in a genetic design. *Psychological Science, 11*(4), 338–342.

Ceballo, R., & McLoyd, V.C. (2002). Social support and parentingin poor, dangerous neighborhoods. *Child Development, 73*(4), 1310–1321.

Chase-Lansdale, P.L., & Gordon, R.A. (1996). Economic hardship and the development of five- and six-year-olds: Neighborhood and regional perspectives. *Child Development,* (67), 3338–3367.

Chase-Lansdale, P.L., Gordon, R.A., Brooks-Gunn, J., & Klebanov, P.K. (1997). Neighborhood and family influences on the intellectual and behavioral competence of preschool and early school-age children. In J. Brooks-Gunn, G.J. Duncan & J.L. Aber (Eds.), *Neighborhood poverty: Vol. 1. Context and consequences for children* (pp. 79–118). New York: Russell Sage Foundation.

Conger, R.D., Ge, X., Elder, G.H., Lorenz, F.O., & Simons, R.L. (1994). Economic stress, coercive family process, and development problems of adolescents. *Child Development, 65,* 541–561.

Cook, T.D., Shagle, S.C., & Degirmencioglu, S.M. (1997). Capturing social process for testing mediational models of neighborhood effects. In J. Brooks-Gunn, G.J. Duncan & J.L. Aber (Eds.), *Neighborhood poverty: Vol. 2. Policy implications in studying neighborhoods* (pp. 94–119). New York: Russell Sage Foundation.

Coulton, C.J., Korbin, J., Chan, T., & Su, M. (2001). Mapping residents' percpetions of neighborhood boundaries: A methodological note. *American Journal of Community Psychology, 29*(2), 371–383.

Coulton, C.J., Korbin, J.E., & Su, M. (1996). Measuring neighborhood context for young children in an urban area. *American Journal of Community Psychology, 24,* 5–32.

Coulton, C.J., Korbin, J.E., & Su, M. (1999). Neighborhoods and child maltreatment: A multi-level study. *Child Abuse & Neglect, 23,* 1019–1040.

Coulton, C.J., Korbin, J.E., Su, M., & Chow, J. (1995). Community level factors and child maltreatment rates. *Child Development, 66,* 1262–1276.

Coulton, C.J., & Pandey, S. (1992). Geographic concentration of poverty and risk to children in urban neighborhoods. *American Behavioral Scientist, 35,* 238–257.

Cubbin, C., LeClere, F.B., & Smith, G.S. (2000). Socioeconomic status and injury mortality: Individual and neighborhood determinants. *Journal of Epidemiology and Community Health, 54*(7), 517–524.

Darling, N., & Steinberg, L. (1997). Community influences on adolescent achievement and deviance. In J. Brooks-Gunn, G.J. Duncan & J.L. Aber (Eds.), *Neighborhood poverty: Vol. 2. Policy implicatons in studying neighborhoods* (pp. 120–131). New York: Russell Sage Foundation.

Deccio, G., Horner, W.C., & Wilson, D. (1994). High-risk neighborhoods and high-risk families: Replication research related to the human ecology of child maltreatment. *Journal of Social Service Research, 18*(3–4), 123–137.

Desai, S., Chase-Lansdale, P.L., & Michael, R.T. (1989). Mother or market? Effects of maternal employment on the intellectual ability of 4-year-old children. *Demography, 26*(4), 545–561.

Diez Roux, A.V., Merkin, S.S., Arnett, D., Chambless, L., Massing, M., Nieto, F.J., et al. (2001). Neighborhood of residence and incidence of coronary heart disease. *The New England Journal of Medicine, 345,* 99–106.

Dubow, E.F., Edwards, S., & Ippolito, M.F. (1997). Life stressors, neighborhood disadvantage, and resources: A focus on inner-city children's adjustment. *Journal of Clinical Child Psychology, 26,* 130–144.

Duncan, G.J., & Brooks-Gunn, J. (Eds.). (1997). *Consequences of growing up poor.* New York: Russell Sage Foundation Press.

Duncan, G.J., Connell, J.P., & Klebanov, P.K. (1997). Conceptual and methodological issues in estimating causal effects of neighborhoods and family conditions on individual development. In J. Brooks-Gunn, G.J. Duncan & J.L. Aber (Eds.), *Neighborhood poverty: Vol 1. Context and consequences for children* (pp. 219–250). New York: Russell Sage Foundation.

Duncan, G.J., & Raudenbush, S.W. (1999). Assessing the effects of context in studies of children and youth development. *Educational Psychologist, 34*(1), 29–41.

Durkin, M.S., Davidson, L.L., Kuhn, L., & O'Connor, P. (1994). Low-income neighborhoods and the risk of severe pediatric injury: A small-area analysis in Northern Manhattan. *American Journal of Public Health, 84*(4), 587–592.

Earls, F., McGuire, J., & Shay, S. (1994). Evaluating a community intervention to reduce the risk of child abuse: Methodological strategies in conducting neighborhood surveys. *Child Abuse & Neglect, 18,* 473–485.

Elder, G.H., Eccles, J.S., Ardelt, M., & Lord, S. (1995). Inner-city parents under economic pressure: Perspectives on the strategies of parenting. *Journal of Marriage and the Family, 57,* 771–784.

Elliott, D.S., Wilson, W.J., Huizinga, D., Sampson, R.J., Elliott, A., & Rankin, B. (1996). The effects of neighborhood disadvantage on adolescent development. *Journal of Research in Crime and Delinquency, 33,* 389–426.

Entwisle, D.R., Alexander, K.L., & Olson, L.S. (1994). The gender gap in math: Its possible origins in neighborhood effects. *American Sociological Review, 59,* 822–838.

Erickson, M.F., Korfmacher, J., & Egeland, B.R. (1992). Attachments past and present: Implications for therapeutic intervention with mother infant dyads. *Development and Psychopathology, 4,* 495–507.

Fauth, R.C., Brady-Smith, C., & Brooks-Gunn, J. (2003). Poverty and education: Children and adolescents. In J.W. Guthrie (Ed.), *Encyclopedia of education* (2nd ed., Vol. 5, pp. 1910–1915). New York: Macmillan.

Fauth, R.C., Leventhal, T., & Brooks-Gunn, J. (in press). Early impacts of moving from poor to middle-class neighborhoods on low-income youth. *Journal of Applied Developmental Psychology.*

Fitzpatrick, K.M. (1993). Exposure to violence and presence of depression among low-income, African American youth. *Journal of Consulting & Clinical Psychology, 61,* 528–531.

Foster, E.M., & McLanahan, S. (1996). An illustration of the use of instrumental variables: Do neighborhood conditions affect a young person's chance of finishing high school? *Psychological Methods, 1*(3), 249–260.

Fuller, B., Coonerty, C., Kipnis, F., & Choong, Y. (1997). *An unfair head start: California families face gaps in preschool and child care availability.* Berkeley, CA: Berkeley-Stanford PACE Center, Yale University, and the California Child Care Resource and Referral Network: Growing Up in Poverty Project.

Furstenberg, F.F. (1993). How families manage risk and opportunity in dangerous neighborhoods. In W.J. Wilson (Ed.), *Sociology and the public agenda* (pp. 231–238). Newbury Park, CA: Sage.

Furstenberg, F.F., Jr., Cook, T.D., Eccles, J., Elder, G.H., & Sameroff, A. (Eds.). (1999). *Managing to make it: Urban families and adolescent success.* Chicago: The University of Chicage Press.

Garbarino, J., & Kostelny, K. (1992). Child maltreatment as a community problem. *Child Abuse and Neglect, 16,* 455–464.

Garbarino, J., & Sherman, D. (1980). High-risk neighborhoods and high-risk families: The human ecology of child maltreatment. *Child Development, 51,* 188–198.

Goering, J., Kraft, J., Feins, J., McInnis, D., Holin, M.J., & Elhassan, H. (1999, September). *Moving to Opportunity for Fair Housing Demonstration Program: Current status and initial findings.* Washington, DC: U.S. Department of Housing and Urban Development.

Goldsmith, H.F., Holzer, C.E., & Manderscheid, R.W. (1998). Neighborhood characteristics and mental illness. *Evaluation and Program Planning, 21,* 211–225.

Gonzales, N.A., Cauce, A.M., Friedman, R.J., & Mason, C.A. (1996). Family, peer, and neighborhood influences on academic achievement among African-American adolescents: One-year prospective effects. *American Journal of Community Psychology, 24,* 365–387.

Gorman-Smith, D., & Tolan, P. (1998). The role of exposure to community violence and developmental problems among inner-city youth. *Developmental Psychopathology, 10,* 101–116.

Greenberg, M.T., Coie, J.D., Lengua, L.J., & Pinderhughes, E.E. (1999). Predicting developmental outcomes at school entry using a multiple-risk model: Four American communities. *Developmental Psychology, 35,* 403–417.

Gross, R.T., Spiker, D., & Haynes, C.W. (Eds.). (1997). *Helping low birth weight, premature babies: The Infant Health and Development Program.* Stanford, CA: Stanford University Press.

Halpern-Felsher, B., Connell, J.P., Spencer, M.B., Aber, J.L., Duncan, G.J., Clifford, E., et al. (1997). Neighborhood and family factors predicting educational risk and attainment in African American and white children and adolescents. In J. Brooks-Gunn, G.J. Duncan & J.L. Aber (Eds.), *Neighborhood poverty: Vol. 1. Context and consequences for children* (pp. 146–173). New York: Russell Sage Foundation Press.

Harvey, E. (1999). Short-term and long-term effects of early parental employment on Children of the National Longitudinal Survey of Youth. *Developmental Psychology, 35*(2), 445–459.

Hernandez, D.J. (1993). *America's children: Resources from family, government, and the economy.* New York: Russell Sage Foundation.

Hill, N.E., & Herman-Stahl, M.A. (2002). Neighborhood safety and social involvement: Associations with parenting behaviors and depressive symptoms among African American and Euro-American mothers. *Journal of Family Psychology, 16*(2), 209–219.

Hinshaw, S.P. (1992). Externalizing behavior problems and academic underachievement in childhood and adolescence: Causal relationships and underlying mechanisms. *Psychological Bulletin, 111,* 127–155.

Jackson, A.P., Brooks-Gunn, J., Huang, C.-C., & Glassman, M. (2000). Single mothers in low-wage jobs: Financial strain, parenting, and preschoolers' outcomes. *Child Development, 71*(5), 1409–1423.

Jargowsky, P.A. (1997). *Poverty and place: Ghettos, barrios, and the American city.* New York: Russell Sage Foundation.

Jarrett, R.L. (1997). Bringing families back in: Neighborhood effects on child development. In J. Brooks-Gunn, G.J. Duncan & J.L. Aber (Eds.), *Neighborhood poverty: Vol. 2. Policy implications in studying neighborhoods* (pp. 48–64). New York: Russell Sage Foundation.

Jarrett, R.L. (1999). Successful parenting in high-risk neighborhoods. *Future of Children, 9*(2), 45–50.

Jencks, C., & Mayer, S. (1990). The social consequences of growing up in a poor neighborhood. In L. Lynn & M. McGeary (Eds.), *Inner-city poverty in the United States* (pp. 111–186.). Washington, DC: National Academy Press.

Johnson, D.L., & Walker, T. (1991). A follow-up evaluation of the Houston Parent–Child Development Center: School performance. *Journal of Early Intervention, 15*(3), 226–236.

Kahlmeier, S., Schindler, C., Grize, L., & Braun-Fahrlander. (2001). Perceived environmental housing quality and wellbeing of movers. *Journal of Epidemiology and Community Health, 55*, 708–715.

Katz, L.F., Kling, J.R., & Liebman, J.B. (2001). Moving to Opportunity in Boston: Early results of a randomized mobility experiment. *Quarterly Journal of Economics, 116*, 607–654.

Klebanov, P.K., Brooks-Gunn, J., Chase-Lansdale, L., & Gordon, R. (1997). Are neighborhood effects on young children mediated by features of the home environment? In J. Brooks-Gunn, G. Duncan & J.L. Aber (Eds.), *Neighborhood poverty: Vol. 1. Context and consequences for children* (pp. 119–145). New York: Russell Sage Foundation.

Klebanov, P.K., Brooks-Gunn, J., & Duncan, G.J. (1994). Does neighborhood and family poverty affect mothers' parenting, mental health, and social support? *Journal of Marriage and the Family, 56*, 441–455.

Klebanov, P.K., Brooks-Gunn, J., McCarton, C., & McCormick, M.C. (1998). The contribution of neighborhood and family income to developmental test scores over the first three years of life. *Child Development, 69*, 1420–1436.

Kohen, D., Brooks-Gunn, J., Leventhal, T., & Hertzman, C. (in press). Neighborhood income and physical and social disorder in Canada: Associations with young children's competencies. *Child Development.*

Korbin, J.E., & Coulton, C.J. (1997). Understanding the neighborhood context for children and families: Combining epidemiological and ethnographic approaches. In J. Brooks-Gunn, G.J. Duncan & J.L. Aber (Eds.), *Neighborhood poverty: Vol. 2. Policy implications in studying neighborhoods* (pp. 65–79). New York: Russell Sage Foundation.

Kornhauser, R. (1978). *Social sources of delinquency.* Chicago: University of Chicago Press.

Lamborn, S.D., Dornbusch, S., & Steinberg, L. (1996). Ethnicity and community context as moderators of the relations between family decision making and adolescent adjustment. *Child Development, 67*, 283–301.

Leventhal, T., & Brooks-Gunn, J. (2000). The neighborhoods they live in: Effects of neighborhood residence upon child and adolescent outcomes. *Psychological Bulletin, 126*, 309–337.

Leventhal, T., & Brooks-Gunn, J. (2004). A randomized study of neighborhood effects on low-income children's educational outcomes. *Developmental Psychology, 40*(4), 488–507.

Leventhal, T., & Brooks-Gunn, J. (2003). Moving to Opportunity: An experimental study of neighborhood effects on mental health. *American Journal of Public Health, 93*(9), 1576–1582.

Liaw, F.-r., & Brooks-Gunn, J. (1994). Cumulative familial risks and low birth weight children's cognitive and behavioral development. *Journal of Clinical Child Psychology, 23*, 360–372.

Logan, J.R., & Spitze, G.D. (1994). Family neighbors. *American Journal of Sociology, 100*(2), 453–476.

Love, J.M., Kisker, E.E., Ross, C.M., Schochet, P. Z., Brooks-Gunn, J., Paulsell, D., et al. (2002). *Making a difference in the lives of infants and toddlers and their families: The impacts of Early Head Start.* Washington, DC: U.S. Department of Health and Human Services.

Lovejoy, M. C., Graczyk, P.A., O'Hare, E., & Neuman, G. (2000). Maternal depression and parenting behavior: A meta-analytic review. *Clinical Psychology Review, 20*(5), 561–592.

Ludwig, J., Ladd, H., & Duncan, G.J. (2001). Urban poverty and educational outcomes. In W.G. Gale & J.R. Pack (Eds.), *Brookings-Wharton papers on urban affairs 2001* (pp. 147–201). Washington, D.C.: Brookings Institution Press.

Ludwig, J.O., & Ladd, H. (1998). *The effects of MTO on educational opportunities in Baltimore: Early evidence* (JCPR Working Paper No. 25). Chicago: Joint Center for Poverty Research.

Malmstrom, M., Johansson, S., & Sundquist, J. (2001). A hierarchical analysis of long-term illness and mortality in socially deprived areas. *Social Science and Medicine, 53*(3), 265–275.

Margolin, G., & Gordis, E.B. (2000). The effects of family and community violence on children. *Annual Review of Psychology, 51*, 445–479.

Martinez, P., & Richters, J.E. (1993). The NIMH Community Violence Project: II. Children's distress symptoms associated with violence exposure. *Psychiatry, 56*, 22–35.

Massey, D.S., & Denton, N.A. (1993). *American apartheid: Segregation and the making of the underclass.* Cambridge: Harvard University Press.

McCulloch, A., & Joshi, H.E. (2001). Neighborhourhood and family influences on the cognitive ability of children in the British National Child Development Study. *Social Science and Medicine, 53*, 579–591.

McKey, R.H., Condelli, L., Granson, H., Barrett, B., McConkey, C., & Plantz, M. (1985). The impact of Head Start on children, families, and communities. In *Final report of the Head Start Evaluation, Synthesis and Utilization Project.* Washington, DC: CSR.

McLoyd, V.C. (1990). The impact of economic hardship on black families and children: Psychological distress, parenting, and socioemotional development. *Child Development, 61*, 311–346.

Molnar, B.E., Buka, S.L., Brennan , R.T., & Earls, F. (2003). A multi-level study of neighborhoods and parent-to-child physical aggression: Results from the Project on Human Development in Chicago Neighborhoods. *Child Maltreatment, 8*(2), 84–97.

O'Donnell, D.A., Schwab-Stone, M.E., & Muyeed, A.Z. (2002). Multidimensional resilience in urban children exposed to community violence. *Child Development, 73*(4), 1265–1282.

Olds, D.L., Eckenrode, J., Henderson, C.R., Jr. , Kitzman, H., Powers, J., Cole, R., et al. (1997). Long-term effects of home visitation on maternal life course and child abuse and neglect: 15-year follow-up of a randomized trial. *Journal of the American Medical Association, 278*, 637–643.

Osofsky, J.D. (1999). The impact of violence on children. *Future of Children, 9*(3), 33–49.

Parke, R.D., & O'Neil, R.L. (1999). Neighborhoods of Southern California children and families. *Future of Children, 9*(2), 58–63.

Pinderhughes, E.E., Nix, R., Foster, E. M., & Jones, D. (2001). Parenting in context: Impact of neighborhood poverty, residential stability, public services, social networks, and danger on parental behaviors. *Journal of Marriage and the Family, 63*(4), 941–953.

Rankin, B.H., & Quane, J.M. (2000). Neighborhood poverty and the social isolation of inner-city African American families. *Social Forces, 79*, 139–164.

Richters, J.E., & Martinez, P. (1993). The NIMH Community Violence Project: I. Children as victims of and witnesses to violence. *Psychiatry, 56*, 7–21.

Rosenbaum, J.E., Kulieke, M.J., & Rubinowitz, L.S. (1988). White suburban schools' responses to low-income black children: Sources of successes and problems. *Urban Review, 20*, 28–41.

Rosenbaum, J.E., Popkin, S.J., Kaufman, J.E., & Rusin, J. (1991). Social integration of low-income black adults in middle-class white suburbs. *Social Problems, 38*(4), 448–461.

Ross, C.E. (2000). Neighborhood disadvantage and adult depression. *Journal of Health and Social Behavior, 41*, 177–187.

Ross, C.E., & Jang, S.J. (2000). Neighborhood disorder, fear, and mistrust: The buffering role of social ties with neighbors. *American Journal of Community Psychology, 28*(4), 401–420.

Ross, C.E., & Mirowsky, J. (2001). Neighborhood disadvantage, disorder, and health. *Journal of Health and Social Behavior, 42*, 258–276.

Ross, C.E., Reynolds, J.R., & Geis, K.J. (2000). The contingent meaning of neighborhood stability for residents' psychological well-being. *American Sociological Review, 65*(4), 581–597.

Sampson, R.J. (1992). Family management and child development: Insights from social disorganization theory. In J. McCord (Ed.), *Facts, frameworks, and forecasts: Advances in criminological theory* (Vol. 3, pp. 63–93). New Brunswick, NJ: Transaction Books.

Sampson, R.J. (1997). Collective regulation of adolescent misbehavior: Validation results from eighty Chicago neighborhoods. *Journal of Adolescent Research, 12*, 227–244.

Sampson, R.J., & Groves, W.B. (1989). Community structure and crime: Testing social-disorganization theory. *American Journal of Sociology, 94*, 774–780.

Sampson, R.J., & Morenoff, J. (1997). Ecological perspectives on the neighborhood context of urban poverty: Past and present. In J. Brooks-Gunn, G.J. Duncan & J.L. Aber (Eds.), *Neighborhood poverty: Vol. 2. Policy implications in studying neighborhoods* (pp. 1–22). New York: Russell Sage Foundation.

Sampson, R.J., Morenoff, J., & Earls, F. (1999). Beyond social capital: Spatial dynamics of collective efficacy for children. *American Sociological Review, 64*, 633–660.

Sampson, R.J., & Raudenbush, S.W. (1999). Systematic social observation of public spaces: A new look at disorder in urban neighborhoods. *American Journal of Sociology, 105*, 603–651.

Sampson, R.J., Raudenbush, S.W., & Earls, F. (1997). Neighborhoods and violent crime: A multilevel study of collective efficacy. *Science, 277*, 918–924.

Schwab-Stone, M.E., Ayers, T.S., Kasprow, W., Voyce, C., Barone, C., Shriver, T. et al. (1995). No safe haven: A study of violence exposure in an urban community. *Journal of the American Academy of Child & Adolescent Psychiatry, 34*, 1343–1352.

Schwab-Stone, M.E., Chen, C., Greenberger, E., Silver, D., Lichtman, J., & Voyce, C. (1999). No safe haven II: The effects of violence exposure on urban youth. *Journal of the American Academy of Child & Adolescent Psychiatry, 38*, 359–367.

Shatz, C.J. (1992). The developing brain. *Scientific American*, 61–67.

Shaw, C., & McKay, H. (1942). *Juvenile delinquency and urban areas*. Chicago: University of Chicago Press.

Shonkoff, J.P., & Phillips, D.A. (Eds.). (2000). *From neurons to neighborhoods: The science of early child development*. Washington, DC: National Academy of Sciences.

Shore, R. (1997). *Rethinking the brain: New insights into early development*. New York: Families and Work Institute.

Shumow, L., Vandell, D. L., & Posner, J. (1999). Risk and resilience in the urban neighborhood: Predictors of academic performance among low-income elementary school children. *Merrill-Palmer Quarterly, 45*(2), 309–331.

Simons, R.L., Johnson, C., Beaman, J.J., Conger, R.D., & Whitbeck, L.B. (1996). Parents and peer group as mediators of the effect of community structure on adolescent behavior. *American Journal of Community Psychology, 24*, 145–171.

Sinclair, J.J., Pettit, G.S., Harrist, A.W., Dodge, K.A., & Bates, J.E. (1994). Encounters with aggressive peers in early childhood: Frequency, age differences, and correlates of risk behaviour problems. *International Journal of Behavioral Development, 17*, 675–696.

Smith, J.R., Brooks-Gunn, J., & Klebanov, P.K. (1997). Consequences of living in poverty for young children's cognitive and verbal ability and early school achievement. In G.J. Duncan & J. Brooks-Gunn (Eds.), *Consequences of growing up poor* (pp. 132–189). New York: Russell Sage Foundation.

Taylor, R.D. (2000). An examination of the association of African American mothers' perceptions of their neighborhoods with their parenting and adolescent adjustment. *Journal of Black Psychology, 26*(3), 267–287.

Tienda, M. (1991). Poor people and poor places: Deciphering neighborhood effects on poverty outcomes. In J. Huber (Ed.), *Macro-micro linkages in sociology* (pp. 244–262). Newbury Park, CA: Sage Publications.

U.S. Department of Health and Human Services. (1999). *Trends in the well-being of America's children and youth 1999.* Washington, DC: Author.

Vandell, D.L., & Shumow, L. (1999). After school child care programs. *Future of Children, 9*(2), 84–90.

Wilson, W.J. (1987). *The truly disadvantaged: The innercity, the underclass, and public policy.* Chicago: University of Chicago Press.

Wilson, W.J. (1991). Studying inner-city social dislocations: The challenge of public agenda research. *American Sociological Review, 56*(February), 1–14.

Wilson, W.J. (1997). *When work disappears.* New York: Alfred J. Knopf.

Zaslow, M.J., & Eldred, C.A. (Eds.). (1998). *Parenting behavior in a sample of young mothers in poverty: Results of the New Chance Observational Study.* New York: Manpower Demonstration Research Corporation.

CHAPTER 8

CHILDREN AS CATALYSTS
FOR ADULT RELATIONS

New Perspectives from Italian
Early Childhood Education

Rebecca S. New and Bruce L. Mallory

INTRODUCTION

The field of early childhood education acknowledges the importance of children's initial interpersonal relationships as one of its core convictions. Supported by attachment theories as well as recent brain research, nurturing relationships with adults are widely regarded as the first of several "irreducible needs of children" (Brazelton & Greenspan, 2000). Related studies highlight the potentially negative consequences for children who are unable to develop positive relationships with family members and other significant adults in their lives. And yet, there is another relationship that receives far less attention, one with an equally powerful role in children's early lives and subsequent development. The underlying premise of this chapter—indeed, this volume—is that respectful and functional relationships with adults, including not only those between parents and teachers

Contemporary Perspectives on Families, Communities, and Schools for Young Children, pages 163–179
Copyright © 2005 by Information Age Publishing

but among parents of classmates and other members of the community, are fundamental to children's well being. The potentials of such relationships for child development become apparent as parents, teachers, and other community members negotiate economic and value-laden decisions regarding early care and education. Active engagement by parents, respect and responsiveness on the part of teachers, and support by the broader community have been identified as key indicators of quality early childhood programs. Unfortunately, in the United States relatively few such programs are available to young children and their families (Kagan & Hallmark, 2001).

The purpose of this chapter is to explore the potentials of more enduring and collaborative relationships among parents, teachers, and other members of the community during the period of early childhood. We begin our exploration with a discussion of findings emerging from a collaborative study of early childhood policies and home-school relations as they have been developed in five different Italian cities. A comparative analysis of the social policies and local practices that characterize Italian early care and education has a twofold purpose. First, Italy has devoted considerable human and financial resources to the lives of its youngest citizens, beginning in the period after World War II and especially since the late 1960s. From this sustained experience, it is possible to observe the results of a national, systemic approach combined with extensive local activism by parents, professionals, and politicians on behalf of young children. Second, the comparative lens inevitably raises questions about what has occurred (or not) in the U.S., where our efforts at creating early childhood education have been less sustained and more a function of the private and nonprofit sectors than collective public action. Thus, the second part of the chapter provides a brief analysis of the rationales and actions surrounding early education in the U.S., vis-à-vis the Italian experience, and concludes with a consideration of what it would take and what it might mean to develop more respectful and collaborative home-school-community partnerships regarding the care and education of young children in contemporary U.S. society.

ITALIAN EARLY CHILDHOOD EDUCATION: A CAUSE AND CONSEQUENCE OF ADULT RELATIONS

Italy is now widely recognized as a place where the well being of young children is both a cultural value and a topic of national concern, as reflected in the 1968 passage of Law 444 proclaiming pre-primary school as a right of all children, beginning at age three. In addition to declaring children's rights as citizens to high quality early childhood services, Law 444 also outlined two features designed to contribute to that quality: the legitimacy of diverse regional and municipal interpretations of early childhood programs (*scuole materna*—or *scuole dell'infanzia*, as they are now often designated); and the critical role of parents in determining the nature of their children's early educational experiences. Although never fully implemented, particularly in the south, the law has insured that well over 90% of Italian three, four, and five-year-old children attend one of three types of *scuole materna*: state-funded, private (often church-affiliated), or municipal (New, 2001). Some of Italy's community-based and funded programs for children are now the focus of global discussion and debate, with the city of Reggio Emilia serving as an exemplar of this triad of cultural values, national policies, and local experimentation and collaboration.

It is not the aim here to review Italian conceptions of and responses to early childhood over the centuries. Rather, the research summarized in this chapter was initiated in an effort to better understand the close parent-teacher relationships observed in Reggio Emilia, an essential but understudied aspect of the internationally acclaimed early childhood program that has evolved during the same years as Head Start developed in the United States. The research soon expanded to include a collaborative study of home-school relations in cities beyond Reggio Emilia, involving parents, teachers, and citizens in 46 early childhood settings in Milan, Trento, Parma, and San Miniato.[1] Research strategies included ethnographic observations, semi-structured interviews with parents and teachers, and questionnaires on educational aims and optimal child development. Additional data include case-study documentation in Reggio Emilia and observations of home-school practices in each of the sample institutions.

Results of this study make clear that Italian conceptions of home-school-community relations in the period of early childhood have roots that reach far into Italy's past. It is impossible to understand the reasons behind the perceived solidarity of Italian parents, teachers, and community members regarding the value of early childhood without first acknowledging the social, economic, and political practices that have contributed to the contemporary phenomena of their working together to create and maintain their early childhood services. The municipal early education programs that served as the foci for our research have as their conceptual origins a coalition of interests, ideologies, and people that have characterized Italian history at least since the *Risorgimento* of the late 19th century.

Among the most important of these ideologies is Italy's deeply embedded ethic of collective action and active political participation at all levels of society. This ethic is particularly evident in northern and central Italy, regions with greater wealth and higher levels of civic engagement than is the case in the south (Putnam, 1987). Today this collective ethic is embodied in what Italians call *partecipazione*—a form of collective democratic action that became the focal point of our inquiry. The particular accomplishments of Reggio Emilia, no less than those of other cities, were made possible following decades of political and economic struggles within this context. Essential to these accomplishments were a close connection between philosophical understandings and program design, the commitments of individual local and regional leaders, and the creation of organizational structures that support involvement of parents and community members in program governance and local political activity. Three features—a philosophical view of the purpose of an early childhood education, a value orientation to society's shared responsibility for children, and an organizational strategy that supports this belief system—combine to create an interpretation of early childhood services that are not-for-children-only.

A PHILOSOPHY OF EARLY EDUCATION: THE ESSENTIAL IMPORTANCE OF A "SYSTEM OF RELATIONSHIPS"

Although early Italian services for children were developed in response to the needs of working parents, the contemporary array of services reveals a more complex view of the Italian child's position in the family and in society. Reflecting, on the one hand, Italy's current low birthrate, and, on the other, its tradition of extended family involvement in the care of young children, Italian early educational settings are regarded as ideal places for children to develop relationships with peers and other adults. Drawing upon attachment theory as well as their own philosophical biases, Italian early childhood services emphasize the potentials of out-of-home care and education for the development of multiple attachments, which, in turn, require close cooperation between caregivers. This is in marked contrast to the sometimes competitive and estranged relationships between parents and caregivers in the U.S. who, as early as the 1930s, were labeled as "natural enemies" (Powell, 1991).

Italian educators work to establish trusting relationships with parents as a basis from which to construct educational experiences for children. This work often begins during the process of *l'inserimento*, (literally an "insertion") in which educators and parents collaborate together to ease both children and adults through this first "delicate moment" of transition from the home to the early childhood setting (Bove, 1999). Whereas the processes of *l'inserimento* vary from city to city, they typically take place during the first days or week(s) of a child's first entry into group care, after which educators create numerous opportunities for parents with teachers and one another in both formal and informal settings. Class meetings, *serate nella cucina* [evenings in the kitchen], parties for grandparents, parent-teacher conferences, school-wide initiatives, and sometimes entire citywide celebrations serve as vehicles to bring parents together and to remind the city of its responsibilities to young children. Although the topic of conversation is often the children, the relationships that develop begin to assume value for what they contribute to adult lives as well as to the educational agenda.

Children as a Shared Responsibility

It has been repeatedly observed that the well-being of Italian children is considered a shared responsibility, one that involves not only the family but also members of the larger community (Moss, 1988). Italy's universal preschool is a testament to this national commitment and cultural value. Strategies for achieving this consensus can be found in the early childhood services themselves. In addition to the numerous occasions by which parents come to know one another and their children's teachers, they are also subject to subtle but persistent reminders that their child's learning and general well-being are dependent upon the quality of experiences that take place with other children. Thus a teacher in Reggio Emilia explains that she rarely if ever uses an image of a single child in creating a documentation display. Teachers in San Miniato purposefully include photographs of other children in each child's individual photo album/portfolio. Teachers in Milan invite groups of mothers to participate in classroom activities as a means by which they can get to know one another—and one another's children. The influence of these efforts to increase a sense of social responsibility is apparent in the remarks made by one mother in Reggio Emilia who noted that, *"at first, I came for my child, and then I began to come so that I could help other children."* Although this mother went on to note that she now participates in school events and activities because of the value that she derives for herself, she made clear that her active role as a mother in her child's *asilo nido* served as a context that introduced her to the lives of other people's children.

Translating Ideologies into Structural and Organizational Supports

The lengths to which Italian educators go to invite and sustain parent participation in early childhood programs was made evident in numerous daily routines and personal encounters such as those described above. And yet the organizational feature that perhaps best illustrates the seriousness with which this principle is interpreted is likely less visible to American educators. Based on the organizational concept of *gestione sociale*, a principal of social management and participation first articulated in regard to civic functions and labor management, each of the programs included in this study benefitted from behind-the scenes working of various advisory committees made up of staff, parents, and members from the community at large. Known generally as *comitati di gestione*, such councils both supported and demonstrated the commitment to collaborative and enduring relationships between children's families, community members, and the early childhood professionals.

This principle of parent and citizen participation was in evidence during Reggio Emilia's nascent efforts at organizing early childhood services. Political leaders and educators in the city also played a leadership role at the regional and national levels in articulating the importance and practical elements of this interpretation of parent involvement, which can be traced back to the factory council movement of the 1920s and the subsequent anti-Fascist resistance movement and associated strengths of the Italian communist and socialist parties. Loris Malaguzzi, the founder of the Reggio Emilia municipal program and active in the political left throughout the postwar period, first spoke in 1970 about the *"comitati di scuola e citta"* (committees of the school and city) as a kind of "welding of the family and school and values." These committees were to be an "urgent correction of the system—a doctrine and a praxis that assume a social role in the same moment in which it assumes and accomplishes an educational role" (Malaguzzi, 1998). Malaguzzi's influence was felt at the national level when, in 1971, Article 6 of law 444 affirmed that daycare centers and preschools *"devono essere gestiti con la partecipazione delle famiglie"* [must be managed with the participation of the families] as well as representatives of social organizations within the region.

Today, each of the municipal programs participating in the research project previously identified has some form of community-wide management council, with varying degrees of authority, responsibility, and status. In every community, there is the recognition that parental participation is an essential ingredient to the determination of program success in meeting the needs of community children and their families. For example, in Milan, the *comitato di gestione* in one preschool program includes four parents, two teachers, one auxiliary staff member (such as a cook or custodian), the principal, and one citizen representative of the neighborhood in which the school is located. In this Italian metropolis (Milan has a population of 13 million inhabitants), each school's *comitato* is responsible for such matters as the promotion of innovative projects within the school (e.g., developing a new library) and meetings with experts on a particular theme, e.g., examining the Montessori method that has influenced these particular municipal programs. Other responsibilities include organizing "moments of reflection" and designing new methods to assure continuity between the school and families.

In other communities, the *comitato* might play a major role in selecting families for admission and setting fees.[2] In the small hill town of San Miniato, for example, the *comitato* facilitated debate and decision-making regarding a move to mixed-age infant-toddler centers for the increasing number of children without siblings. In Parma and Reggio Emilia, the *comitato* often plays a more explicit political role by supporting local or even national political causes and helping parents to become articulate advocates for educational and other social needs. For example, during 1997–98 in Reggio Emilia, the *comitato* organized citywide dialogues on a contemporary theme of "What are the questions of education today?" resulting in a six-month-long process of highly participatory citizen discussion at each of the city schools, followed by a conference open to the community.

In each of the cities involved in this study, it was informative to hear from parents about why they had chosen to be active in the governing process of *gestione sociale*. For some parents, it was described as a means to connect with other parents of young children, and to observe other children in the context of an infant day care or preschool classroom. Some were eager to learn more about local educational services as well as local politics, and wanted to feel more aware of and engaged in their own child's educational experience. Echoing themes we heard often, a mother of an infant in Trento told us, "I like being part of the *consiglio di gestione* because it permits me to follow my children very closely and it is a way of meeting up with other people socially, a way to help each other and to contribute to the good functioning of the *asilo nido*." Two mothers from Milan shared this view, as they both described their satisfaction at feeling more as an "insider" as opposed to an "outsider" in the school's life.

Teachers were also clear about the importance of the *comitati* as sources for deliberation regarding large and small educational decisions. Several noted a historical change in the orientation of the *comitati*, such that, over the years, they have become less political and externally focused in their work and more concerned with the social well being of participating families and children and the logistics of running the schools. While this shift was lamented by some of the veteran teachers (and some parents) of the earlier, highly politicized days of the 1960s and 1970s when the programs were first beginning, others remarked on the dynamic and flexible quality of the organization in responding to the changing needs of society.

This brief summary of the ideological, pedagogical, and structural aspects of home-school relationships in Italian early education programs highlights several themes of interest to U.S. educators. First, we must understand the cultural context of services for young children. Italy's traditions of collective action, first in agriculture and later in industrial and political life, can be clearly traced through the design of national policies as well as local practices in the five cities we studied. The strength of the Italian women's movement in the 1960s and 1970s, and its focus on working families and children rather than individual freedoms (as in the United States), also played an important role in articulating and advocating for services founded on close adult relationships. Second, and perhaps most important, early educational services in Italy are not viewed as only of benefit to the development of children. They are equally sites for adult dialogue and community development. Thus the design of preschool services, as they have evolved over the past 35 years, draws directly upon developmental understandings (as in the importance of the transition from home to school) and a concern for participatory governance (in the *consigli di gestione*). They are, to use the contemporary construct, sites for the building of social capital.

AMERICAN PARENTS, TEACHERS, AND COMMUNITIES: AMBIVALENT GOALS, CHANGING ROLES IN U.S. EARLY CHILDHOOD EDUCATION

Turning to the experience in the United States by way of contrast, we can observe both similar and distinct ideological, pedagogical, and structural forces at work. As is the case with Italy, a brief look at the historical roots of American early education is necessary to understanding the current situation. It might be argued that past and present interpretations of parent, teacher, and community roles and responsibilities in the period of early childhood are inextricably linked to changing images of children themselves—whether as vulnerable dependents, as capable learners, or as citizens of the settings into which they are born (Hwang, Lamb, & Sigel, 1996). It is axiomatic that parents have a critical role in the early development and survival of young children. And yet anthropological records repeatedly demonstrate that the role of parents and other adults in children's early learning has varied as a function of cultural values and conditions, including societal expectations of children and views of parents themselves. As we will argue below, the growing importance assigned to children's early years in the United States eventually, and ironically, contributed to a deficit image of parents and a concomitant unilateral relationship between parents and teachers that has characterized the field for most of the past century.

The origins of U.S. early childhood education can be traced at least as far back as another importation—this time the ideas of Froebel to have a special place outside the home for young children—a *kindergarten*. As is often the case when ideas are transported across cultures, however,

Froebel's kindergarten was appropriated in the United States to address issues particular to its identity as an industrial and multiethnic society. By the late 1880s, Froebel's kindergarten was one of many urban reform efforts in the United States aimed at rescuing children from poor and often immigrant families. The goals of the kindergarten were to teach children the values of industriousness, cleanliness, discipline, and cooperation, particularly those children who came from "unemployed and uneducated poor immigrant families"—children who were otherwise seem as presenting a risk for "an immoral and vice-filled society" (Bloch, 1987). In short, the history of U.S. early childhood education reveals an inextricable link to the social aims, ills, and assets of American society (Beatty, 1995).

This relationship was continued in the 20th century, a period associated with the birth of child development as a field of scientific inquiry. Building on William James' recommendation that the education of a child should be based on the study of children's development, parents and teachers—initially partners with developmental psychologists as they helped to document children's growth and behavior—were soon relegated to consumers of the knowledge deriving from more "objective" forms of child study. As research laboratories gathered scientific data about children, early educational initiatives were linked to social causes and assumptions about which children were most in need of an out-of-home educational experience. Such early programs contributed further to the belief that parents, especially those who were impoverished, were in need of intervention and/or parent education. These assumptions can be found in early descriptions of the charity movement, the kindergarten movement, and the day nursery movement, each of which were created in response to concerns about those children "unlucky" enough to be born of impoverished or uneducated parents (Cahan, 1997, p. 6).

Throughout the first half of the 20th century, a more broadly shared concern with the "at risk" child contributed to expanding concern with how best "to prevent poor developmental outcomes in underprivileged children and families" (Fisher & Osofsky, 1997). This lack of confidence in parents as knowledgeable contributors to children's early development served as a rationale for early childhood programs. This deficit view of parents also informed programs dedicated to the training and development of teachers, who were told in no uncertain terms that one of their roles was "to educate parents" (Lascarides & Hinitz, 2000, p. 338).

Over the next several decades, early childhood institutions continued to develop in response to new professional understandings of children, particularly but not only those considered underprivileged. At the same time, the field of early childhood education made steady progress toward its goal of becoming better respected as both "scientific and professional" (Bloch, 1987). Teacher training institutions and university laboratory schools further distinguished between children's family lives and exemplary educational programs based on empirically derived knowledge of young children (Branscombe, Castle, Dorsey, Surbeck, & Taylor, 2000, p. 374). By the 1940s, the utility of research on child development for children's early care and education was well established and texts on child development were often illustrated with photographs as well as text to insure ease of comprehension by both parents and teachers of young children (cf., Gesell & Ilg, 1943).

The period following World War II saw a major shift in commonly held views of children's needs and parental competencies. Especially in the thriving middle class, mothers were encouraged to become consumers of parent education manuals, as extended families became less common and new parents searched for more "modern" approaches to child-rearing. Harmful child rearing practices were once again associated in the literature with the less educated and less affluent. At the same time, agreement regarding the benefits of attending kindergarten prior to entering public school became increasingly widespread. Prominent research articles touted the kindergarten's "scientifically sound" program of preparing children for a primary education; the maternal role again took second place behind the expertise of the kindergarten teacher.

Research during the 1960s continued to contribute to changing understandings of parental roles and the value of early experiences. Piaget's seminal work contributed to a burgeoning interest in children's cognitive functioning, and the roles of play and object manipulation took on new importance in promoting children's early intelligence. Concurrently, another approach to early childhood education as intervention grew out of shrewd observations that it would be more politically advantageous to help "culturally disadvantaged" children rather than impoverished adults. On this basis, Head Start was established in 1965, consistent with the federal tradition of programs designed specifically to compensate for the presumed deficiencies of parents (Grubb, 1989; New & Mallory, 1996). And yet, Head Start policies included a mandate to involve parents in program governance through the Head Start Policy Council structure—a concrete manifestation of the principle of "maximum feasible participation" which was a key principle of the war on poverty. From the beginning, Head Start regulations required that a majority of members must be parents of children currently enrolled in the program. The two other categories of membership included program staff and community representatives, thus an ecologically sound "model" early education program.

Over the following two decades, early childhood educators increasingly sought to validate their work with young children on the basis of child development research, even as some of this work was used to convince mothers who could afford to do so to stay home with their children for at least the "first three years" (White, 1972). Reflecting the need for scientific validation, the National Association for the Education of Young Children compiled a significant body of research to use as the basis for guidelines for developmentally appropriate practice (Bredekamp, 1987). These guidelines explicitly detailed appropriate and inappropriate practices for early childhood programs, with little acknowledgment of potential differences of opinion in what was by then widely recognized as a multicultural U.S. society. In relatively short order, the guidelines were critiqued (Mallory & New, 1994) and subsequently revised (Bredekamp & Copple, 1997), with increased emphasis on the need to work closely with parents in order to develop shared understandings of—still dominant—scientific research as a basis for high quality and developmentally appropriate educational programs.

Today, parents continue to bemoan the failure of U.S. society to provide early childhood services to all of who need them, even as educators criticize the refusal on the part of some parents to access existing services because they do not reflect the values and beliefs of children's families (Fuller et al., 1996). As conflicts between funding agencies, parents, and professionals increasingly focus on the costs and benefits of preacademic programs, the idea that an early education might be good for *all* children—not just those needing an early intervention—has finally become a part of the collective discourse. And yet the millions of U.S. parents and teachers who value these services have yet to effectively work together with members of their communities to achieve this goal.

IMPLICATIONS OF THE ITALIAN EXPERIENCE FOR ADULT RELATIONSHIPS IN U.S. EARLY CHILDHOOD

Our discussion of adult relations in Italian early childhood programs barely begins to capture the richness of the experiences described to us by parents, teachers, and citizens as they talked about their work together. Throughout the study, we—as the only Americans on the research team—were continually struck by the routine nature of much of what we saw, especially when it contrasted sharply with our own experiences and expectations. Our growing understanding of the role that these early care and educational programs play in promoting adult relations in their respective communities suggests a number of ways in which U.S. early childhood educators might rethink their approaches to partnerships with parents and community members that we have just described.

Moving from Parent Involvement to Civic Engagement

The history of parent involvement in the United States is akin to that of the inclusion of young children with special needs in the educational setting—an educational initiative first labeled as mainstreaming, then integration, then inclusion. Similar shifts in the discourse reflect changing orientations to parents on the part of educators: parent education, parent empowerment, parent involvement—each with limited notions of what parents might actually contribute to the educational exercise. While the notion of parent involvement is likely the closest thing to what has been described in the Italian settings, which, too, has become something of a cliché in that there is "insufficient thought about the nitty gritty mechanics" for what it will take to make it happen (Vincent, 2000, p. ix).

The Italian example is a sharp contrast to the American interpretation of parent-teacher relations. The organizational and structural care with which Italian early childhood programs have been developed and maintained, especially but not only in Reggio Emilia, reveal a wealth of thought given to preparing environments to welcome adults, including but not limited to members of a child's family. And yet the very notion of making specific accommodations for adults is antithetical to some U.S. professionals seeking to create a 'child-centered' environment. This conflict of values was expressed by an Early Head Start professional who rejected the idea of a couch in the classroom because parents "might just sit down and talk to each other instead of playing with the child." Beyond the goal of making adults feel welcome is the notion that their ideas—about children's learning and development—could also be welcome contributions to the learning environment. This sort of partnership goes beyond the principle of involvement and, further, bypasses the patronizing concepts of empowerment and parent education. Instead, it invites parents to engage, with each other and with educators and other community members, in purposeful and ongoing decision-making about how best to respond to the needs and potentials of young children. Such a shift in relations will require not only structural changes; it will also require a major change in attitude regarding parental roles and competencies.

Social Construction of "Good Parent"

The concept of parental engagement implies a level of competency that is not often assumed in U.S. home-school relations. In her analysis of factors that contribute to the social construction of early childhood in Italy and the United States, Saraceno (1984) notes the stigmatizing effects of being identified as a needy parent (she uses, as her example, eligibility for

Head Start) in contrast to Italian families who share, with all other families, the right to what Mantovani calls a *"pedagogia del benessere"* [pedagogy of well-being] as found in their children's early care and educational services (Mantovani, 2001). Within the United States, it is not only low-income families who are regarded as needy. In fact, notions of parent education are so well integrated into U.S. society that few question the hierarchical relationship that is implied by the term. As noted in the previous sections, parents have often been willing consumers of the child development knowledge that is generated and disseminated by scholars and educators—this in spite of the fact that much of what is referred to as foundational to the field of early childhood is based on culturally limited samples of children and families who often fail to adequately represent the diversity of child rearing strategies and developmental pathways that actually characterize childhood in our pluralistic society.

In the Italian settings that we have observed and studied, parents are learning about child development and parenting even as they help teachers to better know and understand their own children. The close partnerships that develop during the processes of *inserimento,* for example, create highly personalized contexts within which both parents and teachers can exchange views, experiences, and expertise. As parents spend time with other parents and observing other children, their own caregiving repertoires and developmental expectations expand. The classroom becomes a setting for individual and group learning—by children as well as adults. This approach to the social construction of knowledge builds confidence even as it contributes to a sense of community. It also reflects a principle cited repeatedly in this study: No one has a monopoly on what is best for children (Spaggiari, 1999).

Professionals as Experts or Partners?

Perhaps the most challenging finding from this study was the interpretation of teachers' roles with respect to children's needs and capabilities. Repeatedly, and especially in Reggio Emilia and Parma, we observed teachers asking parents for information and demonstrations that we felt were clearly within the capabilities of the teachers themselves. After spending a morning in an infant-toddler center in Parma where several parents stayed for the day, not yet ready to leave their child in the hands of the teachers, we shared our sense of confusion with a *pedagogista* whose responsibilities included the professional development of teachers. We described a number of scenes, including one in which the teacher asked the mother to demonstrate how best to feed the child. The *pedagogista* patiently explained to us that "a professional teacher knows when to demonstrate her competencies to parents." She went on to point out that there was nothing artificial about the situation we had described. Certainly, the parent *was* the expert when it came to feeding her infant. And yet such an interpretation of the teacher's role belies efforts, in the US, to standardize professional knowledge and developmentally appropriate teacher behaviors.

Other reasons why teachers in the US resist seeking parental perspectives include a fear of conflict that is associated with controversial topics, or an avoidance of issues that are emotionally charged. By contrast, the Italian conversations that took place during the course of this study were often in the form of serious discussions or debates, whether about the role of religion in the preschool or how best to facilitate exchanges among and between various immigrant groups. In these contexts, every perspective was considered worthy of sharing, and resulting decisions were more widely regarded by the larger community. This interpretation of complementary realms of expertise, with an acceptance of diverse perspectives that may need to be negotiated, is a far cry from current interpretations of child development's power to govern parent [and teacher] decision-making (Bloch, 2000). When teachers are viewed as the distributors of knowledge, classrooms and early childhood programs cannot truly function as learning communities—neither for children nor for adults. Somewhat ironically, given their role in convincing both parents and educators that personal knowledge is of less value than what can be studied scientifically, developmental psychologists have recently turned their attention to how parents think about and make sense of children's development (Goodnow & Collins, 1990). Given the growing number of controversies regarding the aims and processes of early childhood education, perhaps it is time for early childhood educators to take more seriously this source of new ideas and possibilities.

CONCLUSION

In each of the five cities participating in this study, during interviews, on questionnaires, and in casual conversations, parents, teachers, and community members acknowledged the critical role of early childhood programs in helping young children learn how to *stare insieme* [be together] with other adults and other children. This cultural value and educational aim were sometimes attributed to the rapid increase in single-child households in Italy and the declining role of extended-family members in childcare. Others made clear that children simply need more than the family—they need experiences that will introduce them to life in a community (New, 1999). The social policies and early childhood programs found in Italy today insure that children have many such experiences and that the benefits accrue for adults as well.

When cultural values support an interpretation of childhood as a social responsibility, children serve as catalysts for adults to interact and communicate with one another. When adults who know and care about the children being discussed are respected for their particular as well as shared understandings of child development, the relevance of professional knowledge is mediated through processes of social exchange and civic debate. Such an unconventional type of exchange was described, in the abstract, by Bronfenbrenner (1978) when he proclaimed that "the groups most in need of parent education are those who do not yet, no longer, or never will have children" (p. 767).

This interpretation, shared within the context of a discussion of the "profound changes" taking place over decades in structure roles of family in American society, was premeditated by Loris Malaguzzi (1971) when he proclaimed—this time in reference to Italian society—that "the school must be a place where social life is lived, not just a place for lessons about the social life." Malaguzzi was talking about much more than a space for children or a forum for the education of adults—parents and non-parents alike—about children's needs and potentials. Rather, he was advocating for a quality of life for *all* of the community's citizens, not just the youngest—a quality that could and should be found in early childhood educational settings.

Considering the rapid expansion of social policies supporting these services over the three decades subsequent to these remarks, it is clear that Italian preschools and infant-toddler centers have not only contributed to such a social life, but benefitted from it as well. Put another way, the sources of effective home-school-community relations in Italy can be linked, both conceptually and practically, to their consequences. Such a model of early childhood is based on creating conditions whereby adults can become engaged in and committed to working together on behalf of young children—a strategy that U.S. adults might well emulate as we seek ways to rejuvenate some of the social capital essential to a thriving democracy. In such a context, early childhood education moves from being a metaphor for community to a vital means of support for both developing children and a healthy and caring society.

NOTES

1. This research was funded by the Spencer Foundation's Major Grants Program and has taken place in two phases. **Phase I**: *The Sociocultural Construction of Home-School Relations: The Case of Reggio Emilia and Contemporary Italy,*

Principal Investigators Rebecca New and Bruce Mallory (1996–1998). **Phase II**: *Italian Concepts of Community, Social Responsibility, and Civic Participation: Childcare as Metaphor,* Principal Investigators Rebecca New and Susanna Mantovani. (1998–2001).

2.   In each of the five cities participating in this study, demand always exceeds supply for the municipal programs, and eligibility for admission is based on such family characteristics as two working parents, lack of access to grandparents, or having a child with special needs. Fees are very modest, usually covering diapers and food only, adjusted to reflect family income.

REFERENCES

Beatty, B. (1995). *Preschool education in America: The culture of young children from the colonial era to the present.* New Haven: Yale University Press.

Bloch, M.N. (2000). Governing teachers, parents, and children through child development knowledge. *Human Development, 43*(4–5), 257–265.

Bloch, M.N. (1987). Becoming scientific and professional: An historical perspective on the aims and effects of early education. In T.S. Popkewitz (Ed.), *The formation of school subjects* (pp. 25–62). Basingstoke: Falmer.

Bove, C. (1999). *L'inserimento del bambino al nido* [Welcoming the child into infant care]: Perspectives from Italy. *Young Children, 54*(2), 32–34.

Branscombe, N., Castle, K., Dorsey, A., Surbeck, E., & Taylor, J. (2000). *Early childhood education: A constructivist perspective.* Boston: Houghton Mifflin.

Brazelton, T.B., & Greenspan, S.I. (2000). *The irreducible needs of children: What every child must have to grow, learn, and flourish.* Cambridge, MA: Perseus.

Bredekamp, S. (Ed.). (1987). *Developmentally appropriate practice in early childhood programs serving children from birth through age 8.* Washington, DC: National Association for the Education of Young Children.

Bredekamp, S., & Copple, C. (1997). *Developmentally appropriate practice in early childhood programs* (rev. ed.). Washington, DC: National Association for the Education of Young Children.

Bronfenbrenner, U. (1978). Who needs parent education? *Teachers College Record, 79*(4), 767–782.

Cahan, E. (1997). On the uses of history for developmental psychologists or on the social necessity of history. *SRCD Newsletter, 40*(3), 2, 6, 8. Ann Arbor, MI: Society for Research in Child Development.

Fisher, C.B., & Osofsky, J. (1997). Training the applied developmental scientist for prevention and practice: Two current examples. *Social Policy Report, XI*(2), 1–18.

Fuller, B., Eggers-Pierola, C., Holloway, S., Liang, X., & Rambaud, M.F. (1996). Rich culture, poor markets: Why do Latino parents forgo preschooling? *Teachers College Record, 97*(3), 400–418.

Gesell, A., & Ilg, F. (1943). *Infant and child in the culture of today: The guidance of development in home and nursery school.* New York: Harper & Brothers.

Goodnow, J.J., & Collins, W.A. (1990). *Development according to parents: The nature, sources, and consequences of parents' ideas.* Hillsdale, NJ: Erlbaum.

Grubb, W.N. (1989). Young children face the state: Issues and options for early childhood programs. *American Journal of Education*, 358–397.

Hwang, C.P., Lamb, M.E., & Sigel, I.E. (Eds.) (1996). *Images of childhood*. Mahwah, NJ: Erlbaum.

Kagan, S.L., & Hallmark, L.G. (2001). Early care and education policies in Sweden: Implications for the United States. *Phi Delta Kappan, 83*(3), 237–245 .

Lascarides, V.C., & Hinitz, B. F. (2000). *History of early childhood education*. New York: Falmer Press.

Malaguzzi, L. (1998). History, ideas, and basic philosophy: An interview with Lella Gandini. In C. Edwards, L. Gandini, & G. Forman (Eds.), *The hundred languages of children: The Reggio Emilia approach—Advanced reflections* (2nd ed., pp. 49–97). Greenwich, CT: Ablex.

Mallory, B., & New, R. (Eds.) (1994). *Diversity and developmentally appropriate practices: Challenges for early childhood education*. New York: Teachers College Press.

Mantovani, S. (2001). Infant-toddler centers in Italy today: Tradition and innovation. In L. Gandini and C. P. Edwards (Eds.). *Bambini: The Italian approach to infant/toddler care* (pp. 23–37). New York: Teachers College Press.

Moss, P. (1988). *Childcare and equality of opportunity: Consolidated report to the European commission*. London: London University.

New, R. (2001). Italian early care and education: The social construction of policies, programs, and practices. *Phi Delta Kappan, 83*(3), 226–236.

New, R. (1999). What should children learn? Making choices and taking chances. *Early Childhood Research and Practice, 1*(2), 1–25. www.eric.org/ecrp

New, R., & Mallory, B. (1996). The paradox of diversity in early care and education. In E. J. Erwin (Ed.), *Putting children first: Visions for a brighter future for young children and their families* (pp. 143–167). Baltimore, MD: Paul H. Brookes.

Putnam, R. (1997). *Making democracy work: Civic traditions in modern Italy*. Princeton, NJ: Princeton University Press.

Powell, D. (1989). *Families and early childhood programs*. Washington, DC: National Association for the Education of Young Children.

Saraceno, C. (1984). The social construction of childhood: Child care and education policies in Italy and the United States. *Social Problems, 31*(3), 351–363.

Vincent, C. (2000). *Including parents? Education, citizenship and parental agency*. Buckingham: Open University Press.

CHAPTER 9

CULTURAL BELIEFS ABOUT CHILDREARING AND SCHOOLING IN IMMIGRANT FAMILIES AND "DEVELOPMENTALLY APPROPRIATE PRACTICES"

Yawning Gaps!

Jaipaul L. Roopnarine and Aysegul Metindogan

INTRODUCTION

Despite decades of debate about the merit and efficacy of different early childhood education practices (see Beretier & Engleman, 1966; Burts, Hart, Charlesworth, & Kirk, 1990; Elkind, 1981, 1987; Harry, 1995; Holloway, Rambaud, Fuller, & Eggers-Pieorla, 1995; Karnes, Schwedel, & Williams, 1983; Mallory & New, 1994; Miller & Bizzell, 1984; Rescorla, Hyson, & Hirssh-Pasek, 1991; Shonkoff & Phillips, 2000; Stipek, Feiler, Daniels, &

Contemporary Perspectives on Families, Communities, and Schools for Young Children, pages 181–202
Copyright © 2005 by Information Age Publishing

Milburn, 1995; Weikart & Schweinhart, 2005), we are some distance from understanding their appropriateness and currency for guiding the education of immigrant children in the United States. Educational dialogues on what should embody early childhood education foci and curricula have involved considerations of highly structured programs with rigorous assessments of school outcomes to those that are wed to play-based, neo-constructivist principles and tend to shy away from more formal assessments of cognitive and social skills (see Golbeck, 2001; Roopnarine & Johnson, 2005).

Although some key educational figures and researchers have eschewed or recommended movement away from the "either/or" stance regarding the intrinsic benefits of child-centered versus didactic, teacher-centered education (see Golbeck, 2001 for a discussion), a significant divide exists in the early childhood education field. Those aligned with the incorporation of developmentally appropriate, play-enriched practices in early childhood education question the wisdom of subjecting young children to rigorous academic training because of the potential stress and undue anxiety it may impart on them (see Bredekamp & Copple, 1997; Elkind, 1987). Others warn about the lack of school readiness among children and espouse the need for more stringent academic standards (see Early Reading First and Even Start Literacy Programs, U.S. Department of Education, 2002). Greater emphasis is being placed on learning academic skills early in children's lives (see the current "No Child Left Behind" Act, U.S. Department of Education, 2002). To complicate matters further, researchers who focus on the cultural underpinnings of behavioral development and education find designating early childhood education practices as either developmentally "appropriate" or "inappropriate" itself particularly troublesome (LeVine, in press; Roopnarine, Bynoe, & Singh, 2004). It is the latter issue that forms the central concept of this paper. That is, we take a closer look at some core concepts of developmentally appropriate practices in educating children of immigrants in the United States.

With the introduction of the *National Association for the Education of Young Children's* (NAEYC) developmentally-appropriate practices' guidelines for children 0–8 years published in 1987, and in the subsequent revision of the document in 1997 (see Bredekamp, 1987; Bredekamp & Copple, 1997), the impression is conveyed that in the United States groups of young children are pressured to learn narrow academic concepts and skills via the process of "rote memory and whole group instruction" (p. v, preface). The latter are seen as undesirable and less optimal for childhood development. Furthermore, it is suggested that general recommendations on "developmentally appropriate practices" (DAP) offered to educators and practitioners in the United States are driven by "current research and theory" (Bredekamp & Copple, 1997). It is probably worth stating that until fairly recently much of the theoretical knowledge about other "ethnic groups" in the United States (e.g., African Americans, Latinos) has been mired in stereotypes and "myths" about the lack of interest in education and the deficit instructional and parenting styles of families, often disregarding within ethnic group variability evident in these areas (see Moreno & Valencia, 2002, for a discussion of myths about Mexican Americans and the educational process). Likewise, there is simply not enough scientific child development knowledge on new immigrant groups in the United States to make definitive statements about the possible effects of certain caregiving practices at the population level (see LeVine, 2004)

No one would argue with the overall principles outlined in DAP. That is, children should be treated with respect and dignity, accorded the social, emotional, and cognitive supports they require for learning and development, are active learners and are shaped by cultural knowledge and experiences, developmental progression is driven by both biological and environmental experiences and may not be symmetrical or even across developmental domains or children, and development proceeds from the simple to the complex. Accordingly, children's developmental levels should be considered in tailoring cognitive and social experiences to meet their educational needs. Nor is there any denial that home-school partnerships, teacher qualities, knowledge base about curricula, processes of childhood development and learning, cultural consciousness, and different assessment techniques that are geared toward improving curricula and learning are important ingredients in working to enhance the competencies of young children. The academic literature in both areas is vast (see Comer, 1988; Ford, 1995; Harry, 1995; Ladson-Billings, 2000; Marshall, 2001; Stevenson, Chen, & Uttal, 1990). Of concern to cultural and cross-cultural researchers and educators is the full utility of "developmentally appropriate practices" for educating culturally diverse groups of children in the United States—those of recent immigrants in particular whose cultural and childrearing scripts may be far removed from the seemingly unshakeable tenets of DAP (see Hyun & Marshall, 1997; LeVine, 2004; Roopnarine et al., 2004).

Is there a strong empirical basis for judging how developmentally appropriate practices actually work with children of immigrants or children in diverse populations in general? Are early childhood professionals aware of the varied adjustment patterns of immigrant families in this country? Do childrearing practices and conceptual frameworks about childhood development among diverse immigrant groups coincide or collide with those articulated by DAP? What beliefs do immigrant parents hold about what constitutes exemplary early childhood education practices? For example, do they embrace more academically inclined programs that emphasize the learning of basic skills (e.g., literacy, mathematics) and assign homework, or those that are embedded in play-based neo-constructivist principles? What are immigrant parents' beliefs about involvement in their children's schooling and how is parental involvement manifested?

In addressing these questions, we refer to, but do not limit our discussion to, the developmental and curricula concepts laid out in the 1997 NAEYC document (Bredekamp & Copple, 1997). Several authors (e.g., Hyun & Marshall, 1997; Spodek & Brown, 1993) have provided feedback on different aspects of developmentally appropriate practices, and a few (LeVine, 2004) have pointed to the duality that exists between "an ideological advocacy movement for the humane treatment of children and a scientific endeavor seeking knowledge and understanding of child development." As LeVine (2004) suggests, "this combination can narrow and distort scientific exploration in the interest of promoting a moral cause" (p. 151). What follows is in the spirit of prior attempts to define "culturally sensitive" practices for diverse groups of children (e.g., Developmentally and Culturally Appropriate Practice—DCAP) in the contemporary field of early childhood education. In a way, it offers to build on what NAEYC believes is fundamental to improving early education for all children—"to be dynamic and changing in response to new knowledge as well as to benefit from the shared experiences of and interactions among professionals." It is perhaps necessary to first understand beliefs about early education and behavioral training, the links between beliefs and school involvement practices and the structuring of educational activities at home, and the prioritization of educational and socialization goals among immigrant families before we continue our efforts to design culturally relevant early childhood curricula.

In line with concerns raised by other educators, cultural psychologists, and anthropologists (e.g., Fuligni, 2001; LeVine, 2004; Ogbu, 1991; Suarez-Orozco, 2001), we aspire to cast further light on educating children of immigrants and immigrant children during the early childhood years. There is good consensus that this is a critical period when conceptions about the functions and benefits of schools and schooling are starting to take shape, and solid partnerships with immigrant parents can have an enabling effect on school success. As we build a sound knowledge base on childhood development, family practices, and adjustment patterns of recent immigrants in the United States (e.g., those of color in particular; see entire issue of *Harvard Educational Review*, Fall, 2001) and modify our views on acculturation to a new society (see Foner, 1997, 2001; Zhou, 1997), it is an opportune time to bridge the "voices" and educational needs of immigrant parents with discussions of developmentally appropriate practices. In the same vein, newer theoretical and research developments (see Arnett, 2002; Chao, 1994, 2001; Greenfield, 1997; Ladson-Billings, 2000; Lamb, 2004; Roopnarine et al., 2004; Roopnarine & Gielen, 2005; Sharma & Fischer, 1998; Shweder et al., 1998; Super & Harkness,

1997; Suarez-Orozco, 2001) in the field of cultural psychology and education can assist in broadening NAEYC's recommendations for appropriate practices with immigrant children—especially when it comes to parental beliefs and practices and parents as partners in the educational enterprise. From a growing literature, there is strong indication that conceptions of what are minimally or maximally optimal for childhood development and education vary considerably across and within cultures (Super & Harkness, 1997).

Whereas some of the topics we single out in this paper may very well apply to children across immigrant groups, our emphasis is on children from Latin America, the Caribbean, and South and South East Asia, the sources of most new immigrants in the United States today. It is imperative to stress that even though these families may share common views about the academic content of early childhood education, there is tremendous cultural heterogeneity in childrearing and parental aspirations for children.

WHO ARE THE NEW IMMIGRANTS?

Today, a majority of the immigrants in the United States come from Latin America and the Caribbean, followed by Asia (see Adler & Gielen, 2003). By some estimates, one in five children in the United States lives in an immigrant household (Suarez-Orozco, 2001). There are more than 14 million children of immigrants and in some public school systems such as New York City, 48% of the children are from immigrant households—forming what Foner (2001), in her analysis of Caribbean immigrants to New York, has called *"Islands in the City."* Comparable scenarios exist in other major metropolitan areas (e.g., Los Angeles, Miami, Houston) as well. The number of new immigrants (documented and undocumented) continues to increase in the face of a downturn in our national economy, with a majority of states with large concentrations of immigrants (e.g., New York, California) reporting deficits in revenues. Add to the budgetary crises the fact that disproportionate numbers of immigrant children of color are placed in "special education classes," and children of immigrants on the whole are more likely to attend substandard schools in poorer urban neighborhoods (Suarez-Orozco, 2001). The responsibility of providing culturally appropriate early childhood educational experiences to young children of immigrants remains daunting.

CONCEPTUAL CONSIDERATIONS FOR EARLY CHILDHOOD EDUCATION PRACTICES FOR CHILDREN OF IMMIGRANTS

Before moving on to a consideration of developmentally appropriate practices and early childhood education for children of immigrants, it might be advantageous to lay out some interrelated issues identified by researchers as important in educating diverse groups of children in the twenty-first century. Four of them appear pertinent to our deliberations here: the benefits of structured versus less-structured early childhood programs, conceptions of social and cognitive competence, processes of changes that are occurring simultaneously in immigrant families and the school systems in the United States, and increasing globalization and its possible impact on young children of immigrants living here. We begin with an overall, albeit brief, evaluation of some of the findings on the salubrious effects of early childhood education programs that are more structured and teacher-guided (didactic-instruction) and those that are more child-centered (developmentally appropriate). Mind you, little data exist on programs that adopt a blend of both approaches (see Marcon, 1999; Rescorla et al., 1991; Stipek et al., 1995).

An analysis of data gathered over several decades on both child-centered and teacher-centered early childhood programs provides little room for tidy conclusions about the relative long-term effectiveness of either educational approach. Furthermore, some of the conceptual frameworks (e.g., cultural disadvantage; deficit structure) that guided research in prior decades may not be relevant for the education of children of immigrants in the twenty-first century. As Moreno (2002) articulated, "only by examining the personnel, task demands, values and beliefs, scripts, and purposes and motives are we in a position to better understand the nature of instruction" (p. 192). Even so, we find the intervention data on children from the last four decades of the previous century quite instructive. They speak to the potential value of direct instruction for economically disadvantaged groups.

With the above caveats aside, in highly structured early childhood programs (e.g., DISTAR, DARCEE), favored by some immigrant groups, initial gains were recorded on standardized tests and achievement ratings (e.g., I.Q., arithmetic, sentence construction). By second grade, DISTAR children scored higher on reading achievement compared to DARCEE children and those who were enrolled in a traditional preschool program, whereas DARCEE children scored higher on divergent thinking relative to DISTAR and children from the traditional program. Interestingly, children who were exposed to the Montessori approach—viewed by some as more structured in the sense that it is not play-based and relies on interactions with specified materials—outperformed the other groups of children on different measures through the grade school years. Later assessments conducted in the seventh and eight grades showed that a small number of the DARCEE and DISTAR children exceeded the 50th percentile in academic performance (Miller & Bizzell, 1983). Additional work from the same period indicates that children enrolled in an Ameliorative program and in DISTAR did far better on tests of reading achievement at the end of first-grade than those enrolled in a traditional program (Karnes et al., 1983). In the cognitively oriented High Scope Program that is more child-centered, children did not accrue superior benefits to children in the more structured DISTAR model until they were about age 15 (Schweinhart, Weikart, & Larner, 1986).

Studies conducted in the 1990s revealed better letter/writing achievement among kindergartners in didactic instruction than their counterparts in child-centered programs (Stipek et al., 1995). However, there are drawbacks associated with more structured early childhood programs. Higher levels of stress, as manifested in daydreaming, teeth grinding, ear pulling, stuttering and so on, were observed, especially in boys (Burts et al., 1990; Burts et al., 1992), and lower perceptions of school success and related abilities, dependency on adults, and worries about school were more common in children enrolled in structured than child-centered programs (developmentally appropriate) (Stipek et al., 1995). Greater structure has also been shown to have negative consequences on academic and motivational skills during the preschool years (Stipek et al., 1998).

How do we interpret these mixed results on the "effects" of didactic instruction and child-centered educational programs in the context of children of immigrants and immigrant children? Research findings demonstrate that face-to-face, direct-instruction is most consistent with the teaching practices that Mexican Americans (Moreno, 2002), diverse Asian immigrant groups (Parmar, Harkness, & Super, in press), and English-speaking Caribbean immigrants employ with children at home (Roopnarine, 1999; Roopnarine et al., 2004). These parents are more likely than not to have been involved themselves in educational programs in the natal culture that are structured and guided by direct-instruction. A number of families enroll their children in early childhood programs that require school uniforms, demand compliance, and stress learning basic skills. For them, structured education and rigor in the early childhood curriculum are the sine-qua-non of quality education. On a common sense level, improving instructional continuity between the home and school has the potential of making the learning experiences of children and parent-teacher relationships more sanguine. Possibly more structure during the transition to formal schooling is essential to setting some children of immigrants off on a successful path. This may also provide opportunities for immigrant parents and their children to broker cultural scripts about schooling.

Tied to immigrant parents' push for more educational content in the preschool years, are parental ethnotheories about what constitutes intellectual and social competence. Data gathered across cultures suggest that parents have different ideas about "developmental milestones" and different formulas for what signifies competence (Super & Harkness, 1997). While recent immigrants in the United States seem aware of general developmental patterns in their children (e.g., onset of walking, speaking in sentences and so on), some (e.g., Caribbean immigrants) are not aware of what developmental appropriateness means or the desired practices outlined in DAP that are clearly delineated along ages/stages of development (see Roopnarine et al., 2004). For some groups, maturity in social and intellectual skills may entail listening to adults, compliance, knowing the alphabet and counting, and these attributes are expected at early ages. In addition, preferences for social and intellectual development are hierarchically arranged across cultural groups (Roopnarine, 1999).

Along with their reluctance to embrace less direct instructional philosophies for young children is the ability of immigrant parents to adjust to changes in their own lives as immigrants to a new society, and to simultaneously deal with the different waves of school reforms in the United States. In the natal cultures—Caribbean, Latin America, and parts of Asia— there is greater stability in methods of instruction, and changes in the school system occur at a much more measured, slower pace. Parents entrust their children to schools without much involvement in shaping curricula. The concurrent tides of changes that are occurring among immigrant families in terms of psychological adaptation (e.g., acculturation stress and coping, adaptation, shedding cultural values) and within the school systems in the United States can create a specter of discontinuity between the home and school environments (Roopnarine et al., 2004). During the post immigration period, immigrants and their children must contend with language barriers, finding housing and stable employment, job training/retraining, ethnic identity issues, and discrimination among a multitude of other daily struggles. At this time of transition, they are implicitly required to comprehend and accept the capricious nature of school reforms laced with highstakes testing (see "No Child Left Behind Act, U.S. Department of Education, 2002). In the absence of adequate community/familial support and financial resources, transitional difficulties may become exacerbated—affecting the calibration of parent–child relationships, the parent-school interface, and children's social adjustment and school functioning (see Roopnarine et al., 2004). Of course, not all immigrant parents and children experience persistent transitional difficulties. Immigrants enter the United States with varying levels of knowledge about the prevailing cultural mores here, educational training, and language skills (Rumbaut, 1997). For families who experience economic and social hardships, dealing with changes in the schools in the United States (e.g., reduced funding for bilingual education, less support for after-school programs) can only add to the burden of coping with the competing demands of meeting obligations and responsibilities within the family and those annexed to children's schooling.

A final point on early childhood education for immigrant children bears stating. The increase in global and cultural consciousness (see Arnett, 2002) has led to convergences in childhood experiences within and across societies (see Brown, Larsen, & Saraswathi, 2002; Roopnarine & Gielen, 2005). Because of technological, media, and to a lesser extent interpersonal contact, children across the globe are exposed to the same television programs (e.g., Barney, Bugs Bunny, Sesame Street, Mister Rogers Neighborhood, The Cosby Show), movies (e.g., Disney films, the sensation of Harry Potter), and video games (e.g., Sega, Play Station), and they communicate through the Internet. The point is this: children from diverse cultural backgrounds are sharing similar cultural information more than ever before. Could this lead to the development of hybrid or transnational identities? It has already been hinted that immigrant groups in the New York City area develop transnational or hybrid identities rooted in childrearing practices in the natal and immigrant cultures (see Foner, 2001; Roopnarine, 1999). In other words, some immigrant parents in the United States adopt pan-cultural childrearing techniques. This does not negate the fact that deep cultural differences remain among peoples. What it does suggest, however, is that currently we are in uncharted territory when it comes to designing early childhood curricula for young children of immigrants.

IMMIGRANT ADJUSTMENT—MULTIPLE PATHWAYS

Several hotly contested positions have been proffered about the adjustment patterns of immigrants to a new society (see Adler & Gielen, 2003; Berry, 1998; DeWind & Kasinitz, 1997; Foner, 2001; Gordon, 1964; Rumbaut, 1997; Zhou, 1997). As suggested already, immigrants enter the United States with different levels of training/educational and language skills, and economic resources. Few societies around the world have no knowledge about life in the United States. Consider for a moment that a large number of Caribbean immigrants are English-speaking, have easy access to "American cultural values" through the media, communicate with relatives here who send remittances and goods to them, and travel to the United States as either guest workers or visitors. The same can be said for non-English speaking immigrants from Mexico and other Latin American countries, and to a lesser extent Asian countries. In other words, compared with immigrants of prior periods, people who come to settle in the United States in this postmodern period are quite savvy about life here. Consequently, the acculturation or adjustment of immigrant families and children in the United States is far from homogeneous. With greater expressions of cultural pride and focus on ethnic identity and socialization, what values do immigrant groups move toward during the acculturation process? (See Laosa, 1999 for a discussion of intercultural change and intercultural transition.)

Building on the work of other social science (e.g., Berry, 1998; Foner, 1997, 2001; Laosa, 1999; Zhou, 1997) and educational researchers (e.g., Fuligni, 2001; Suarez-Orozco, 2001), in another paper (Roopnarine et al., 2004) several typologies of immigrant adjustment that fall along a continuum were laid out. Due to the ebb and flow and volatility of immigrant community life and adjustment, the typologies are hardly exhaustive and adjustment should not be taken as a linear process. It was proposed that some immigrant families show a *synchronous pattern* of adjustment in which they blend socialization and education values from the natal culture with those in their new society. They reorganize elements of their internal working models about childhood education and care as they increasingly come into contact with those that predominate in their new society. Beliefs and practices that are of lower adaptive value may be replaced by others that are of greater utility for life in the new community (see Berry, 1998). In general, among this group, the pacing of parent child relationships is smoother and more harmonious as parents and children negotiate their way through the school system. Children receive a good deal of support from parents for their educational efforts and parent-teacher communications and educational goals are more closely aligned and primed to optimize school success. By contrast, there are families who show a *staggered pattern* of adjustment, holding on to entrenched natal childrearing and education beliefs during the initial adjustment period but relinquishing and/or modifying them gradually as they become more firmly planted in life here. Under these circumstances, the socialization values and principles that children pick up through schooling and from the community at large may cause some dissonance for parents, forcing them to reflect on and subsequently change some childrearing practices and belief systems regarding schooling, health, and childrearing (see Berry, 1998). Nonetheless, there is a tendency for parents to emphasize the values they were brought up with. Expectations about schooling and parent-teacher partnerships evolve over time.

In the other two adjustment patterns—*asynchronous* and *disorganized/disoriented*, parents and children experience more difficulties in telescoping and adjusting to life in their new country. In the asynchronous adjustment pattern, families are dogmatic in keeping individual members in line with childrearing values and beliefs (e.g., strong hand in discipline, traditional husband-wife roles, etc.) that served them "well" in the old country and strongly urge that they be transferred and implemented here. They are only too eager to recite the "pitfalls" of life in America—parents being too lax, children have more rights than parents, and lack of enforcement of parental authority. It is not unusual for these parents to use ad hoc strategies in childrearing and to find themselves busy warding off challenges from their children about the inherent ills of the natal culture value systems (e.g., harsh discipline; unilateral respect for older members of the family; total obedience). Discrepancies may exist between the family and school systems as parents become progressively alienated from their children and the schooling process. The fate of *disorganized/disoriented parents* and children seems much worse. These families experience extreme adjustment and acculturation difficulties. They may become disenfranchised from the immediate community, possibly becoming a permanent member of the urban "underclass" (see Portes & Zhou, 1993). Parent–child relationships are strained and parents are disconnected from schools and may be referred for social service or psychological help. School outcomes are poor or unpredictable.

These classifications are largely untested and are not meant to be conclusive. They provide a preliminary effort to move away from umbrella characterizations that have been used to describe immigrant adjustment to American society. Some families do quite well upon arrival here and elude traditional paths to upward mobility—from "inner city to suburb" and "the mailroom to the boardroom." Others must balance economic needs and cultural/linguistic differences with modes of childrearing and schooling practices that emphasize democratic principles, less-structure, and non-punitive methods of disciplining children. Increasing numbers establish residences in more than one culture, moving children back and forth for schooling and cultural identity reasons (e.g., parachute children in Los Angeles, Asian Indians, African-Caribbean). A few succumb to their own inability to meet the daily needs of their families and children and may become disenfranchised, dropping out from mainstream society altogether (Zhou, 1997).

PARENT–CHILD BELIEFS AND PRACTICES
IN IMMIGRANT FAMILIES

There have been several attempts to draw attention to the childrearing practices and styles of diverse immigrant groups in the United States. For example (Chao, 1994, 2001; Darling & Steinberg, 1993; Moreno, 2002; Roopnarine, 1999; Roopnarine et al., 2004) questions have been raised about parenting style typologies and their meaning for childhood social and intellectual competence among children of immigrants. Similarly, variations in parent–child interactions and childrearing beliefs and their meaning for childhood development across immigrant groups in the United States and other cultures have been captured in several authoritative reviews and books (see Brown et al., 2002; Greenfield & Cocking, 1994; LeVine, 2004; Roopnarine & Gielen, 2005; Shweder et al., 1998; Suarez-Orozco, 2001; Super & Harkness, 1997; United Nations Development Report, 2001; Weisner, 1998). What can be derived from both bodies of research is that beliefs and practices about the care and education of young children at times appear inimical to NAEYC's definitions of what is "developmentally appropriate." The dilemma is obvious: how does one reconcile yawning gaps in beliefs about the care/education of young children in immigrant families and those outlined by DAP?

In this segment of the paper, we turn our attention to: (a) parental cultural belief systems and their relationships to educational outcomes and social behaviors, and (b) the importance of understanding parental beliefs for educating young children of immigrants. Recall that the NAEYC manual has empirically dichotomized behaviors, and specified those that are superior to others and touted as invariably producing better social and intellectual outcomes in children. Summarily, during the pre-kindergarten and kindergarten years, play is implemented as a central part of the early childhood curriculum, rigorous academic work and testing are discouraged, and so is harsh discipline. Other areas of behavioral training such as adult control, direct correction of errors, indulgence, and inhibition as opposed to self-reliance and assertiveness may be considered inappropriate in the language of developmental appropriateness. By its very nature, dichotomy is problematic. So many things in the educational field are not straightforward. It is not difficult to envision the confusion these categorical distinctions may cause for immigrant families and early childhood teachers who work with children of immigrants.

Determining the empirical relationships between parental belief systems about childrearing and childhood development improves our ability to speak more convincingly about their significance for early childhood education practices. That parental beliefs are connected to diverse aspects of children's growth and development and schooling has been demonstrated for diverse cultural groups (see Harkness & Super, 1996; Sigel & McGillicuddy-De Lisi, 2002). For example, parental beliefs about children's abilities and competencies are linked to children's perceptions of their own competencies in academic subjects and directly or indirectly to academic performance (see Andre, Whigham, Hendrickson, & Chambers,

1999; Hortacsu, 1995; Jacobs, 1991; Li Pan, Yi, & Xia, 1999; McGillicuddy-De Lisi & Subramanian, 1994; Sonnenschein et al., 1997), to social skills—aggression (Hastings & Rubin, 1999), control and discipline (Grusec, Rudy, & Martini, 1997; Leo-Rhynie, 1997), and to health and physical well-being (Engle, Zeitlin, Medrano, & Garcia, 1996; Pebley, Hutardo, & Goldman, 1999).

Having established these associations, let us turn to cultural and cross-cultural investigations on childrearing beliefs and practices in the natal cultures of immigrant groups in the United States. It is important to repeat that parental beliefs provide a template for organizing daily routines of family life and structuring social and cognitive activities for children (see Super & Harkness, 1997). Some cultures (e.g., Taiwanese, Koren, Thai, East Indian) that are based in Confucian and Buddhist religious traditions emphasize equanimity, self-restraint, behavioral inhibition, obedience to adults, and parental control of childhood activities—all of which are viewed by parents as appropriate for the acquisition of childhood social competence (see Chao, 1994; Shin, 2001; Tulananda & Roopnarine, 2001). In other cultural settings (e.g., Caribbean), parents use harsh discipline (Roopnarine et al., 2004) and shaming to regulate childhood behaviors. Again, even though there is a worldwide push to abolish the physical punishment and humiliation of children (United Nations General Assembly, 1989) and excellent reviews (e.g., Baumrind, Larzelere, & Cowan, 2002) have questioned the harmfulness of physical punishment, these methods of disciplining children are still prevalent in a number of cultural groups (see Gopaul-McNicoll, 1993).

Divergent cultural beliefs have also been recorded about the value and meaning parents accord to play for early childhood development (see Roopnarine, Shin, Jung, & Hossain, 2003), the importance of learning academic content during the early childhood years, and the assignment of copious amounts of homework to preschoolers, kindergarteners, and children in the early grades of elementary school (Roopnarine et al., 2004). More specifically, parents in the developing countries (e.g., Caribbean, Latin America) place far less emphasis on play as important for the development of early social and cognitive skills (see Roopnarine et al., 2003 for a review). Both immigrant (Farver, Kim, & Lee, 1995; Farver & Shin, 1997; Holloway et al., 1995; Parmar & Harkness, in press; Roopnarine, 1999) and non-immigrant parents in the United States (Haight, Parke, & Black, 1997) stress the benefits of academic activities such as reading, learning the alphabet, and rudimentary mathematics content over those purportedly attributed to play by child development experts. Some immigrant parents (e.g., those from the English-speaking Caribbean) even believe that pre-school-aged children should be given daily homework assignments so that they can sharpen academic skills already learned in school. Lest you think these beliefs are limited to immigrant parents, several researchers (e.g., Stipek, 1991; Stipek et al., 1995) have argued that there is much confusion about employing any singular approach to educating young children, and teachers already use a blend of strategies in programs that are intended to be play-based and serve European-American children.

Clearly, the cultural scripts about early education and curricula among some immigrant groups are at odds with those recommended by NAEYC—particularly in areas of child guidance and the content of early childhood curricula. It would be a mistake to assume that all parents within a particular immigrant group or across immigrant groups hold identical beliefs about childrearing and early education. What is relevant is whether these "inappropriate" methods of caregiving are as harmful for children's intellectual and social development as has been professed by NAEYC. As LeVine (2004) wrote regarding his work with children in other cultures, it may be disconcerting to some "that young children can grow up normally without the kind of enthusiastic and energetic maternal support for their self-esteem, individuality, exploratory tendencies and personal autonomy that has become standard in the United States and some other Western countries during the last half century. In fact, children grew up without that kind of support at earlier times and still do in other parts of the world. Their parents had a different set of moral values to guide and foster their development, not a way of thwarting them" (p. 162). Obviously, we run the risk of exaggerating the dangers of more structured educational philosophies and controlling childrearing practices that do not fit neatly into what is considered by NAEYC as appropriate. The last point bears emphasis. No one is recommending the less than optimal treatment of children. Simply put, there are many paths to the same developmental outcomes. The "degree of appropriateness" of specific behaviors may fall along a continuum and their importance in guiding and educating young children may wax or wane over time.

PARENTAL INVOLVEMENT IN SCHOOLING—MANY FACES

The Goals 2002: Educate America Act and the reauthorized Elementary and Secondary Education Act (ESEA) have brought further attention to the importance of parental involvement in children's schooling at all levels. Research data lend credence to the role of parental involvement in their children's academic achievement (see Epstein, 1990; Kim, 2002; Lopez, 2001; Moreno, 2002). Be this as it may, cultural scripts regarding parental involvement range from being physically involved in children's school activities and curricula to the reinforcement at home of the virtues of educational achievement. For quite a few immigrant parents, "parents as partners" in the schooling process is a foreign concept, and they may rarely, if ever, contemplate being in the classroom with their children. Thus, using conventional definitions of parental involvement would certainly portray these families as uninterested bystanders in the educational process.

Our main aim is to feature other facets of parental involvement that move beyond physical presence in the classroom and at children's extra-curricular activities. Admittedly, these components are vitally important for children's schooling and shoring up home-school connections. The problem is that their relative importance in the education of immigrant children is now being recorded. Generally speaking, education is a primary index of success and immigrant parents use several means of reinforcing the importance of schooling other than through physical participation in the classroom. They lay out educational expectations, emphasize the importance of education daily (e.g., "education provides a third eye to the world"), provide daily assistance and guidance in matters of schooling (e.g., hiring tutors), expose children to models and symbols of success in the family and community, and stress the value of hard work within the immigrant experience (see Keith, Troutman, Trivette, & Singh, 1993; Kim, 2002; Lopez, 2001). Intrapersonal and sociodemographic factors such as family background (e.g., physical capital—finances, human capital-parental education, and social capital—human relationships, parenting skills, knowledge about schooling), linguistic and cultural barriers (Kim, 2002; Roopnarine et al., 2004), level of acculturation (Moreno & Valencia, 2002), and the interplay among these variables (e.g., the influence of physical capital and its direct and indirect relationships to children's well-being) have also been ascertained as significant in parental involvement (see Coleman, 1988; Epstein, 1990; Kim, 2002; Moreno & Valencia, 2002; Roopnarine et al., 2004; Teachman, Paasch, & Carver, 1997).

Last, but not least, are the partnerships that teachers and other school personnel develop with parents and the immigrant community at large. By most counts, "passive parental involvement," as in lack of contact with teachers, is seen as a drawback to the teaching-learning process. But strong parental involvement is contingent, in part, on the joint partnerships that parents and teachers cultivate. A prerequisite to this partnership is a commitment on the part of early childhood teachers and school personnel to acquire a deep understanding of different childrearing practices and beliefs, develop multilingual skills, practice culturally relevant pedagogy, and avoid punctuating parent–child conversations with the use of educational jargon (see Marshall, 2001; Roopnarine et al., 2004). Teachers and school personnel may need to assume a good deal of responsibility in informing parents about their efforts to improve schooling for immigrant children, how they will eliminate intentional and unintentional biases and "myths" about immigrant families, while empowering parents to share their cultural scripts about educational support for children (Ladson-Bill-ings, 2002; Moreno & Valencia, 2002).

CONCLUDING REMARKS AND RECOMMENDATIONS

As the number of immigrant children and children of immigrants contin-ues to climb in the United States, there is an urgent need to both define and chart pathways to education that are sensitive to parental beliefs and practices. Immigrant families bring cultural scripts on childrearing and education that are sometimes at odds with those that prevail in the school systems in the United States. In the early childhood education field, NAEYC recommends a set of behaviors and practices that are labeled "appropriate" and seen as optimal for working with young children, and used for the accreditation of early childhood programs. Let us reiterate that the basic tenets of DAP appear sound. However, it is our contention that the categories of behaviors designated as "appropriate" by NAEYC could imply that some practices that are valued and implemented by new immigrants are inferior. The scientific child development and early child-hood education data on immigrant families do not permit conclusive gen-eralizations about what is optimal for childhood development in these groups.

Today, it is necessary but not sufficient to just learn about the child's cul-tural frame of reference. To keep abreast with the educational needs of a changing multicultural democracy that continues to accept immigrants mainly from Asia, Latin America, and the Caribbean, it behooves us to con-sider the range of childrearing and behavioral practices rooted in the child's culture that may be seen as optimal. A wide array of cultural theories and research on childhood development and education in diverse disci-plines can be instructive in this regard. Although NAEYC has acknowledged the role of cultural-contextual issues in the education of young children, early childhood professionals may want to ponder the following:

1. Processes of psychological adaptation remain a key issue in influenc-ing school success among children of immigrants. Immigrant chil-dren and their parents enter the United States with different educational, social, and economic capital. Thus, their respective adjustment patterns may not follow a linear trajectory or uniform processes.

2. Immigrant parents' ethnotheories about childrearing and early edu-cation may reflect pancultural or transnational practices that affect not only the demands and expectations about school and schooling, but also the choice of early childhood programs in which children

are enrolled, and subsequently, the level of parental investment in such programs. While highly imbued in the natal culture, definitions of desired childhood behaviors and skills, conceptions of parental involvement in schooling, and parental ethnotheories about child-rearing and schooling (e.g., homework, value of play as an educational tool) do not remain static. They are likely to be modified or revised as families increasingly come in contact with cultural values and practices espoused in the United States and as children mature and act as cultural brokers for their parents.

3. Children of immigrants may develop hybrid cultural identities with social and cultural ties to multiple ethnic groups who live adjacent to them and to those in the natal and the evolving global culture. The complexities of their development defy traditional theoretical conceptions of social-cognitive processes.

4. The search for cross-ethnic and cross-cultural equivalence in parental ethnotheories about childhood development and education and involvement in children's schooling can be elusive. By categorizing behavioral practices into "appropriate" and "inappropriate" categories we run the risk of negating the rich tapestry of behaviors that are the heart of a multicultural society. When it comes to curricula, it may be better to speak about diverse cultural practices and their adaptive values in non-universal terms.

REFERENCES

Adler, L., & Gielen, U. (2003). (Eds.). *Immigration, emigration, and migration in international perspective.* Westport, CT: Praeger.

Andre, T., Whigham, M., Hendrikson, A., & Chambers, S. (1999). Competency beliefs, positive affect, and gender stereotypes of elementary students and their parents about science versus other school subjects. *Journal of Research in Science Teaching, 36,* 719–747.

Arnett, J.J. (2002). The psychology of globalization. *American Psychologist, 57,* 774–783.

Baumrind, D., Larzelere, & Cowan, P.A. (2002). Ordinary physical punishment: Is it harmful. *Psychological Bulletin, 128,* 580–589.

Beretier, C., & Engelmann, S. (1966). *Teaching disadvantaged children in the preschool.* Englewood Cliffs, NJ: Prentice-Hall, Inc.

Berry, J.W. (1998). Acculturation and health: Theory and research. In S.S. Kazarain & D.R. Evans (Eds.), *Cultural clinical psychology: Theory, research, and practice* (pp. 39–57). New York: Oxford University Press.

Bredekamp, S. (1987). *Developmentally appropriate practice in early childhood programs serving children from birth through age eight.* Washington, DC: NAEYC.

Bredekamp, S., & Copple, C. (1997). (Eds.). *Developmentally appropriate practice in early childhood programs* (rev. ed.). Washington, DC: NAEYC.

Brown, B.B., Larson, R., & Sarsawathi, T.S. (Eds.). (2002). *The world's youth: Adolescence in eight regions of the globe.* New York: Cambridge University Press.

Burts, D., Hart, C., Charlesworth, R., Fleege, P., Mosley, J., & Thomason, R. (1992). Observed activities and stress behaviors in classrooms with developmentally appropriate versus developmentally inappropriate kindergarten classrooms. *Early Childhood Research Quarterly, 7,* 297–318.

Burts, D., Hart, C., Charlesworth, R., & Kirk, L. (1990). A comparison of stress behaviors observed in kindergarten children in classrooms with developmentally appropriate versus developmentally inappropriate instructional practices. *Early Childhood Research Quarterly, 5,* 407–423.

Chao, R. (1994). Beyond parental control and authoritarian parenting style: Understanding Chinese parenting through the cultural notion of training. *Child Development, 72,* 1832–1843.

Chao, R. (2001). Extending research on the consequences of parenting style for Chinese Americans and European Americans. *Child Development, 72,* 1832–1843.

Coleman, J.S. (1988). Social capital in the creation of human capital. *American Journal of Sociology, 94,* 95–120.

Comer, J.P. (1988). Educating poor minority children. *Scientific American, 259,* 42–48.

Darling, N., & Steinberg, L. (1993). Parenting style as context: An integrative model. *Psychological Bulletin, 113,* 487–496.

DeWind, J., & Kasinitz, P. (1997). Everything old is new again? Processes and theories of immigrant incorporation. *International Migration Review, 31,* 1096–1111.

Elkind, D. (1987). *Miseducation: Preschoolers at risk.* New York: Alfred Knopf.

Elkind, D. (1981). *The hurried child.* Reading, MA: Addison-Wesley.

Engle, P.L., Zeitlin, M., Medrano, Y., & Garcia, L. (1996). Growth consequences of low-income Nicaraguan mothers theories about feeding 1-year olds. In S. Harkness & C. Super (Eds.), *Parents cultural belief systems: Their origins, expressions, and consequences* (pp. 428–446). New York: Guildford Press.

Epstein, J.L. (1990). School and family connections: Theory, research and implications for integrating sociologies of education and family. *Marriage and Family Review, 15,* 99–126.

Farver, J.A.M., Kim, Y.K., & Lee, Y. (1995). Cultural difference in Korean- and Anglo-American preschoolers social interaction and play behaviors. *Child Development, 66,* 1088–1099.

Farver, J.A.M., & Shin, Y.I. (1997). Social pretend play in Korean- and Anglo-American preschoolers. *Child Development, 68,* 544–556.

Foner, N. (1997). The immigrant family: Cultural legacies and cultural changes. *International Migration Review, 31,* 961–974.

Foner, N. (2001). *Islands in the City: West Indian migration to New York.* Berkeley: University of California Press.

Ford, B. (1995). African American community involvement process and special education: Essential networks for effective education. In B. Ford, F. Obiakor, &

J. Patton (Eds.), *Effective education for African American exceptional learners* (pp. 235–273). Austin, TX: Pro-ED.

Fuligni, A. (2001). A comparative longitudinal approach to acculturation among children from immigrant families. *Harvard Educational Review, 71*, 566–578.

Golbeck, S. (2001) (Ed.). *Psychological perspectives on early childhood education: Reframing dilemmas in research and practice.* Mahwah, NJ: Erlbaum.

Gopaul-McNicoll, S. (1993). *Working with West Indian families.* New York: Guilford.

Gordon, M.M. (1964). *Assimilation in American life: The role of race, religion, and national origins.* New York: Oxford University Press.

Greenfield, P. (1997). Culture as process: Empirical methods for cultural psychology. In J. Berry, P. Dasen, & T.S. Saraswathi, (Eds.), *Handbook of cross-cultural psychology: Basic processes and human development* (pp. 301–346). Needham, MA: Allyn & Bacon.

Greenfield, P., & Cocking, R. (1994). (Eds.). *Cross-cultural roots of minority child development.* Hillsdale, NJ: Erlbaum.

Grusec, J.E., Rudy, D., & Martini, T. (1997). Parenting cognitions and child outcomes: An overview and implications for children's internalization of values. In J.E. Grusec & L. Kuczynski (Eds.), *Parenting and children internalization of values: A handbook of contemporary theory* (pp. 259–282). New York: Wiley.

Haight, W.L., Parke, R.D., & Black, J.E. (1997). Mothers and fathers beliefs about and spontaneous participation in their toddlers pretend play. *Merrill-Palmer Quarterly, 43*, 271–290.

Harkness, S., & Super, C. (1996). (Eds.), *Parents' cultural belief systems: Their origins, expressions, and consequences.* New York: Guildford Press.

Harry, B. (1995). African American families. In B. Ford, F. Obiakor & J. Patton (Eds.), *Effective education for African American exceptional learners* (pp. 211–234). Austin, TX: Pro-ED.

Hastings, P., & Rubin, K.H. (1999). Predicting mothers' beliefs about preschool-aged children social behavior: Evidence for maternal attitudes moderating child effects. *Child Development, 70*, 722–741.

Holloway, S., Rambaud, M.F., Fuller, B., & Eggers-Pieorla, C. (1995). What is appropriate practice at home and in child care? Low-income mothers' view on preparing their children for school. *Early Childhood Research Quarterly, 10*, 451–473.

Hortacsu, N. (1995). Parents education levels, parents beliefs, and child outcomes. *Journal of Genetic Psychology, 156*, 373–383.

Hyun, E., & Marshall, J.D. (1997). Theory of multiple/multiethnic perspective-taking ability for teachers in developmentally and culturally appropriate practice (DCAP). *Journal of Research in Childhood Education, 11*, 188–199.

Jacobs, J.E. (1991). Influence of gender stereotypes on parent and child mathematics attitudes. *Journal of Educational Psychology, 83*, 518–527.

Karnes, M., Schwedel, A.M., & Williams, M.B. (1983). A comparison of five approaches of educating children from low-income homes. In *As the twig is bent: Lasting effects of preschool programs* (pp. 133–170). Hillsdale, NJ: Erlbaum.

Keith, T., Keith, P., Troutman, G.C., Brickley, P.G., Trivette, P.S., Singh, K. (1993). Does parental involvement affect eight grade student achievement? Structural analysis of national data. *School Psychology Review, 22*, 474–496.

Kim, E. (2002). The relationship between parental involvement and children's educational achievement in the Korean immigrant family. *Journal of Comparative Family Studies, 33*, 529–542.

Ladson-Billings, G. (2000). Fighting for our lives: Preparing teachers to teach African American children. *Journal of Teacher Education, 51*, 206–214.

Lamb, M.E. (Ed.). (2004). *The role of the father in child development* (4th ed.). New York: Wiley & Sons.

Laosa, L.M. (1999). Intercultural transitions in human development and education. *Journal of Applied Developmental Psychology, 20*, 355–406.

Leo-Rhynie, E. (1997). Class, race, and gender issues in childrearing in the Caribbean. In J.L. Roopnarine & J. Brown (Eds.), *Caribbean families: Diversity among ethnic groups.* (pp. 25–55). Norwood, NJ: Ablex.

LeVine, R. (2004). Challenging expert knowledge: Findings from an African study of infant care and development. In U.P. Gielen, & J.L. Roopnarine (Eds.), *Childhood and adolescence.* Westport, CT: Praeger.

Lopez, G.R. (2001). The value of hard work: Lessons of involvement from an (Im)migrant household. *Harvard Educational Review, 70*, 417–437.

Li, L., Pan, L., & Xia, Y. (1997). Structure and influencing factors of parental belief of mothers of 2–6 year-old children. *Psychological Science* (China), *20*, 243–247.

Marcon, R.A. (1999). Differential impact of preschool models on development and early learning of inner-city children. *Developmental Psychology, 35*, 358–375.

Mallory, B.L., & New, R.S. (Ed.). (1994). *Diversity and developmentally appropriate practices: Challenges for early childhood education.* New York: Teachers College Press.

Marshall, J.A. (2001) *Minority learning disabled students in segregated and integrated classes.* Dissertation Abstracts International, (University Microfilms No. 99-92356).

McGillicuddy-De Lisi, A.V., & Subramanian, S. (1994). Tanzanian and United States mothers' beliefs about parents' and teachers' roles in children knowledge acquisition. *International Journal of Behavioral Development, 17*, 209–237.

Miller, L.B., & Bizzell, R.P. (1984). Long-term effects of four preschool programs: Ninth and tenth grade results. *Child Development, 55*, 517–530.

Moreno, R.P. (2002). Teaching the alphabet: An exploratory look at maternal instruction in Mexican American families. *Hispanic Journal of Behavioral Science, 24*, 191–205.

Moreno, R.P., & Valencia, R.R. f(2002). Chicano families and schools: Myths, knowledge, and future directions for understanding. In R.R. Valencia (Ed.), *Chicano school failure and success: Past, present, and future* (pp.227–248). New York: Falmer Press.

Ogbu, J. (1991). Immigrant and involuntary minorities in comparative perspective. In M. Gibson & J. Ogbu (Eds.), *Minority status and schooling: A comparative study of immigrant and involuntary minorities* (pp. 3–33). New York: Garland Publishing.

Parmar, P., Harkness, S., & Super, C. (in press). Asian and European American parents ethnotheories of play and learning: Effects on home routines and children's behavior. *International Journal of Behavioral Development.*

Pebley, A., Hurtado, E., & Goldman, N. (1999). Beliefs about children's illness. *Journal of Biosocial Science, 31*, 195–219.

Portes, A., & Zhou, M. (1993). The new second generation: Segmented assimilation and its variants. *Annals of the American Academy of Political and Social Science, 530*, 74–96.

Rescorla, M.L., Hyson, M., & Hirsh-Pasek, K. (Eds.). (1991). Instruction in early childhood: Challenge or pressure. In *New directions in child development* (Vol. 53). San Francisco: Jossey-Bass.

Roopnarine, J.L. (1999, February). *Parental involvement, ethnotheories about development, parenting styles, and early academic achievement in Caribbean-American children.* Paper presented in the Department of Applied Psychology, New York University.

Roopnarine, J.L., & Johnson, J.E. (Eds.). (2005). *Approaches to early childhood education* (4th ed.). Columbus, OH: Merrill/Prentice Hall.

Roopnarine, J.L. & Gielen, U. (in press). *Families in global perspectives.* Boston: Allyn & Bacon.

Roopnarine, J.L., Bynoe, P.B., & Singh, R. (2004). Factors tied to the schooling of English-speaking immigrants in the United States. In U. Gielen, & J.L. Roopnarine (Eds.), *Childhood and adolescence.* (pp. 319–349). Westport, CT: Praeger.

Roopnarine, J.L., Shin, M., Jung, K., & Hossain, Z. (2003). Play and early education and development: The instantiation of parental belief systems. In O. Saracho & B. Spodek (Eds.), *Contemporary issues in early childhood education.* Westport, CT: New Age Publishers.

Rumbaut, R.G. (1997). Assimilation and its discontents: Between rhetoric and reality. *International Migration Review, 31*, 923–960.

Schweinhart, L.J., Weikart, D.P., & Larner, M.B. (1986). Consequences of three preschool curriculum models through age 15. *Early Childhood Research Quarterly, 1*, 15–45.

Sharma, D., & Fischer, K. (Eds.). (1998). *Socioemotional development across cultures. New Directions in Child Development* (pp. 69–85). San Francisco: Jossey-Bass.

Shin, M. (2001). *Beyond independent children and authoritative parenting: Korean mothers' perspectives.* Unpublished doctoral dissertation, Syracuse University, Syracuse.

Shonkoff, J., & Phillips, D. (2000). *From neurons to neighborhoods: The science of early childhood development.* Washington, DC: National Academy Press.

Shweder, R., Goodnow, J., Hatano, G., LeVine, R., Markus, H., & Miller, P. (1998). The cultural psychology of development: One mind, many mentalities. In R. Lerner (Vol. Ed.), *Theoretical models of human development: Vol 1. Handbook of child psychology* (pp. 865–937). New York: Wiley.

Sigel, I., & McGillicuddy-De Lisi, A. (2002). Parental beliefs as cognitions: The dynamic belief systems model. In M. Bornstein (Ed.), *Handbook of parenting* (vol. 3, 2nd ed.). Mahwah, NJ: Erlbaum.

Sonnenschein, S., Baker, L. Serpell, R., Scher, D., Truitt, V.G., & Munsterman, K. (1997). Parental beliefs about ways to help children learn to read: The impact of an entertainment or a skills perspective. *Early Child Development and Care, 127–128*, 111–118.

Spodek, B., & Brown, P.C. (1993). Curriculum alternatives in early childhood education. In B. Spodek (Ed.), *Handbook of research on the education of young children* (pp. 91–104). New York: Macmillan.

Stevenson, H.W., Chen, C., & Uttal, D.H. (1990). Beliefs and achievement: A study of Black, White, and Hispanic children. *Child Development, 61,* 518–523.

Stipek, D.J. (1991). Characterizing early childhood programs. In L. Rescorla, M.C. Hyson, & K. Hirssh-Pasek (Eds.), Instruction in early childhood: Challenge or pressure. *New Directions for Child Development, 53,* 47–55.

Stipek, D., Feiler, R., Daniels. D., & Milburn, S. (1995). Effects of different instructional approaches on young children's achievement and motivation. *Child Development, 66,* 209–223.

Stipek, D.J., Fieler, R., Byler, P., Ryan, R., Milburn, S., & Salmon, J.M. (1998). Good beginnings: What difference does the program make in preparing young children for school. *Journal of Applied Developmental Psychology, 19,* 41–66.

Suarez-Orozco, M. (2001). Globalization, immigration, and education: The research agenda. *Harvard Educational Review, 71,* 345–365.

Super, C., & Harkness, S. (1997). The cultural structuring of child development. In J. Berry, P. Dasen, & T.S. Saraswathi, (Eds.), *Handbook of cross-cultural psychology: Basic processes and human development* (pp. 1–39). Needham, MA: Allyn & Bacon.

Teachman, J.D., Paasch, K., & Carver, K. (1997). Social capital and dropping out of school early. *Journal of Marriage and the Family, 58,* 773–783.

Tulananda, O., & Roopnarine, J.L. (2001). Mothers' and fathers' interactions with preschoolers in the home in Northern Thailand: Relationships to teachers' assessments of children's social skills. *Journal of Family Psychology, 15,* 676–687.

United States Department of Education. (2002). *No child left behind.* Washington, DC: Author.

United Nations Development Programme. (2001). *Human development report.* New York: Oxford University Press.

United Nations General Assembly. (1989. November). *Adoption of a convention on the rights of the child* (U.N. Doc. A/Resolution 44/25). New York: United Nations.

Weikart, D., & Schweinhart, L. J. (2005). The High Scope Curriculum for early child care and education. In J.L. Roopnarine & J.E. Johnson (Eds.), *Approaches to early childhood education* (4th ed.). Columbus, OH: Merrill/Prentice Hall.

Weisner, T. (1998). Human development, child well-being, and the cultural project of development. In D. Sharma, & K. Fischer (Eds.), *Socioemotional development across cultures. New directions in child development* (pp. 69–85). San Francisco: Jossey-Bass.

Zhou, M. (1997). Segmented assimilation: Issues, controversies, and recent research on the new second generation. *International Migration Review, 31,* 975–1008.

CHAPTER 10

MEXICAN AMERICAN FAMILIES

Cultural and Linguistic Influences

Olivia N. Saracho and Frances Martínez-Hancock

INTRODUCTION

The family is the context into which children are born and are socialized to become productive citizens in their society. Family members belong to multiple cultures (Culturally and Linguistically Appropriate Services, CLAS, 2002). By virtue of the children's genetic background, they are unique individuals within their family of origin and cultural heritage. The National Association for the Education of Young Children (NAEYC), a highly respected early childhood organization, published a book titled, *Developmentally appropriate practices in early childhood programs* (Bredekamp & Copple, 1997), that advocates appropriate practices in the education of young children. The NAEYC book presents a set of principles that state that there are individual differences within the norms of development and recognizes culturally appropriate practices (Bredekamp & Copple, 1997) in the education of young children. The previous year NAEYC (1996) had

Contemporary Perspectives on Families, Communities, and Schools for Young Children, pages 203–224
Copyright © 2005 by Information Age Publishing
203

published a position paper titled, *Responding to linguistic and cultural diversity—Recommendations for effective early childhood education*, which provided recommendations that addressed the linguistic and cultural needs of young children including their social factors.

Social factors affect the children's development including child rearing practices, family roles, sociolinguistic patterns, historical, political, and economic systems as well as the individual's family socialization and behavior patterns. Given the complexity of influences on the development of children, educators need to recognize, understand, respect, and accept cultural differences (Saracho & Martínez-Hancock, 1983).

MEANING OF CULTURE

Culture represents the values, beliefs, and behaviors of a group of people. It is part of the group's language, customs, and traditions (Saracho & Martínez-Hancock, 1983). There are many definitions of culture. Franz Boas began to use the term "culture" at the end of the nineteenth century, to refer to the distinct body of customs, beliefs, and social institutions that seemed to characterize each separate society (Goodenough, 1971). According to Goodenough (1957), a society's culture is the knowledge individuals need to know or believe to be able to function in an appropriate way and assume a worthy role that is accepted by its members. Culture is an individual's mode of thinking, perceiving, relating, and otherwise interpreting. Recently Goodenough (2001) refers to culture as an "information pool." Authentic culture is in the mentalities of the culture messengers. Thus, culture is the information that individuals must know about their heritage to function successfully within their society.

Saracho and Martínez-Hancock (1983) use culture in reference to life style elements, such as language, diet, dress, social patterns, and ethnicity. Another definition of culture includes the set of values, assumptions, customs, physical objects, clothing, houses, food, tools, and art that a group of people have established to give structure to their daily life (Stassen-Berger & Thompson, 2000). Other cultural components are geography, history, architecture, religion, folk medicine, music, dance and socialization practices. According to Stassen-Berger and Thompson (2000), culture and ethnicity are analogous and overlap. An ethnic group is a body of people who have similar antecedent characteristics (including national origin, religion, upbringing, and language) and who possesses comparable beliefs, values, and cultural experiences.

Cultural Differences

The complexity of influences on the development of children requires that cultural differences be recognized, understood, respected, and accepted by early childhood education teachers (Saracho & Martínez-Hancock, 1983). Luis Laosa (1980) points out the differences associated with social class within ethnic and immigrant populations in his study of Mexican American mothers and their child-rearing interactions with their young children. Bowman (1994) also makes the distinction about the variation and difficulty with generalizations about minority groups and adds that poverty causes further complexity when discussing culture. She asks to what extent are group differences explained by adaptation to their environment vis-à-vis social class or are these differences part of their cultural norms as members of an ethnic group. Educators and researchers need to make this distinction.

According to Robinson (1993), gender, class, race, and culture are core components that develop a person's identity. Payne (1995) in her book, *Poverty: A Framework for Understanding and Working with Students and Adults from Poverty,* provides a framework for understanding how poverty affects conceptions about time such as living for the present to meet survival needs versus living for the future. She provides details for learning the rules of the middle class. She does not blame students for their own problems but instead identifies ways for educators to build relationships with students as a way to provide them the support they need to succeed. She claims that students of poverty have limited choices. The Spencer Foundation sponsored a conference on culture, child development, and education (New et al., 1998; Thomas et al., 1999). In this conference, a group of interdisciplinary scholars convened to discuss the place of cultural research on young children's development. From the discussions of small groups emerged the idea that there are differences between schools' and families' beliefs and, to some degree, their goals for children. NAEYC advocates consideration and respect for the family when it identifies and supports the concept of "culturally appropriate practices" in early childhood education (Bredekamp & Copple, 1997; NAEYC, 1996). Peña (2000) shows in her study on parent involvement that teachers fail to acknowledge the Mexican American families' contributions to the school and have different role expectations from those families. One assumption proposes that Mexican American children fail to succeed in the classroom because they confront styles of language socialization that disagree with those at home (Delgado-Gaitán, 1990). Saracho (1986) concludes that children in this situation may function in one of the following levels:

Level 1 (lowest level):   Students become confused when they experience a drastic difference between the two language and cultures.

> **Example:**   A series of charts is used to teach the unit of the family. The father usually is blond, has blue eyes, wears a suit and holds a black attaché case. Dalia, who does not speak or understand English, sees the charts and discovers that the family on the chart does not resemble her family. Her father has black hair and wears greasy overalls, because he is a mechanic. This experience confuses her.

Level 2:   Students deny their language and culture, pretending that their language and culture is the same as the school's.

> **Example:**   Miguel Jiménez, a Spanish-speaking student, changes his name to Michael and may even go a step further and change the pronunciation of his name to "Geemenes."

Level 3:   Students adapt to those new or different customs in the culture in which they perceive to have more advanced patterns. Children will assess each language and culture to adapt only the best patterns or customs to make them their own.

> **Example:**   Juan José enjoys eating the food from his culture. He makes it a point to celebrate birthdays and holidays with his family and friends, because he usually gets to eat and has a good time. However, when he is with his English-speaking friends, he refuses to speak his native language and only listens to English-speaking stations on the radio.

Level 4 (highest level):   Students are able to make the transition back and forth from one language and culture to another language and culture with ease.

> **Example:**   Juanita is a fluent bilingual student. She speaks her native language and the school's language. She carries a conversation in the language that is used in the group. Her behavior is appropriate in the different situations or settings such as at home, school or gatherings (pp. 53–54).

Sheets (2002) and Wortham and Contreras (2002) support these results. In Sheets' (2002) qualitative study students felt alienated. Wortham and Contreras (2002) show similar experiences with adolescent students to Saracho's (1986) Spanish-speaking six-year-olds. Wortham and Contreras (2002) describe how the adolescent students arrive the first day of school and usually encounter that culture shock that is being transplanted into a different lingual and cultural environment. They feel that the mainstream American life is sterile and boring.

Diversity

One out of seven children nationwide is from a different culture. The size and characteristics of the different cultural groups have been increasing which affects the population of young children. Culturally different children between the ages ranging from birth to four-years-old have increased from 1.8 million in 1976 to a projected 1.6 million in 1990, whereas those in the ages between five and 14 increased from 3.6 million to 5.1 million in the year 2000 (Oxford, 1984). Presently, there are more than two million culturally different children in this young population (Macias, 2000) in the public schools. It is estimated that by the year 2020 there will be more than five million culturally different people where the majority will be Spanish speakers whose number will triple by the year 2050 (National Coalition of Advocates for Students, 1988; Natriello, McDill, & Pallas, 1990). Among these Spanish speakers and other cultural groups, one of the largest cultural groups in the United States is the Mexican American group. They view themselves as America's forgotten minority. Although society has identified them as passive, their constitutive role continues to increase in the industrial, agricultural, artistic, intellectual, and political life of the country.

An understanding of the Mexican American families' cultural influence can enhance the early childhood teachers' sensitivity to what Mexican American children bring to school. Vásquez, Pease-Alvarez, and Shannon (1994), in their independent studies of Mexican immigrants in northern California, urge the adoption of a perspective that recognizes young children's assets which need to be identified and appreciated in order to provide an appropriate learning environment and curriculum that are relevant to the children's lives. This is what Bredekamp and Copple (1997) and NAEYC (1996) advocate in their concept of "culturally appropriate practices." However, it is still a challenge for all teachers to discover the children's strengths as they get to know them and their families through the building of relationships, focused observation, communication, and a commitment to move toward more family-centered practices after examining their own attitudes, bias and stereotypes. This process begins with teachers who have an ethical commitment to provide child-centered and family-centered practices. Teachers can take the initiative by identifying their own attitudes, biases, prejudices, and stereotypes in order to transform their curriculum to reflect an "integrated" multicultural and anti-bias education for all children (York, 1998). The family-centered practice acknowledges the importance of the family system on child development, respects families as decision-makers, and supports families in their role as parents (McBride, 1999).

Culture in Mexican American Families

Culture is vigorous within the Mexican American families. It changes as immigrants adapt to societal challenges and they become acculturated into the American mainstream. Some become acculturated, whereas others may choose to become bicultural. Martínez (2001) portrays the lives of a family of Mexican immigrants, the detachments from their families, and the adjustments they had to endure in the United States to be able to survive. He also delineates their effort to "assimilate," not to assimilate, or to conform to become "American." The book that was written by Valdés (1996) titled, *Con Respeto: Bridging the Distances between Culturally Diverse Families and Schools, An Ethnographic Portrait,* describes a study of ten first-generation Mexican American working-class families. It documents the strategies that families use to survive, including the children's role as active participants. In these families, children are taught respect (*respeto*) and to obey parents, to take care of siblings, and to concentrate on family goals rather than self-centered individual goals. Nevertheless, Valdés (1996) criticizes these socialization practices which interfere with the values of the school culture. This is a social class issue and a gap between the values and goals of the school and family.

Ricardo Muñoz (2002), through his Latino Outreach program at the University of California-San Francisco, has discovered that Mexican American individuals find that the adaptation to the mainstream American culture is stressful. He claims that clinical depression in the Mexican American population is 13% in comparison to 17% of the general population. It is 14.4% for those born in the United States and 3% for recent immigrants. He contends that the longer they reside in the United States (13 years or longer), their life becomes more stressful. He asserts that immigrants have more ties with their families, but when their support system breaks down, it affects their mental health. Also, there is a stigma attached to mental health services and mental health professionals in Latino communities. Muñoz (2002) adds that maintaining family ties conflicts with the American mainstream's view of the development of independence. First generation Mexican American families may become confused when they lose their culture, their roots, and their levels of acceptance. He maintains that those who are born in the United States are adopting the mainstream American culture and that their psychological distress varies across time and cultural context. Each person's identity is closely related to the family. The traditional Mexican American families are becoming less common as families adapt to a more technological society.

One of the major obstacles which has impeded the development of a coherent educational policy for Mexican Americans is the idea that this population is a homogenous one, characterized by low economic status and low educational achievement. A limited focus only on economic status and educational achievement has distorted the heterogeneity of the Mexican American group in many important spheres of life. There are still biases and stereotypes that need to be dispelled. In addition, social scientists and educators need to conduct more research that describes the diversity of the Mexican Americans' socialization practices for their families and their young children, their effects on the individuals' personality and behavioral development, and how these are influenced by social class. Results from these studies are vital for those attempting to develop educational programs and/or policy for the education of Mexican Americans.

Presently, the Early Childhood Research Institute on Culturally and Linguistically Appropriate Services (CLAS, 2002), a federally-funded collaborative effort of several institutions (including the University of Illinois at Urbana-Champaign, Council for Exceptional Children, University of Wisconsin-Milwaukee, ERIC Clearinghouse on Elementary and Early Childhood Education, ERIC Clearinghouse on Disabilities and Gifted Education), "identifies, evaluates and promotes effective and appropriate early intervention practices and preschool practices that are sensitive and respectful to children and families from culturally and linguistically diverse backgrounds." It acknowledges that "cultures are multifaceted and dynamic and that individuals and families are members of multiple cultures."

PROGRESSION OF THE MEXICAN AMERICAN FAMILIES

The historical, genetic, and cultural background of Mexican American families are heterogenous. According to Ramírez and Castañeda (1974), the Spanish and Indian heritage of Mexican American families may range from none to 100%. The Spaniards who came to Mexico varied in cultural origin. They included individuals of Iberian, Greek, Latin, Visigoth, Moroccan, Phoenician, Carthaginian, and other backgrounds. In 1848, after the Mexican-United States War, the Treaty of Guadalupe Hidalgo ceded California, Nevada, Utah, parts of Colorado, Arizona, and New Mexico to the United States. The treaty stipulated that Mexicans could stay in the United States or return to Mexico. For those who chose to stay and become United States citizens, it was expected that they would assimilate to the mainstream American culture, like other immigrant groups. Unlike other immigrant groups who were separated by oceans or great distances, Mexican American families live near their country of origin.

In a special edition of *Time Magazine* that focused on the United States and Mexican border, the article titled "Welcome to Amexica" (Gibbs, 2001) states, "there is no customs station for customs—for ideas and tastes, stories and songs, values, instincts, attitudes, and none of those stop in El Paso, Texas, or San Diego, California, anymore." The *Time Magazine* issue identifies Mexicans as the predominant segment and the largest minority group of Hispanics in the United States. Vigil's (1998) book titled, *From Indians to Chicanos: The Dynamics of Mexican-American Culture*, outlines four eras in our history: pre-Columbian, Spanish Colonial, the period of Mexican Independence from Spain and the United States victory in the Mexican American War (Treaty of Guadalupe 1848). Terms used to describe this group's members vary from one region of the country to another. Vigil (1998) uses the term "mestizaje" which refers to the racial mixing of Mexican Indians and Spaniards. This would make Mexican Americans "mestizos." The Resource Center for the Americas (1996) identifies the term "Chicano" as one adopted in the late 1960s by advocates of the Civil Rights Movement. Some Mexican Americans favor this term, because it recognizes their Indian, African, and Spanish roots; while others prefer the term "La Raza" over mestizo; because it characterizes those of Mexican origin or Mexican Americans whose heritage has an Indian-Spanish blend.

Those of Mexican descent in northern New Mexico and southern Colorado call themselves Spanish Americans; while others call themselves Latin Americans, Chicanos, Hispanos, Spanish-speaking, La Raza, and Americans of Mexican descent (Ramírez & Castañeda, 1974). Gratton et al. (2003) examine family and household relationships of Mexican origin Americans between 1880 and 1990. They compare Mexican American families to several other immigrant origin groups (such as the Irish, Italians, Poles, Chinese, and Puerto Ricans) and assess the effects of ethnicity on family structure, particularly the household situations with children. They show that presently Hispanic families have rising rates of unmarried female-headed families with children rather than the idealized nuclear family. This occurred after 1970, because Mexican origin individuals controlled the Hispanic population. An examination of the children's family experiences with their mothers show the development of female-headed households and at intermarriage theoretical issues that emerge in the assimilation patterns of immigrant groups.

The native Mexicans represent distinct groups that differ physically, socially, economically, and culturally from one another. However, Trueba (1999) in his book titled, *Latinos Unidos: From Cultural Diversity to the Politics of Solidarity*, concludes that in spite of the diversity, Latinos are united by "common experiences in the United States." The National Council of La Raza (2001) report titled, *Beyond the Census: Hispanics and an American Agenda*, indicates that most Hispanics live in California, Texas, New York, Florida, Illinois, Arizona, and New Jersey. It also shows that Hispanic communities have moved to Georgia, North Carolina, and Tennessee. The Mexican population primarily lives in the urban areas of Los Angeles, Chicago, and Houston, although there is migration to the Midwest, to the East coast, and to other geographic areas that offer them employment opportunities that will help them to support their families.

Socioeconomic Factors of Mexican American Families

The statistics indicate that 41% of Hispanic workers are employed in service occupations or as operators and laborers (United States Census Bureau, 2000). An analysis of the socioeconomic status of Hispanics in general reveals that only 14% were employed in managerial or professional occupations, with only 11% of Hispanics over 25 years of age who have earned at least a bachelor's degree. The census also shows that home ownerships by Hispanics is at 46% with Cubans and Spaniards having the highest rates. In 1997 there were only 472,000 businesses that were owned by Mexican origin individuals. Those of Mexican descent owned the highest number of Hispanic-owned businesses (United States Census Bureau, 2000). Mexican Americans are considered hard-working, although they are generally undereducated and, thus, receive low wages. Many Mexican Americans have raised their socioeconomic status to middle class, but many are still considered working class or poor.

The culture of the school reflects a middle class orientation. As such, a gap exists between schools and the poor or working class families in relation to their goals for life and the education of their children. Mehan, Hubbard, and Villanueva (1994) claim that schools and other "symbolic institutions" devise a curriculum that reward the "cultural capital" of the dominant classes and "systematically devalues that of the lower classes." They add that children who read good books and go to museums, concerts, and the theater become familiar with the dominant culture in society that the educational system requires and rewards.

Teachers have been heard to say, "If Mexican American children are to be successful in this society, they must be competitive, assertive, and learn to look out for themselves." However, their family ties focus on cooperation rather than competition. Traditionally, the culture of the Mexican American families instills in the child a strong sense of extended family ties, including all relatives. They firmly believe that the family is sacred. Each person's identity is closely related to the family and their culture. Traditional Mexican American families are becoming less common and most of the children are growing up in transitional families.

Roles, Values, and Interdependence of Mexican American Families

The family's fundamental human needs as well as their perceptions and roles of the family determines the Mexican Americans' family functions. Bigner (1994) states that roles are used in family systems to explain acceptable behavior and to regulate the functioning of the system. The roles of

Mexican American families are based on the family's basic human needs, and on the family's perceptions and functions. The Mexican American families' most important values are the family relationships, leisure time activities, and the Catholic church. Rituals associated with religious or national holidays, as they were celebrated in Mexico are often retained. Many Mexican American families maintain their folkways and characteristic patterns of action such as the acceptance of authority in the home, church, and state; maintaining personal loyalty to friends; being sensitive to praise and criticism; and practicing folk medicine. They differ to a great extent in their economic condition and social status (Saracho & Martínez-Hancock, 1983).

Mexican American families are generally sensitive to others' feelings and observe their rules of conduct such as respect for the status of others. Age and sex are important determinants of roles and status in their culture. Older people hold more status and are afforded more respect than others in the community. They are respected for their knowledge of the history of the community, culture, and ethnic group as well as for having more experience in life (Ramírez & Castañeda, 1974). Children learn early in life to give parents a special respect and to respect all elders.

Within the family, roles are assigned by age. The eldest child is given more responsibility and status is determined by how well the child fulfills responsibilities. In larger families, older children may be responsible for socializing younger ones. Many Mexican American children may be socialized to teach or tutor younger brothers and sisters. Classroom teachers may view this socialization practice as a positive, because it facilitates their instructional organization of learning experiences. Culturally competent Mexican American children and young adults who have learned their social roles and behaviors are often perceived to be well educated. Mexican American families consider being socially well educated to be more important than being academically well educated. Those who fulfill their roles and know how to behave properly bestow honor on their family in the eyes of the community.

Many of the values in the traditional Mexican American culture resemble those of other ethnic groups and differ considerably from values typically proclaimed by school. The term "traditional values" refer to those values that are characteristic of communities that are (1) rural, (2) situated near the Mexican border, and (3) found where most of the population is Mexican American. Assimilation and external variables may have an impact on these traditional values because they resemble the core of values that influence the behavior of Mexican American families regardless of any transformations that have transpired (Ramírez & Castañeda, 1974; Saracho & Martínez-Hancock, 1983). Valdés (1996) points out that Mexican American children have active roles in the family. Children in these families are expected to respect and obey their parents, to assume care of their siblings, and to focus on family goals. Valdés (1996) faults these socialization practices, because he believes that they interfere with the values of the school culture. This is a social class issue and only members in those circumstances know what they need to do to survive. Honoring their parents is one of the Ten Commandments for Mexican American Catholic families. This is an important commandment since faith in their religion is important.

The Faith of Mexican American Families

The Mexican Catholic ideology represents a blend of European and Indian religious ideas and practices. Mexican Catholicism supports and reinforces the values of the Mexican American culture. Identification with the ethnic group is reinforced through the worship of the Virgin of Guadalupe, the religious symbol of La Raza (literally the race). Furthermore, the emphasis on religious ceremonies that are built on close family ties reinforces the Mexican American's identification with the community. Parents and other adults are viewed as representatives of God; to disobey them is a transgression against God (Ramírez & Castañeda, 1974). Families select for their children different sets of godparents for each religious ritual such as baptism, first communion, and confirmation. God parents serve as co-parents—*comadres* (co-mothers) and *compadres* (co-fathers)—and are considered to be special persons in the families' lives and become part of the extended family because they were specifically selected by the families. They become second parents to the children and ideally are responsible for the moral upbringing of their god children.

Mexican American families also celebrate several religious rituals and holidays. Religious rituals consist of baptism, first communion, confirmation, marriage, Silver and Golden Anniversary weddings, and birthdays like Quinceañeras. When girls reach 15 years of age, the families have a Quinceañeara celebration with a party that includes a mass and/or dance, based on the families' resources. Some families invite members of their social network to make financial contributions to this event. Those who contribute are referred to as godparents.

In addition to baptisms, first communions, marriages, and quinceañeras, Mexican American families celebrate the Day of the Dead on November 1, Virgin of Guadalupe Day on December 12 (the day Juan Diego saw Our Lady of Guadalupe in Tepeyac, México), and the day Jesus Christ was born on December 25 (Christmas Day). Many Mexican American families value the authority of the home, church, and state as well as their personal loyalty to friends. These distinct elements in the culture of the Mexican American families contribute to their religious ideas, celebrations, and practices.

Role Expectations

Within the traditional Mexican American family, roles are defined according to age and gender. Ideally, family members believe that male dominance (concept of machismo) insures family survival. The extended family includes aunts, cousins, grandparents, godparents, and other relatives. Family means extended family members with specific roles and responsibilities with the male being the head of the family and the female being the nurturer. Embedded in these roles are the concepts of machismo (male dominance), sex, and age status as well as family orientation. The male has the authority to make decisions and the women are nurturers and child bearers, while the young listen to and respect the elderly. The family is a source of support and a socialization agent. Traditional Mexican American ideals and values are drawn from an agrarian society in Mexico. However, these ideals and values have changed due to political and economic circumstances that families encounter in the United States. As men have left their families to go to war or to seek work in the United States, women have taken over as heads of the household. Also, many Mexican American women have joined the labor force, especially in the United States. Becerra (1998) points out that patriarchal values did not disappear despite these economic or political pressures. However, the family continues to be a support system for most Mexican Americans with its basic values of sharing and cooperation. Family members help by providing child care, monetary loans, transportation, care for the sick and elderly, and housing. Most encouraging is the knowledge that the Mexican American family has endured. Its history in the United States suggests a tenacious ability to survive, to overcome adversity, and to adapt to change.

Belief System

The Mexican Catholic Church represents a blend of European and Indian religious ideas and practices. During the conquest of Mexico, the Spaniards brought the Catholic religion with its calendar of saints' days (Ancona, 2002). Mexican Catholicism supports and reinforces the values of the Mexican American culture. Identification with the ethnic group is reinforced through the worship of the Virgin of Guadalupe, who represents the religious symbol of La Raza (literally the race). Our Lady of Guadalupe is the patron saint of Mexico and traditionally many children (both boys and girls) are named after her and would go by the endearing and shortened version of "Lupita" (female name) or "Lupito" (male name). This is changing with the level of assimilation, with more families giving their children English names.

The rapid growth of the Mexican American population in the United States has raised researchers' interest in the issue of assimilation. They want to investigate the possibility that new immigrant groups can assimilate, and the length of time they will take to assimilate. Rosenfeld (2002) used census data from 1970, 1980, and 1990 to examine the behavior of Mexican Americans and Mexican immigrants in the United States marriage market. He shows that Mexican Americans are assimilating with non-Hispanic whites over time.

Holidays and Celebrations

While Mexican American families celebrate religious holidays year round, they also celebrate saints' days and patriotic holidays. These celebrations are observed throughout Mexico; therefore, they influence the celebrations that immigrants bring to the United States. More traditional Mexican American families have many additional religious celebrations such as baptisms, first communions, marriages, Day of the Dead (November 1), and Virgin of Guadalupe Day on December 12. In the year 2002, the Mexican peasant Juan Diego was canonized (Our Lady of Guadalupe Patroness of the America, 2003). He became the first indigenous Saint.

Mexican American families also celebrate other holidays such as birthdays and Quinceañeras, which were briefly introduced before. Quinceañeras are celebrated to announce that girls are making a transition from childhood to adulthood. It is a manner of providing 15-year-old girls a formal introduction to society. This type of celebration includes a party with a mass and a dance depending on the family's resources. Some families use their social networks to contribute to the event. The members of these social networks will contribute for the expense of the celebration. For example, a close family member can pay for the mass or contribute money that will pay for dance expenses such as the dance hall or music group. Some friends may pay for the dress. All of the contributors are members of the social network and are considered god parents. The number of members of the social network will depend on how many need to contribute to pay for the full cost of the event.

More recently immigrated Mexican American families celebrate Mexican patriotic holidays such as Cinco de Mayo (May 5), the defeat of French forces at Puebla, México. They also celebrate Mexico's Independence Day on September 16 (Mexican Independence from Spain). Los Angeles, California, has an all citywide celebration to commemorate this holiday with singing, dancing, and eating traditional foods. In the United States, many Catholic Mexican American families celebrate Christmas as the birth of Jesus Christ. This celebration begins on December 16 through December 24. During this time, they celebrate Las Posadas, which is the traditional procession of Mary and Joseph's search for a place to stay (a posada) in Bethlehem. This event is reenacted every day during this time of the year in many Mexican American communities, especially by those families who have closer ties to Mexico. However, many Mexican American families have modified this celebration, celebrating Christmas with a tree, the arrival of Santa Claus, and a sharing of gifts. Many of their traditions are being lost as immigrants adapt or accept new traditions as part of modern society. Today's Mexican American family has developed a unique culture in American society that maintains elements of both the Mexican and American culture, but it is not fully characterized by either the Mexican culture or the American culture (Becerra 1998).

EDUCATIONAL IMPLICATIONS

A child's self-image is also based on culture. The child raised in the traditional Mexican American community has been socialized within a language, heritage, set of cultural values, and predominant teaching style unique to that system (Laosa, 1980). Children will develop communication, learning, and motivational styles consistent with their socialization practices. When Mexican American children first enter an early childhood program, they may be expected to function in a sociocultural system whose practices relating to language and heritage, cultural values, and teaching styles are different from those they experience at home. They must be given time and sufficient opportunities to explore and to understand a new cultural world.

Mexican American children are required to function effectively in the mainstream American cultural world while simultaneously continuing to function in and contributing effectively to thier own cultural world. Mexican American children learn from their families socially meaningful behaviors, one of which is language. Language (Spanish and its variants) helps children to integrate the family patterns that they use every day in their life. Children learn appropriate ways to interact with others. Without being directly taught, they learn by looking, by touching, and by others reactions. The active process of building the new on the old is a form of self -regulation. Children assume active roles throughout this process by imitating others and practicing what they observe.

Lower school achievement and fewer years of schooling in many Mexican Americans can be attributed to three complex and interrelated sets of factors:

1. The nature of the diverse Mexican American subcultures and the socialization afforded Mexican American children;
2. The kind and quality of formal education available to Mexican Americans; and
3. The nature of the local and regional social systems and the equal or unequal opportunity they afford the minority group (Carter, 1971, p. 275).

Ogbu (1995a,b) refers to Mexican Americans and other minorities 'involuntary minorities.' He claims that they equate schooling with assimilation into the dominant group, which creates a cause for resistance. They are cognizant of the fact that there is inequality of opportunity and prejudice. However, he tends to blame them for their problems.

Most educators emphasize only the socialization factor in explaining the low status of Mexican American families. They blame the group's culture for the lack of assimilation and acculturation, because these lead to school failure. This assumption is widely accepted because it exonerates society and school. However, the low status and the continued foreignness of minority groups are situations caused by many social and economic factors within society as well as by cultural characteristics of the minority group. Nevertheless, American society generally blames minority groups as the cause of their own problems (Carter, 1971). Nieto and Rolón (1997) believe that change can only occur when schools stop blaming Mexican American students and their families for their lack of success. Arciniega (1971) views culture as persistent and self-perpetuating with family patterns being transmitted from one generation to the other. He suggests the following fundamental modifications to integrate the Mexican American students' culture in their educational programs.

1. Schools need to develop a commitment to a pluralistic model of society. Schools have advocated the myth of a melting pot and the rhetoric of equal opportunities, creating failure in the education of the Mexican American students.
2. Schools need to be organized as a microcosm of the ideal society in which diversity is perceived as a source of strength.
3. In designing programs, schools need to focus on the teacher's and family's influence on the student. Teachers need to accept the children's cultural and family background to enhance their positive self-concept. On the other hand, the teacher's rejection may diminish

the students' self-concept. The interactions and learning experiences provided within the curriculum needs to be responsive to the student's family and cultural background.

4. Schools need to recognize that children from both low and high socioeconomic backgrounds benefit from an education that is integrated and in an inter-ethnic setting. Such a setting would allow genuine communication across social, racial, and ethnic boundaries.

5. Schools need to use the wide range of cultural resources, including human resources, in planning and implementing the young child's learning experiences. When aspects of the Mexican American culture are incorporated into the school experience, the educational goals of the school become more relevant to children from that culture.

6. Most Mexican Americans have not been integrated into the dominant society. Schools can take the initiative in working with other social agencies to develop systems that will open opportunities for Mexican Americans to become equal members of our society.

Some groups may resist many of these suggested changes. Educators who strongly believe in providing equal educational opportunities will be challenged in overcoming this resistance. Schools will change when teacher education programs modify the prospective and practicing teachers' perspectives and attitudes. Schools must make philosophical, pedagogical, and organizational changes to respond to the needs of these families and their children. Nieto and Rolón (1997) suggest centering pedagogies that match the concepts of culturally compatible, culturally congruent, culturally responsive, and culturally relevant pedagogy. They define "centering pedagogies" as the development of a cultural environment in which students are allowed to explore and affirm their own social and individual factors that affect their identity and the social contexts of their lives. Hyun and Marshall(1997) argue that teacher preparation programs should also prepare prospective teachers to understand themselves and their individual family and ethnic cultures to understand the similarities and differences in their cultures. They propose a Developmentally and Culturally Appropriate Practices (DCAP) model to guide teaching and instructional thinking. This model resembles the Derman-Sparks' (1989) self-education guide on the anti-bias curriculum that goes beyond multicultural education goals to include a more activist approach for the education and empowerment of young children. Wortham and Contreras (2002) affirm that cultural relevant pedagogy may be of some value. For example, they describe the pedagogies of Margaret, an ESL teacher.

Margaret's ESL (English as a Second Language) room resembled a Latino family in at least three ways. First, Margaret herself was maternal. She had high standards, but she cared for her students. Second, she encouraged students to be close to one another. In her room, other students were not seen as competition or as distractions, but as *resources* to help others succeed academically and develop pride in their home cultures. Third, Margaret allowed more fluid spatiotemporal boundaries around activities. Students often participated in more than one activity, in the same place and at the same time. This third characteristic was perhaps the most striking, because of the contrast between the extreme spatiotemporal compartmentalization of activities in a typical United States school and the fluidity of Margaret's ESL room. (p. 137)

It is essential that teachers accept and use the student's cultural and linguistic experiences in establishing educational goals (Saville-Troike, 1973). They need to understand and appreciate the nature of specific languages and cultural attitudes that influence the students' cognitive growth and socialization process. Teachers must accept children and their language system to promote learning. Winsler, Díaz, Espinosa and Rodríguez (1999) advocate the potential advantages of being bilingual. They conclude that learning a second language does not mean losing the first. They acknowledge the need to identify the social, cultural, economic, educational, and temporal contexts for the development of "balanced bilingual" children, which are those children who show high and relatively equal levels of competence in two languages. Winsler and Associates (1999) claim that most of the studies have been conducted with middle class, language majority children who receive strong support for their native language. Unlike these students, Mexican American children in the United States learn a second language in a remedial, deficit model that does not value their heritage's first language.

The children's language provides the key in their development of a socially adequate identity. Children learn their parameters, that is, what they can do and how others interpret what they can do. Respect for the children's family cultural and language practices that they share in the school setting should be the basis for building a learning environment that will motivate children to learn. Zamora (1976) analyzed the cultural problem in the traditional school which values conformity and acculturation and fails to recognize the beauty of cultural diversity. Generally, teachers often do not know how to provide cultural reinforcement. Schools must become sensitive to the culture of their students. Teachers need to develop skills that include:

1. knowing how to reinforce the home culture,
2. knowing how to adapt curriculum materials to make them more relevant to the families and community they serve,
3. knowing how to build a curriculum based on the children's lives and language experiences, and
4. knowing how to involve parents in the educational experience.

The traditional curriculum is oriented to an ethnic group and culture incompatible with the Mexican American culture. Children who have been called culturally disadvantaged in reality have been culturally different. Comer (1988) urges educators to recognize the students' social development and social needs. Their importance is equivalent to their academic abilities. Mexican American children differ in their preparation for the school's academic setting; therefore, they should not be required to perform according to school expectations.

Approaches that need to be developed for the education of Mexican American children should be consistent with the children's cultural background. Vásquez, Pease-Alvarez and Shannon (1994) document the role of Mexican American immigrant parents in their study of two preschool children where parents stimulated, corrected, and guided language socialization. They describe the children's active involvement in communicating with adults, and assert that both children and families have rich resources to acquire a second language.

Discontinuities exist between the early home environments of Mexican American children and the environments they encounter in the school which appear to explain their early academic failure. Laosa's (1977) study revealed that children's environments possessed many unique characteristics depending on the children's membership in particular sociocultural groups and even within these groups there was much variability. Laosa (1977) discovered that Mexican American and Anglo-American mothers of the same socioeconomic background used very different teaching strategies. For example, Mexican American mothers did more teaching by modeling, while Anglo American mothers did more teaching verbally.

Ethnic differences that reflect cultural values are closely related to teaching strategies. Ramírez and Castañeda (1974) suggested that helping teachers understand the cultural values of Mexican Americans is not enough. They stressed the importance of familiarizing teachers with the teaching styles of Mexican American parents for them to be able to match their own teaching strategies to the learning styles of Mexican American children.

Young children need to be educated in the context of cultural pluralism where their individual differences are respected and their education is based on their own family's life history and unique characteristics. They need to learn in education programs that are built on cultural pluralism to maintain their rights and their personal dignity. This will guarantee that schools will provide the cornerstone of a real democracy (Saracho & Martínez-Hancock, 1983).

REFERENCES

Ancona, G. (2002). Saints' days. In *Viva Mexico! The fiestas*. New York: Marshall Cavendish.

Arciniega, T. (1971). *Toward a philosophy of education for the Chicano: Implications for school organizations*. Paper presented at the Conference on Mexican-Americans, Austin, Texas, November 3–5, 1971.

Becerra, R.M. (1998). The Mexican-American family. In C.H. Mindel, R.W. Habenstein, & R. Wright (Eds.), *Ethnic families in America, Patterns and variations* (4th ed., pp. 153–171). Upper Saddle River, NJ: Prentice Hall.

Bigner, J.J. (1994). *Individual and family development: A lifespan interdisciplinary approach*. Englewood Cliffs, NJ: Prentice Hall.

Bredekamp, S., & Copple, C. (Eds.) (1997). *Developmentally appropriate practices in early childhood programs* (rev. ed). Washington, DC: NAEYC.

Bowman, B.T. (1994). *Cultural diversity and academic achievement*. Retrieved on September 14, 2003, from http://www.ncrel.org/sdrs/areas/issues/educatrs/leadrshp/le0bow.htm

Carter, T. (1971). Where to from here? In J.C. Stone & D.P. Denevi (Eds.) *Five heritages: Teaching multicultural populations*. (pp. 197–246). New York: Van Nostrand-Reinhold.

Comer, J.P. (1988). Educating poor minority children. *Scientific American, 259*(5).

Culturally and Linguistically Appropriate Services. (CLAS, 2002). *Early Childhood Research Institute on Culturally and Linguistically Appropriate Services*. Retrieved December 3, 2002, from http://clas.uiuc.edu/aboutclas.html

Delgado-Gaitán, C. (1990). *Literacy for empowerment: the role of parents in children's education*. Basingstoke: Falmer Press.

Derman-Sparks, L., & the A.B.C. Task Force (1989). *Anti-bias curriculum: Tools for empowering young children*. Washington, DC: NAEYC.

Gibbs, N. (2001). Welcome to Amexica. *Time Magazine, 157*(23), 38–47.

Goodenough, W. (1957). *Cultural Anthropology and Linguistics*. In Report of the Seventh Annual Round Table Meeting on Linguistics and Language Study. Monograph Series on Languages and Linguistics, no. 9. Washington, DC: Georgetown University.

Goodenough, W. (1971). *Culture, language and society*. Module in Anthropology, no. 7. Reading, MA: Addison-Wesley.

Goodenough, W. (2001). *Theory and methodology. Lecture 17: Cognitive anthropology*. Retrieved June 30, 2003, from Web site: http://www.neurognosis.com/54.310/Lecture%2017%20-%20Cognitive20Anthropology.rft

Gratton, B., Gutmann, M.P., Skop, E., Hirman, J.W., & Wildsmith, E. (2003). *Mexican American trajectories. Family geography, and intermarriage across the century.* Retrieved on October 11, 2003, from http://www.icpsr.umich.edu/ATMAF/overview.html

Hyun, E., & Marshall, J.D. (1997). Theory of multiple/multiethnic perspective-taking ability for teachers' developmentally and culturally appropriate practice. *Journal of Research in Childhood Education, 11*(2), 188–198.

Laosa, L.M. (1980). Maternal teaching strategies in Chicano and Anglo-American families: The influence of culture and education on maternal behavior. *Child Development, 51,* 759–765.

Laosa, L.M. (1977). Socialization, education, and continuity: The implications of the sociocultural context. *Young Children, 32*(5), 21–27.

Macias, R. (September 2000). *Summary report of the survey of the states' limited English proficient students and available educational programs and services.* Washington, DC: National Clearinghouse for Bilingual Education. Retrieved on September 9, 2003, from http://www.ncela.gwu.edu/ncbepubs/seareports/97-98/index.htm

Martínez, R. (2001). *Crossing over, a Mexican family on the migrant trail.* New York: Henry Holt and Company.

McBride, S.L. (1999). Family-centered practices. *Young Children, 54*(3), 62–68.

Mehan, H., Hubbard, L., & Villanueva, I. (1994). Forming academic identities: Accommodation without assimilation among involuntary minorities. *Anthropology and Education Quarterly, 25*(2).

Muñoz, R. (December, 2002). *Cultural psychology* [Television Broadcast]. New York and Washington, DC: Publication Broadcasting Service.

National Association for the Education of Young Children. (1996). NAEYC Position Paper: Responding to linguistic and cultural diversity—Recommendations for effective early childhood education. *Young Children, 52*(2), 4–12.

National Coalition of Advocates for Students. (1988). *New voices: Immigrant students in U.S. public schools.* Boston: Author.

National Council of La Raza (NCLR). (2001). *Beyond the census: Hispanics and an American agenda.* Retrieved on December 15, 2002, from http://www.nclr.org

Natriello, G., McDill, E., & Pallas, (1990). *Schooling disadvantaged children: Racing against catastrophe.* New York: Teacher's College Press.

New, R., Snow, C., Quiroz, B., Sheinberg, N., Thomas, R., & Barr, R. (1998). *Report on the Conference Culture, Child Development and Education* (Spencer Foundation). Retrieved on June 29, 2003, from http://www.spencer.org/Conferences/Culture/Report.html

Nieto, S., & Rolón, C (1997). Preparation and professional development of teachers: a perspective from two latinas. In J.J. Irvine(Ed.), *Critical knowledge for diverse teachers and learners* (pp. 89–121). Washington, DC: American Association of Colleges for Teacher Education.

Ogbu, J.U. (1995a, Dec.). Cultural problems in minority education: Their interpretations and consequences-part one. *Urban Review, 27,* 189–206.

Ogbu, J.U. (1995b, Dec.). Cultural problems in minority education: Their interpretations and consequences-part one. *Urban Review, 27,* 271–297.

Our Lady Of Guadalupe Patroness of the Americas. (2003). *Saint Juan Diego: A model of humility.* Retrieved on June 27, 2003, from http://sancta.org/

Oxford, C. (1984). *Demographic projections of non-English background and limited English proficient persons in the Unites States in the year 2000.* Rossyln, VA: Inter-America Research Associates.

Payne, R. (1995). *Poverty: A framework for understanding and working with students and adults from poverty.* Baytown, TX: RFT Publishing.

Peña , D.C. (2000). Sharing power? An experience of Mexican American parents serving on a campus advisory council. *School Community Journal, 10*(1)61–84.

Ramírez, M., III, & Castañeda, A. (1974). *Cultural democracy, bicognitive development, and education.* New York: Academic Press.

Resource Center of the Americas. (Fall, 1996). *The power of names.* Minneapolis: Author.

Robinson, T.L. (1993). The intersections of gender, class, race, and culture. *Journal of Multicultural Counseling and Development, 21*, 50–58.

Rosenfeld, M.J . (2002). Measures of assimilation in the marriage market: Mexican Americans 1970–1990. *Journal of Marriage and Family, 64*(1), 152–162.

Saracho, O.N. (1986). Teaching second language literacy with computers. In D. Hainline (Ed.), New developments in language CAI, (pp. 53–68). Beckenham, Kent (London): Croom Helm.

Saracho, O.N., & Martínez-Hancock, F.M. (1983). The culture of the Mexican Americans. In O.N. Saracho & B. Spodek (Eds.), *Understanding the multicultural experience in early childhood education* (pp. 3–15). Washington, DC: National Association for the Education of Young Children.

Saville-Troike, M. (1973). *Bilingual children: A resource document.* Arlington, VA: Center for Applied Linguistics.

Sheets, R.H. (2002). "You're just a kid that's there"–Chicano perception of disciplinary events. *Journal of Latinos and Education, 2*(1), 105–122.

Stassen-Berger, K., & Thompson, R.A. (2000). *Developing person through the life span* (5th ed.). New York: Worth Publishers.

Thomas, R., Barr, R., Halverson, R., Synder, L., & Wiebe, M. (1999). *Report on the conference collaborative research for practice.* Retrieved on October 11, 2003, from http://www.spencer.org/publications/conferences/Practice/report.htm

Trueba, E.T. (1999). *Latinos Unidos: From cultural diversity to the politics of solidarity.* Boulder, CO: Rowman & Littlefield.

United Sstates Census Bureau. (2000). *Facts and features.* Retrieved on November 25, 2002, from http://www.census.gov/PressRelease/www/2002/cbo2ff15.html

Valdés, G. (1996). *Con respeto: Bridging the distances between culturally diverse families and schools, an ethnographic portrait.* New York: Teachers College Press.

Vásquez, O.A., Pease-Alvarez, L., & Shannon, S.M. (1994). *Pushing boundaries: Language and culture in a Mexican community.* Cambridge: Cambridge University Press.

Vigil, J.D. (1998). *From Indians to Chicanos: The dynamics of Mexican-American culture.* Prospect Heights, IL: Waveland Press.

Vygotsky, L.S. (1978). *Mind in society.* Cambridge, MA: Harvard University Press.

Winsler, A., Díaz, R.M., Espinosa, L., & Rodriguez, J.L. (1999). When learning a second language does not mean losing the first: Bilingual language development in low-income, Spanish-speaking children attending bilingual preschool. *Child Development, 70*, 349–362.

Wortham, S., & Contreras, M. (2002) . Struggling toward culturally relevant pedagogy in the Latino diaspora. *Journal of Latinos and Education, 2*(1),133–144.

York, S. (1998). *Big as life, the everyday inclusive curriculum.* St. Paul, MN: Red Leaf Press.

Zamora, G. (1976). Staff development for bilingual bicultural programs: A philosophical base. In F. Cordasco (Ed.). *Bilingual schooling in the United States: A sourcebook for educational personnel* (pp. 243–245). New York: McGraw-Hill.

CHAPTER 11

INVOLVEMENT OF AMERICAN INDIAN FAMILIES IN EARLY CHILDHOOD EDUCATION

Laura Hubbs-Tait, David Tait, Charley Hare, and Erron Huey

INTRODUCTION

The education and socialization of American Indian[1] children have been contested issues since the beginning of contact between Europeans and indigenous peoples. When early childhood education is considered today, history is inescapable. The dominant American culture has frequently rejected Indian cultures in general and Indian educational and parenting practices in particular. In the pages that follow, we offer (a) an overview of the history of United States policies concerning Indian education and their impact on contemporary involvement of American Indian families in their children's education. Next, we review studies of (b) roles of American Indian parents and communities in their children's education, (c) involvement desired by American Indian parents, and (d) barriers to involvement by American Indian parents and communities. Finally, we discuss (e)

Contemporary Perspectives on Families, Communities, and Schools for Young Children, pages 225–246
Copyright © 2005 by Information Age Publishing
225

model programs of American Indian family and community involvement in children's education. Our thesis throughout is that displacement of American Indian peoples and removal of their children to boarding schools left a legacy of alienation and distrust. This legacy and continuing cultural differences between American Indian families and educational institutions inhibit parental involvement in education.

EDUCATION, FAMILIES, AND FEDERAL POLICIES

Prior to European contact, American Indians provided education informally through parents, relatives, and elders. Although there was great variety among Indian educational systems, tribal history, the natural world, religious training, and respect for elders were commonly important. American Indian leaders generally preferred their time-tested methods to European ones. In 1744 an Iroquois spokesman politely but firmly declined an offer by the colonial Virginia legislature to educate six youths at the College of William and Mary. Several Iroquois had attended northern colleges before, but they returned home unable to fulfill customary roles in their society or even to speak its language properly (DeJong, 1999). Some other Eastern tribes, however, valued European education, and members who received it often attained a general education equal to that of their non-Indian contemporaries (Hale, 2002).

Early in the nineteenth century, the United States War Department began to organize educational programs to introduce American Indians to the ways of Euro-American society in order to assimilate them (Adams, 1988). In 1838, the government sponsored 87 boarding schools and six manual training schools staffed mostly by missionaries (Reyhner & Eder, 1992). The emerging education system featured four tenets of colonial education described by Lomawaima: (a) a requirement that Indians be civilized; (b) a link between civilization and Christian conversion; (c) the subordination of Indian communities, often effected by resettlement; and (d) a conviction that special pedagogical methods were needed in light of moral, mental, or physical deficiencies (Lomawaima, 1999). By the 1870s the federal government allocated funds to day and boarding schools that taught fundamental skills in English and arithmetic while devoting half the day to vocational education. Indian Bureau regulations issued in 1880 mandated English-only instruction. In the 1880s some educators recommended that special textbooks be developed for Indian education, but decades would pass before the federal government authorized such materials (Adams, 1995; Reyhner & Eder, 1992).

A new chapter in federal education policy began in 1879 with the opening of the first off-reservation government-sponsored boarding school in

Carlisle, Pennsylvania. Carlisle's founder declared that the function of the school was to "kill the Indian in him and save the man" (Adams, 1995, p. 52). To this end, the school separated children from parents and communities to break their ties with tribal cultures. Educators and public officials were contemptuous of American Indian cultures; their plan was to destroy and replace them with what they called civilization (Reyhner & Eder, 1992). The key to this plan was education for the children (Adams, 1988).

To become civilized in the United States of the 1880s meant embracing Christianity, replacing community loyalty with an individual orientation, and becoming self-sufficient, acquisitive, and success seeking (Adams, 1988). Two education systems tried but failed to get American Indian children to adopt these values: reservation day schools and reservation boarding schools. Government-sponsored day schools on reservations were inexpensive, and parents were less likely to oppose this kind of schooling than boarding schools. Children, however, did not change as educators wanted them to do. They left school each day to return to unaltered homes in an unchanged culture, and seemed to retain nothing from their schooling. If parents were hostile to the school, high absenteeism further undermined the program (Adams, 1995).

The reservation boarding school provided more separation between school and community, and was expected to have greater potential to achieve assimilationist goals than the day school. While some educators welcomed parental visits as an opportunity to introduce them to the school, others thought visits disrupted school life and awakened in the children a desire for home. Some parents sabotaged the school by discouraging the use of English and encouraging runaways. As a result of parental and community influences, boarding school students abandoned the school's "civilized habits" and returned to traditional ways (Adams, 1995).

The off-reservation boarding school provided a third option. In 1879 Carlisle stood alone; by 1902 there were 25 off-reservation boarding schools. Educators hoped that boarders would replace their parents with the Christian home provided by the schools (Hale, 2002). Such schools implemented a comprehensive program that addressed clothing, grooming, manners, religion, academic learning, and vocational preparation. A military style of discipline replaced allegedly poor parental discipline at home (Adams, 1995; Child, 1998). To increase their capacity to shape their charges, schools soon began to restrict students' visits to their home communities, or even to keep them at the school year round until the course of studies was completed (Child, 1998). Yet the off-reservation boarding school also failed. Reformers had overestimated the power of schools to break children's ties with their own culture. Students returning to reservations found the transition difficult, but usually they adjusted to community norms. In 1901 the Commissioner of Indian Affairs acknowledged that most Indians still lived on reservations and maintained traditional ideas and practices. Change could not come, he added, without "improvement" in the home (Adams, 1995). The intense effort to assimilate American Indian children through boarding school education, often against the desires of parents, had failed.

Although off-reservation boarding schools did not meet the federal government's expectations, they did affect parent–child relationships. Children maintained contact with their parents through letters and rare visits home, but experienced terrible homesickness (Child, 1998). Parents resented the disruption of their relationship with their children (Adams, 1995). After a generation of students returned from school, however, the faraway institution did not seem quite so alien (Adams, 1995; Child, 1998). Sometimes children preferred the school to troubled situations at home (Adams, 1995). Families also used the schools for their own purposes, to obtain education and, during the Great Depression, food and shelter for their offspring (Child, 1998). At their worst, however, boarding schools deprived students of parental role models, leaving them ill equipped to raise their own children (DeJong, 1993).

The failure of day and boarding schools to assimilate children into mainstream society did not bring down the system but did prepare the way for yet another option. Education for American Indian children became mandatory in 1891. Parents who did not cooperate could be denied government-provided rations or even jailed (Adams, 1995). In the 1890s Congress began to fund local school districts that agreed to educate American Indian children. In 1900 only 246 pupils were enrolled in public schools, but by 1925 the total was 34,452, while reservation and off-reservation government schools counted only 23,761 pupils (Adams, 1995).

After 1893, children could not be sent to off-reservation boarding schools without parental consent, but they were required to attend a public or reservation school. Many parents, and occasionally entire communities, resisted. Some parents disappeared for a few weeks at the school roundup time in the fall. When children attended boarding schools, some parents returned their children late after vacations. On occasion parents removed children en masse from reservation boarding schools, especially if they heard of widespread sickness there. Student resistance at school, sometimes encouraged by parents, ranged from arson to running away to stubborn non-responsiveness. During the summer months, tribal elders continued to teach traditional culture to the young (Adams, 1995; Child, 1998).

By the 1920s, the majority of American Indian children attended public, private, or government-operated schools. Even if some students benefited in various ways from what they learned, the record of resistance indicates that Indian communities were not satisfied. Educators had retreated somewhat from a goal of rapid and total assimilation, but the basic pattern of government schools did not change. They denied communities and parents any meaningful role. English remained the sole language of instruction. There was little or no room for any aspect of indigenous cultures in the curriculum. Public schools were similar, with the added disadvantage that American Indian children often suffered from prejudicial treatment (Szasz, 1999).

Policy changes during the New Deal of the 1930s modified federal schools and provided funds for public schools, but left the structure of Indian education intact. American Indian culture received greater attention in the classrooms and a few textbooks were written in Indian languages. Special summer institutes equipped teachers to work with American Indian students. Soon, however, the Second World War reduced funding, bringing an effective end to change. But, two legislative achievements of the New Deal had important implications for Indian education. The Indian Reorganization Act of 1934 stopped land allotment, protected religious freedom, and allowed a degree of tribal government. The Act did not address education at length, but by opening the door to tribal government, it anticipated the self-determination in education that would begin in the 1960s. The Johnson-O'Malley Act (JOM) of 1934 was specifically concerned with American Indian education. It allowed the Secretary of the Interior to enter into contracts with states, rather than with a myriad of local governments, for educational and social welfare purposes. Because this money was effectively controlled by the states, it was normally used in the general operating funds of the schools rather than applied to the specific needs of Indian students. The Act did not, therefore, empower Indian communities or individual parents to shape education for their children. Decades later, however, federal law was revised to require that JOM funds be spent on supplemental programs for Indian students with the approval of an advisory committee of Indian parents (Reyhner & Eder 1992; Szasz, 1999).

A breakthrough came in the 1960s as increasingly powerful American Indian leaders took advantage of Great Society programs and federal legislation to begin to assert Indian control over education. The Rough Rock Demonstration School in northeast Arizona on the Navajo Nation (Dick, Estell, & McCarty, 1994) was the first twentieth-century school to be directed by an all-Indian elected board.[2] It was also the first to provide systematic teaching in Navajo language and culture. In the fall of 1966 the Rough Rock School enrolled 216 elementary school-age children in a program intended to provide them with a Navajo education that would also equip them to function in the dominant society (McCarty, 1989, 2002).

The example of Rough Rock inspired the opening of additional schools and, soon, junior colleges as well. Several important pieces of legislation helped to establish a new framework in which Indian-controlled education was feasible. The Indian Education Act of 1972 provided money for programs for Indian students in urban and reservation school systems. The funds could not be used for operational expenses. Parents had to be involved in all aspects of projects funded under this Act. In addition, the Act made direct grants available to Indian tribes and organizations, state departments of education, and colleges and universities. The Indian Self-Determination and Education Assistance Act of 1975 required the Bureau of Indian Affairs (BIA) to contract with tribes for the administration of schools (Hale, 2002; Warner, 1999). The Bilingual Education Act of 1968 provided funding for bilingual teaching assistants, new materials, and parent involvement (McCarty, 2002). The Native American Languages Act of 1990 required the federal government to cooperate with American Indians communities to preserve their cultures and languages (Hale, 2002; Warner, 1999).

An Indian-controlled education system is emerging in primary, secondary, and higher education. However, 90% of American Indian children attend public elementary schools, which are not subject to Indian control (Tippeconnic, 1999). In 1900, American Indian parents and communities had no say over their children's education. At the beginning of the 21st century, they are better positioned to participate in, or even direct, education for their offspring. Yet many challenges remain for parent and community involvement in early childhood education.

MODERN INVOLVEMENT OF PARENTS AND COMMUNITIES WITH SCHOOLS

Roles of American Indian Parents and Communities in Their Children's Education

A recent review of the educational literature identified five categories of parental involvement: (a) communication about educational issues between schools and families; (b) parental aspirations and expectations; (c) parental participation in school events and activities; (d) parental participation in school policy making; and (e) home learning environment (Keith et al., 1998). The early childhood literature is consistent with most of these categories, but adds the parent–child relationship to the definition of involvement (e.g., Culp, Hubbs-Tait, Culp, & Starost, 2000; Parker et al., 1999). Because there are relatively few studies of American Indian parental and community involvement with children of any age, we include some research on older children and adolescents below. For the same reason we include educational and developmental outcomes within the definition of school-related adjustment.

Communication and aspirations.   Keith et al. (1998) found that communication and aspirations mattered twice as much to American Indian high school students as to the entire national sample in their study. These researchers defined "aspirations" as the number of years of education parents expect children to complete and "communication" as how often parents and children discuss school activities, classes, high school plan of study, and post-high school plans. Using the National Education Longitudinal Study (NELS) data set, Keith et al. examined the relation of communication and aspirations when students were in 8th grade to students' 10th-grade grade point average (GPA). For the whole sample, an increase of 1 standard deviation (SD) in communication and aspirations in 8th grade led to a .25 SD increase in 10th grade GPA. For American Indian students, a 1 SD increase in communication and aspirations led to a .43 SD increase in GPA, almost double the impact. Consistent with the NELS sample, the proportion of American Indian students in the study was small (1% or 126 students). Thus, the results must be interpreted cautiously, particularly in light of the structural equation modeling technique used to evaluate the data (see Fan, Thompson, & Wang, 1999). However, they do suggest aspirations and communication may play an even more important role in the school success of American Indian students than of European, Hispanic, African, and Asian American students.

Research by Robinson-Zañartu and Majel-Dixon (1996) reveals that American Indian parents' definition of communication differs from that of Keith et al. (1998) in that American Indian parents place some of the responsibility for communication on the schools. Robinson-Zañartu and Majel-Dixon administered their American Indian Relationships with Schools Survey to 234 adults from 55 tribes or bands attending meetings of the National Congress of American Indians or the National Indian Education Association. Adults were parents or concerned community members reporting on children (13.4% between the ages of 4 and 7; 38.1% between the ages of 8 and 11) attending school. Involvement varied as a function of the type of school in which children were enrolled, with Indian-controlled schools being viewed as the most responsive to American Indian parents. On two communication items (e.g., "the school values my input about the education of my children"), adults reporting on children in Indian-controlled schools indicated greater involvement than adults reporting on children in BIA or public schools. Across all schools, American Indian parents perceived their role in children's education to be very important. However, they did not find it easy to fulfill this role in contacts with schools. In reply to two open-response questions asking what parents wanted to know from schools or what they thought schools should know about educating their children, the third most frequently mentioned theme was concerns about the schools' shortcomings in communication with or inclusion of American Indian parents (Robinson-Zañartu & Majel-Dixon, 1996).

Willeto (1999) confirmed the positive relation between parental aspirations and American Indian student achievement in an investigation of 450 9th- through 12th-grade Navajo students attending 11 high schools on the Navajo Nation. Students' reports of their parents' educational aspirations for them were significantly related to students' own college aspirations. The relation between parent and student aspirations was significant even when parental education, family income, family size, and family residential history were controlled in the statistical model.

Summary of communication and aspirations. American Indian parents and educational researchers appear to share definitions of aspirations but not of communication. Greater communication problems in non-Indian-controlled schools suggest cultural differences in the meaning or process of communication and may also reflect historical alienation of Indian parents from government-operated schools.

Home learning environment. Research suggests the home learning environment for American Indian children may differ from that of middle class European American children. The first difference is a greater emphasis on nonverbal than verbal communication (Long & Christensen, 1998; Seideman et al., 1994). The importance of particular types of nonverbal activities varies among nations, with an emphasis on traditional dance among the Lakota (Zimiga, 1982), a visual approach to learning among Navajo, Yaqui, Kwakuitl, and Pueblo children (Swisher & Deyhle, 1989), an observation-practice-demonstration method of learning among Navajo, Lakota, and Yaqui children (Swisher & Deyhle, 1989), and a nonverbal modeling and gesturing approach used by parents of Papago (Tohono O'odham) children (Macias, 1987). Such cultural differences may develop into academic strengths when incorporated into curricula (Swisher & Deyhle, 1989). However, research evaluating nonverbal curricular approaches for American Indian children is sparse. Approaches suggested by research or practice include visual learning activities, particularly demonstration-observation-practice methods (Plank, 1994; Swisher & Deyhle, 1989) and activity-based instruction (Zwick & Miller, 1996), the latter resulting in significant increases in science achievement scores for American Indian children over traditional textbook learning methods (Zwick & Miller, 1996).

The second difference in home learning environments is an emphasis on oral storytelling over reading (Levin et al., 1997). For example, whereas only 40% of Yaqui parents participating in an Even Start program read books, approximately 80% told stories to children (Levin et al., 1997). Strengths of such oral storytelling from parent to child have been successfully incorporated into some early literacy curricula (see an account of Yup'ik kindergarten children in Akaran & Fields, 1997).

The third difference in home learning environments is non-English home language (Macias, 1987; McCarty et al., 1997; Reyhner, 1992; Watahomigie & McCarty, 1994). Moreover, until late in the 20th century, some tribes and nations did not have a written symbol system with which to transcribe their language (e.g., Boseker, 1994; Watahomigie & McCarty, 1994), which rendered reading books to children impossible. Programs that supplant home language and culture with the language and culture of instruction (i.e., subtractive language programs; Cummins, 1992), like those found in many public and BIA schools, are likely to reduce language scores during the early school years. Such discontinuities between home and classroom language have been linked to the interruption of parent–child communication and difficulties in language proficiency (National Association for the Education of Young Children, 1996). Although the political climate at the beginning of the new millennium is not favorable, additive language programs for American Indian children appear to be related to their school success (e.g., Watahomigie & McCarty, 1994).

The fourth difference in home learning environments is a warmer, non-punitive approach to child rearing by American Indian than European American parents (e.g., Seideman et al., 1994). MacPhee, Fritz, and Miller-Heyl (1996) examined social networks and parenting among 500 American Indian (mostly Ute, but also Navajo and Laguna Pueblo), Hispanic, and European American parents or guardians of 2- to 5-year-old children. Compared to the other groups, American Indian parents were significantly less likely to use physical punishment. Such warm, supportive parenting has been associated with school success among American Indian children. For example, Whitbeck, Hoyt, Stubben, and LaFramboise, (2001) measured the school success of 212 American Indian children (ages 9 to 16) on three reservations in the upper Midwest by grades and positive school attitudes. The researchers measured supportive maternal parenting by children's reports of how often their mother encouraged them (e.g., talks with you about things that bother you). Supportiveness predicted child school success in all analyses. The unique variance explained by maternal supportiveness (9%) corresponds to other calculations of the unique variance in children's cognitive scores explained by maternal emotional support (Hubbs-Tait, Culp, Culp, & Miller, 2002), underscoring the importance of emotional support in the home learning environment of American Indian children.

The fifth difference is lower promotion of autonomy by American Indian than European American parents (Abraham, Christopherson, & Kuehl, 1984; MacPhee et al., 1996). Research on school-related correlates of American Indian autonomy promotion is nonexistent. We suspect that the most important issue is cultural divergence in the meaning of autonomy. Autonomy promotion for Papago (Tohono O'odham) parents, for instance, is defined as not forcing the child to accede to adult demands but respecting the child as an individual (Macias, 1987). This definition differs from autonomy promotion as urging children to try new things (Abraham et al., 1984). The impact of curricula incorporating respect for the individual child or other aspects of Indian autonomy promotion on school success needs to be investigated.

Summary of home learning environment. Differences in home learning environments are differences *between* American Indian and European American children. However, associations between variations in home learning environments (e.g., supportive parenting) and school success of American Indian children are associations *within* groups of American Indian children. The differential impact of variations in home and classroom learning environment on American Indian versus European American children has not been examined (but see Zwick & Miller, 1996, for an evaluation of differential impact of classroom learning environments). However, a complex understanding of American Indian parent and community involvement recognizes that inter-nation, inter-tribe, and inter-band variations in beliefs and practices may be as quantitatively great and as qualitatively meaningful as differences between majority culture and American Indian parents (Littlebear, 1992). Associations between inter-nation, inter-tribe, or inter-band differences in parenting and school success need to be studied.

Parental participation in school activities. Involvement of American Indian parents is higher in Indian-controlled than public or BIA schools (Robinson-Zañartu & Majel-Dixon, 1996). The bilingual/bicultural curriculum of Indian-controlled schools emphasizes incorporation of American Indian culture and families across the curriculum and at all levels of the school. For example, Reyhner (1992) emphasizes parent participation in the success of the Rock Point Community School in the Navajo Nation in northeast Arizona. Reyhner reports an 80% parent attendance rate at conferences with teachers after the implementation of the bilingual/bicultural curriculum. Student test performance also improved after the implementation of the new curriculum (Benjamin, 1987; Reyhner, 1992). Research has not yet evaluated the independent contributions of parent and community involvement and the bilingual/bicultural curriculum. One reason for high parent participation appears to be parent-oriented community and cultural events held by the school and a parent-advisory committee with some power (Reyhner, 1992). Such high parent and community involvement in Indian-controlled community schools (e.g., McCarty, 2002) diverges sharply from descriptions of alienated parents in public schools with European American teachers (e.g., see Deyhle & Margonis, 1995, on Navajo mothers).

Summary of parental participation.   Differences between public and Indian-controlled schools include variations in curriculum, community involvement, parent participation, and student test performance. It is not known which of the first three factors, alone or in combination, is responsible for the differences in student test performance.

Involvement Desired by American Indian Parents

Incorporation of American Indian culture and values.   Robinson-Zañartu and Majel-Dixon (1996) reported parent concerns about schools' insensitivity to American Indian culture and values. Items were "the school understands Indian cultures," "the school values Indian cultures," "the school helps build pride in my children about their Indianness," and "the school is open to learning and including more about Indian cultures." These items were viewed as least likely to be present in the parent-school relationship for the 70% of the sample with a child in BIA or public schools. Replies to two open-response questions confirmed this concern, because absence of American Indian culture in schools was the theme mentioned most frequently.

Importance of incorporation of American Indian culture and values.   Traditional American Indian culture has been linked with American Indian children's school success (Coggins, Williams, & Radin, 1997; Ward, 1998; Whitbeck et al., 2001; Willeto, 1999). Coggins et al. (1997) found a positive association between American Indian values of Ojibwe mothers of the Michigan Upper Peninsula and their children's performance at school. Ojibwe parents of 17 3- to 11-year-old children completed an index of traditional American Indian values developed by Coggins (an Odawa) and a former Ojibwe tribal judge. Values included attitudes toward sharing, other-centeredness, harmony with nature, non-interference, patience, circular time, non-confrontation, and broad view of the family. Teachers reported child grades, cognitive and socioemotional functioning, behavior problems, attributes of American Indian Adaptive Functioning (AIAF, a measure developed by American Indian graduate students), and expectations for the child regarding his/her potential to become a community leader. The latter two measures are more consistent with American Indian values than the former three measures. Mothers' traditional attitudes were significantly related to grades, behavior problems, cognitive and social functioning, AIAF attributes, and likelihood of becoming a future community leader (Coggins et al., 1997). Thus, mothers' traditional values are important to Ojibwe children's school success, as defined by American Indian values or by conventions such as report card grades.

Willeto's (1999) research likewise supports the importance of traditional values for academic success, but suggests such values overlap with parenting. Willeto operationalized academic success among Navajo youth in Arizona as students' grades, commitment to school, and college aspirations. She operationalized traditional values of 450 high school students as three components: (a) ritual behavior (Navajo healing ceremonies); (b) cultural conventions (e.g., Navajo rug weaving, silversmithing); and (c) Navajo language use. Students reported on their adherence to ritual behavior, cultural conventions, and language; several parenting variables, including parental cultural practices and educational aspirations for the student; and family background variables. Students' adherence to Navajo cultural conventions predicted two types of school success. The first was commitment to school. The second was college aspirations. This second effect was revealed in the initial ordinary least squares multiple regression models. Once parenting variables were entered into the models, however, students' adherence to cultural conventions no longer predicted college aspirations. Instead, as noted previously, parents' aspirations predicted students' aspirations. This suggests students with traditional Navajo values had parents with higher aspirations for their education. Thus, students' cultural conventions are embedded in a system that includes Navajo parents' aspirations for their academic success.

Consistent with the results for Ojibwe children and Navajo youth, Ward (1998) reported that among 296 Crow and Cheyenne students attending three high schools in Montana, traditional culture and coming from a reservation with high levels of contact in the community was associated with better student academic performance. Because residential community and traditional values were not independent, the results for the Cheyenne and Crow students must be treated with some caution. In particular, students from the traditional community (Cheyenne) attended a tribal school (Cheyenne), which had high community support and parent involvement. Thus, the better academic performance of the Cheyenne students is best interpreted as due to a particularly advantageous combination of traditional values, parent involvement, and community support. In fact, the Northern Cheyenne Tribal Schools board recently voted to instigate a year-round school program for kindergarten through 12th grade, after a parent survey indicated majority support for the change. One essential component of the new curriculum is Cheyenne culture. Thus, the integration of traditional values, parent involvement, and community support is a continuing effort of the Northern Cheyenne Tribal Schools (Olp, 2002).

In the study of the relation of maternal supportiveness to the school success of American Indian children in the upper Midwest discussed above, Whitbeck et al. (2001) also measured enculturation, defined as participation in traditional cultural activities (e.g., ceremonies, language), cultural identity (e.g., self-rated success in own culture), and traditional spirituality (extent and importance of participation). School success was positively related to maternal supportiveness, participation in clubs and extracurricular activities, and enculturation. In fact, the results suggest that enculturation constitutes a unique pathway to school success for American Indian students. There was no interaction between student self-esteem and enculturation, which would have suggested that self-esteem and enculturation could each compensate for the effects of the other.

Summary of incorporation of culture and values. These four investigations of the importance of traditional American Indian values and practices for academic competence are quite consistent in their findings. The consistency is particularly important in light of variations in geographical location (Southwest, Upper Peninsula, upper Midwest, and Montana) and tribes or nations studied. Nonetheless, all students were living on or near reservation communities offering opportunities for involvement with the respective tribe or nation. Whether traditional American Indian values, customs, and practices would be effective for off-reservation American Indian children is not clear. However, Cheshire's (2001) qualitative study reveals agreement across 10 off-reservation mothers and their children on the importance of cultural transmission. Taken together with the four previous studies, Cheshire's work suggests the need for research on the impact of adding American Indian values to curricula in off-reservation schools serving American Indian children.

Need for more American Indian professionals in education. The need for American Indian teachers and administrators emerged in answers to Robinson-Zañartu and Majel-Dixon's (1996) questionnaire. Replies to their open-response questions raised these issues, with several mentioning the need for American Indian teachers and counselors. This theme also surfaces in the literature on Indian-controlled schools. Successful bilingual/bicultural schools report they had to develop their own faculty by supporting paraprofessional staff through the process of getting certified (Dick et al., 1994; Reyhner, 1992; Watahomigie & McCarty, 1994; Watahomigie, 1995).

Importance of more Indian professionals. If American Indian children and parents are to feel that the school welcomes their culture and language, the school has to have professionals who are experts in that culture and language. The fact that bilingual/bicultural Indian-controlled schools, which include as teachers and administrators native speakers of American Indian languages, have higher attendance rates suggests the inclusion of American Indian educational professionals in the classroom and administration is related to children's school success (e.g., Benjamin, 1987; Reyhner, 1992; Watahomigie & McCarty, 1994).

Barriers to Involvement by American Indian Parents and Communities

Previous paragraphs suggest barriers to involvement by American Indian parents and communities. The biggest is the relocation of Indian nations and the boarding school movement with their contemporary legacies in parent and community alienation from schools (Charleston, 1994). A modern barrier is the disparity between definitions of involvement by the educational community and American Indian parents and communities. There are other barriers as well.

Teacher–child relationship. Several studies suggest problems in the relationship between American Indian children and majority culture teachers. Dion, Gotowiec, and Beiser (1998) compared depression and conduct disorder in 603 American Indian and First Nations children with that of 245 non-Native children. Seventy-two percent of this U.S. and Canadian sample were in 2nd grade; the rest were in 4th grade. For each child, the teacher, a parent, and the child completed ratings of depression and conduct disorder. Although both non-Native children and parents rated non-Native children as significantly higher on depression than American Indian or First Nations children, teachers rated Native children as more depressed than non-Native children. Similarly, although non-Native children and parents did not differ from Native children and parents in ratings of children's conduct disorder, teachers rated Native children significantly higher on conduct disorder than non-Native children. Thus, teachers viewed Native children as more problematic than non-Native children, even though parents and children in both ethnic groups disagreed with this assessment. Comparison of non-Native and Native teachers' ratings revealed that non-Native teachers evaluated Native children negatively. For ratings of both depression and conduct disorder there was a significant difference between the Native and non-Native teachers. Non-Native teachers rated Native children significantly higher on both types of behavior problems than Native teachers (Dion et al., 1998). Such differences could be due to misunderstandings arising from cultural differences or to prejudice.

A study of 67 American Indian and 51 European American 5th and 6th graders on a reservation in Montana also reveals estrangement between majority culture teachers and American Indian students (Bolls, Tan, & Austin, 1997). Compared to their European American classmates, American Indian children rated European American teachers as significantly lower on "good will communication competence," which consisted of such items as: "my teacher understands me" (Bolls et al., 1997, p. 200). American Indian children also rated European American teachers as significantly lower on "delivery communication competence," which consisted of "my teacher's voice is boring to listen to" and "my teacher's facial expressions are boring to look at" (Bolls et al., 1997, p. 200). Because of the correlational nature of the study, it is not possible to determine how much of the difference between groups is due to disparity in teacher treatment, cultural differences in perceptions, or a combination of both.

Summary and implications of teacher–child relationship. The two studies reviewed in this section provide differing viewpoints but yield the same conclusion. Dion et al.'s (1998) research suggests non-Native teachers evaluate American Indian and First Nations children negatively. Bolls et al.'s (1997) research suggests American Indian children regard European American teachers negatively. Both studies substantiate American Indian parents' concerns (Robinson-Zañartu & Majel-Dixon, 1996) about communication problems between schools and American Indian families. Regardless of whether communication problems are rooted in historical alienation and distrust, in cultural differences in meaning, or both, interventions to change attitudes of teachers, students, and parents may yield increased parent involvement.

Culture of teachers versus American Indian parents. Although investigators have mentioned differences in learning style between majority and American Indian culture and their impact on children's adjustment to school (e.g., Swisher & Deyhle, 1989; Tharp, 1994), systematic research on teachers and American Indian parents has yet to be conducted. However, research on cultural differences in social networks of American Indian and non-Native parents suggests how such differences may hinder communication between American Indian parents and non-Native teachers. For American Indian parents, satisfaction with social networks is related to network density (number of people in the network who know each other) and to frequency of contact between the parent and network members (MacPhee et al., 1996). For European American parents, satisfaction is related to degree of perceived intimacy (high = "so close it is hard to imagine life without them" [p. 3283]) with network members. For Hispanic parents, satisfaction is related to network size. Frequency of contact with network members is related to intimacy for American Indian parents, but not for any of the other groups (MacPhee et al., 1996).

The pertinence of these findings for the current chapter lies in the fact that interactions of non-Indian teachers (whether Hispanic or European American) and American Indian parents are grounded in entirely different systems of meaning (see Greenfield, 1997). Although intimacy is important to both American Indian and European American parents, actual contact with interconnected network members is part of intimacy only for American Indian parents. For Hispanic and European American parents (and by extension, teachers), interconnectedness and contact are unrelated to satisfaction with social networks. Thus, although non-Native teachers and American Indian parents may both express a desire to meet with each other, the meaning and preferred content of such meetings is not the same for teachers and parents.

Summary of culture of teachers versus American Indian parents.   Meeting with a teacher who is completely independent of one's social network may not be as satisfying to an American Indian parent as it is to a European American teacher. Moreover, meeting with an American Indian parent who inherently values more contact with kin than is comfortable for a European American teacher is not likely to lead to successful communication between the two. Whether the findings of MacPhee et al. (1996) can be generalized beyond the participating Ute, Navajo, and Laguna Pueblo parents is not known. However, such widely divergent views about social contact and interaction may underlie communication problems between American Indian families and non-Native teachers. Becoming aware of and respecting these differences may aid in removing barriers to involvement by American Indian parents and communities.

Model Programs of American Indian Family and Community Involvement in Children's Education

As mentioned previously, the Indian-controlled community school movement introduced bilingual/bicultural curricula. Two programs illustrate how principles of bilingual and bicultural education were integrated with developmentally and individually appropriate practice as well as family and community involvement.

Rough Rock Community School (Navajo).   From the inception of the Rough Rock Community School (in 1966 as mentioned earlier in this chapter), parents and community members were involved at all levels of the school. Community parents were hired as dorm parents (McCarty, 2002) and also functioned as assistants in classrooms. Traditional grade distinctions were eliminated to emphasize individually appropriate instruction and remove concerns about student promotion. To further include the community, the school hired Navajo artists and artisans to instruct adults in traditional arts and crafts (McCarty, 2002).

In 1983, Rough Rock began collaborating with the researchers and teachers of the Kamehameha Early Education Program in Hawaii (Vogt, Jordan, & Tharp, 1987) to incorporate reading and writing, speaking and listening within a culturally and linguistically compatible framework through 3rd grade. The Rough Rock English-Navajo Language Arts Program (RRENLAP) resulted in 1987 (Dick et al., 1994). Evaluations of RRENLAP revealed significant student progress with mean scores on English literacy comprehension increasing from 58% in kindergarten in 1989–1990 to 91% four years later (McCarty, 2002). However, low funding and a recent push for standardized tests and accountability have decreased the emphasis on the Navajo-English curriculum. Teaching to the standards takes time away from the curriculum. Such changes jeopardize the influence of parents, elders, and community (McCarty, 2002).

Peach Springs School District No. 8 (Hualapai).   Peach Springs School is located in Peach Springs, Arizona, on the Hualapai reservation (Watahomigie & McCarty, 1994). The Hualapai Bilingual/Bicultural Program was funded in 1975, but had its roots in an earlier collaboration between one of the community's elders and a linguist. The resulting writing system and two storybooks constituted the only transcription of the Hualapai language before 1975. Watahomigie (1995) speaks of the importance of parent and community involvement to counteract the effects of majority culture, educate parents about the importance of their own language and culture, and include elders in the development of curricula in Hualapai ethnobotany and other subjects. As of 1995, Peach Springs School included children from kindergarten through 8th grade (Watahomigie, 1995) and emphasized a child-centered curriculum of consistent culture and language across home, school, and community (Watahomigie & McCarty, 1994). After the introduction of this curriculum, test scores showed improvement of 8.06 normal curve equivalents on the California Test of Basic Skills (Watahomigie & McCarty, 1994). Only two students dropped out from 8th grade, with all 8th-grade graduates completing high school (Watahomigie, 1995).

The development of written Hualapai, training of teachers, and creation of the Hualapai curriculum was nurtured by the American Indian Language Development Institute (AILDI), conceived by Watahomigie and currently located at the University of Arizona. The emphasis of AILDI is on an additive approach to language and culture and to community involvement and control (McCarty et al., 1997). The success of the Hualapai Bilingual/Bicultural Program is measured not only by the individual success of Hualapai students but also by the export of its fundamental principles to more than 30 American Indian nations and tribes (McCarty et al., 1997).

Summary of models of family and community involvement.   The success of the Indian-controlled community school movement emphasizes three principles: community and parent involvement, individually appropriate practice, and bilingual/bicultural education. The success of Peach Springs and Rough Rock schools has also depended on the ability of school administrators to secure sufficient funding to implement these principles. Whether these principles can be adapted to the majority of American Indian children and families served by the public schools, has not yet been explored.

CONCLUSIONS AND IMPLICATIONS FOR RESEARCH AND PRACTICE

Indian-controlled schools promoting parental involvement and changes in federal law since the 1960s have led to increased involvement of American Indian families in their children's education. But the legacy of the past, including the displacement of American Indian peoples and the boarding school experience, combined with cultural differences between Indian families and both BIA and public schools, inhibits greater parental participation.

Aspects of parental involvement linked to American Indian children's school success include parental aspirations and supportiveness. We have suggested a need for research into most aspects of American Indian parent and community involvement. The limited research to date has focused on older children. The need for research on the early childhood period is pressing. Recent research emphasizes the importance of features of both home and classroom learning environments as early as preschool (e.g., Hubbs-Tait, Culp, Huey, et al., 2002). Thus, we recommend programmatic investigations of best practices for American Indian children from different home learning environments, from families with differing degrees of parental participation, and from families with differing educational aspirations.

American Indian parents have urged the incorporation of Indian culture and values into the curriculum and Indian teachers into the classroom and administration. We encourage schools to promote such modifications in curriculum and hiring, and teachers to make such fundamental changes in practice.

ACKNOWLEDGMENT

We thank Janet Scott for research assistance. The first author's contribution to this chapter was supported by funds from the John and Sue Taylor Professorship in Human Environmental Sciences.

NOTES

1. In this chapter, we adhere to the terminology recommended by the *Journal of American Indian Education*. "American Indians" refer to the indigenous populace of the continental United States; "First Nations" refer to the indigenous populace of Canada. When referring to individuals of both countries, we use the term "Native" or "indigenous."
2. Rough Rock was not, however, the first school ever to be directed by American Indians. The Cherokee and Choctaw tribes ran highly effective schools in the 19th century (Tippeconnic, 1999).

REFERENCES

Abraham, K.G., Christopherson, V.A., & Kuehl, R.O. (1984). *Journal of Comparative Family Studies, 15*, 372–388.

Adams, D.W. (1988). Fundamental considerations: The deep meaning of Native American schooling, 1880–1900. *Harvard Educational Review, 58*, 1–28.

Adams, D.W. (1995). *Education for extinction: American Indians and the boarding school experience, 1875–1928.* Lawrence: University Press of Kansas.

Akaran, S.E., & Fields, M.V. (1997). Family and cultural context: A writing breakthrough. *Young Children, 52*(4), 37–40.

Benjamin, S. (1987). Low-cost learning strategies produce high-quality education on the Navajo Indian reservation. *Performance & Instruction, 26*(5), 12–15.

Bolls, P.D., Tan, A., & Austin, E. (1997). An exploratory comparison of Native American and Caucasian students' attitudes toward teacher communicative behavior and toward school. *Communication Education, 46*, 198–202.

Boseker, B.J., (1994). The disappearance of American Indian languages. *Journal of Multilingual and Multicultural Development, 15*(2–3), 147–160.

Charleston, G.M. (1994). Toward true Native education: A treaty of 1992. Final report of the Indian Nations At Risk Task Force Draft 3. *Journal of American Indian Education, 33*(2), 1–23.

Cheshire, T.C. (2001). Cultural transmission in urban American Indian families. *American Behavioral Scientist, 44*, 1528–1535.

Child, B.J. (1998). *Boarding school seasons: American Indian families, 1900–1940.* Lincoln: University of Nebraska Press.

Coggins, K., Williams, E., & Radin, N. (1997). The traditional tribal values of Ojibwa parents and the school performance of their children: An exploratory study. *Journal of American Indian Education, 36*(3), 1–15.

Culp, A., Hubbs-Tait, L., Culp, R.E., & Starost, H-J. (2000). Maternal parenting characteristics and school involvement: Predictors of kindergarten cognitive competence among Head Start children. *Journal of Research in Childhood Education, 15*, 5–17.

Cummins, J. (1992). The empowerment of Indian students. In J. A. Reyhner (Ed.), *Teaching American Indian students* (pp. 3–12). Norman: University of Oklahoma Press.

DeJong, D. H. (1993). *Promises of the past: A history of Indian education.* Golden, CO: North American Press.

Deyhle, D., & Margonis, F. (1995). Navajo mothers and daughters: Schools, jobs, and the family. *Anthropology and Education Quarterly, 26*, 135–167.

Dick, G.S., Estell, D.W., & McCarty, T.L. (1994). Saad naakih bee'enootíi̱_jí na'alkaa: Restructuring the teaching of language and literacy in a Navajo community school. *Journal of American Indian Education, 33*(3), 31–46.

Dion, R., Gotowiec, A., & Beiser, M. (1998). Depression and conduct disorder in Native and non-Native children. *Journal of the American Academy of Child and Adolescent Psychiatry, 37*, 736–742.

Fan, X., Thompson, B., & Wang, L. (1999). Effects of sample size, estimation methods and model specification on structural equation modeling fit indexes. *Structural Equation Modeling, 6*, 56–83.

Greenfield, P.M. (1997). You can't take it with you: Why ability assessments don't cross cultures. *American Psychologist, 52,* 1115–1124.

Hale, L. (2002). *Native American education: A reference handbook.* Santa Barbara: ABC-CLIO.

Hubbs-Tait, L., Culp, A.M., Culp, R.E., & Miller, C.E. (2002). Relation of maternal cognitive stimulation, emotional support, and intrusive behavior during Head Start to children's kindergarten cognitive abilities. *Child Development, 73,* 110–131.

Hubbs-Tait, L., Culp, A.M., Huey, E., Culp, R.E., Starost, H.-J., & Hare, C. (2002). Relation of Head Start attendance to children's cognitive and social outcomes: moderation by family risk. *Early Childhood Research Quarterly, 17,* 539–558.

Keith, T.Z., Keith, P.B., Quirk, K.J., Sperduto, J., Santillo, S., & Killings, S. (1998). Longitudinal effects of parent involvement on high school grades: Similarities and differences across gender and ethnic groups. *Journal of School Psychology, 36,* 335–363.

Levin, M., Moss, M., Swartz, J., Khan, S., & Tarr, H. (1997). *National evaluation of the Even Start family literacy program: Report on Even Start projects for Indian tribes and tribal organizations.* Bethesda, MD: Abt Associates, Inc.; Fu Associates, Ltd. (Eric Document Reproduction Service No. ED415084)

Littlebear, D. (1992). Getting teachers and parents to work together. In J.A. Reyhner (Ed.), *Teaching American Indian students* (pp. 104–111). Norman: University of Oklahoma Press.

Lomawaima, K.T. (1999). The unnatural history of American Indian education. In K.G. Swisher & J.W. Tippeconic III (Eds.), *Next steps: Research and practice to advance Indian education* (pp. 1–31). Charleston, WV: ERIC Clearinghouse on Rural Education and Small Schools.

Long, E.E., & Christensen, J.M. (1998). Indirect language assessment tool for English-speaking Cherokee Indian children. *Journal of American Indian Education, 37*(3), 1–14.

Macias, J. (1987). The hidden curriculum of Papago teachers: American Indian strategies for mitigating cultural discontinuity in early schooling. In G. Spindler & L. Spindler (Eds.), *An interpretive ethnography of education: At home and abroad* (pp. 363–380). Hillsdale, NJ: Erlbaum.

MacPhee, D., Fritz, J., & Miller-Heyl, J. (1996). Ethnic variations in personal social networks and parenting. *Child Development, 67,* 3278–3295.

McCarty, T.L. (1989). School as community: The Rough Rock demonstration. *Harvard Educational Review, 59,* 484–503.

McCarty, T.L. (2002). *A place to be Navajo: Rough Rock and the struggle for self-determination in indigenous schooling.* Mahwah, NJ: Erlbaum.

McCarty, T.L., Watahomigie, L.J., Yamamoto, A.Y., & Zepeda, O. (1997). School-community-university collaborations: The American Indian Language Development Institute. In J.A. Reyhner (Ed.), *Teaching indigenous languages* (pp. 85–104). Flagstaff: Northern Arizona University.

National Association for the Education of Young Children. (1996). NAEYC position statement: Responding to linguistic and cultural diversity— Recommendations for effective early childhood education. *Young Children, 51*(2), 4–12.

Olp, S. (2002, July 10). Busby school to operate year-round: Northern Cheyenne Tribal School hopes to improve test scores. *Billings Gazette*. Retrieved November 2, 2002, from NewsBank database.

Parker, F.L., Boak, A. Y., Griffin, K.W., Ripple, C., & Peay, L. (1999). Parent–child relationship, home learning environment, and school readiness. *School Psychology Review, 28*, 413–425.

Plank, G.A. (1994). What silence means for educators of American Indian children. *Journal of American Indian Education, 34*(1), 3–19.

Reyhner, J.A. (1992). American Indian cultures and school success. *Journal of American Indian Education, 32*(1), 30–39.

Reyhner, J., & Eder, J. (1992). A history of education. In J. A. Reyhner (Ed.), *Teaching American Indian students* (pp. 33–58). Norman: University of Oklahoma Press.

Robinson-Zañartu, C., & Majel-Dixon, J. (1996). Parent voices: American Indian relationships with schools. *Journal of American Indian Education, 36*(1), 33–54.

Seideman, R.Y., Williams, R., Burns, P., Jacobson, S., Weatherby, F., & Primeaux, M. (1994). Culture sensitivity in assessing urban Native American parenting. *Public Health Nursing, 11*(2), 98–103.

Swisher, K., & Deyhle, D. (1989). The styles of learning are different, but the teaching is just the same: Suggestions for teachers of American Indian youth. *Journal of American Indian Education, 28*(Special Issue), 1–14.

Szasz, M. C. (1999). *Education and the American Indian: The road to self-determination since 1928* (3rd ed). Albuquerque: University of New Mexico Press.

Tharp, R.G. (1994). Intergroup differences among Native Americans in socialization and child cognition: An ethnogenetic analysis. In P.M. Greenfield, & R.R. Cocking (Eds.), *Cross-cultural roots of minority child development* (pp. 87–105). Hillsdale, NJ: Erlbaum.

Tippeconnic, J.W., III. (1999). Tribal control of American Indian education: Observations since the 1960s with implications for the future. In K.G. Swisher & J.W. Tippeconic III (Eds.), *Next steps: Research and practice to advance Indian education* (pp. 33–52). Charleston, WV: ERIC Clearinghouse on Rural Education and Small Schools.

Vogt, L.A., Jordan, C., & Tharp, R.G. (1987). Explaining school failure, producing school success: Two cases. *Anthropology and Education Quarterly, 18*, 276–186.

Ward, C. (1998). Community resources and school performance: The Northern Cheyenne case. *Sociological Inquiry, 68*, 83–113.

Warner, L.S. (1999). Education and the law: Implications for American Indian/Alaska Native students. In K.G. Swisher & J.W. Tippeconic III (Eds.), *Next steps: Research and practice to advance Indian education* (pp. 53–80). Charleston, WV: ERIC Clearinghouse on Rural Education and Small Schools.

Watahomigie, L.J. (1995). The power of American Indian parents and communities. *The Bilingual Research Journal, 19*(1), 189–194.

Watahomigie, L.J., & McCarty, T.L. (1994). Bilingual/bicultural education at Peach Springs: A Hualapai way of schooling. *Peabody Journal of Education, 69*(2), 26–42.

Whitbeck, L.B., Hoyt, D.R., Stubben, J.D., & LaFromboise, T. (2001). Traditional culture and academic success among American Indian children in the upper Midwest. *Journal of American Indian Education, 40*(2), 48–60.

Willeto, A.A.A. (1999). Navajo culture and family influences on academic success: Traditionalism is not a significant predictor of achievement among young Navajos. *Journal of American Indian Education, 38*(2), 1–21.

Zimiga, A.W. (1982). The influence of traditional Lakota thought on Indian parent group involvement on the Pine Ridge Indian Reservation: A case study. *Dissertation Abstracts International, 42*(8), 3488A. (UMI No. 8125501)

Zwick, T.T., & Miller, K.W. (1996). A comparison of integrated outdoor education activities and traditional science learning with American Indian students. *Journal of American Indian Education, 35*(2), 1–9.

CHAPTER 12

CONTEMPORARY TRANSFORMATIONS IN FAMILIES, COMMUNITIES, AND SCHOOLS

Olivia N. Saracho and Bernard Spodek

INTRODUCTION

The 20th century brought about radical changes in the lives of American families, communities, and school settings. Among the forces that created these changes were two world wars along with a number of smaller international conflicts, a major depression, changes in forms of transportation and technology which saw the country move from the horse and buggy era to the era of automobiles, jet planes, and interstellar travel. Other technological changes brought us electricity, the telephone, radio, televison, computers and a host of other changes. This allowed for ease of movement from place to place, the creation of large suburbs outside of cities, and an increase in nuclear families. Each generation was challenged with a series of unique historical occurrences, which contributed to new situations in their lives and livelihood as well as shaped, and formed our cultural understandings.

Contemporary Perspectives on Families, Communities, and Schools for Young Children, pages 247–256
Copyright © 2005 by Information Age Publishing
All rights of reproduction in any form reserved.

Not all the changes of the century were positive and supportive of families. Everywhere (including cities, suburbs, rural areas) families, communities, and schools came up against a socially toxic environment that included ingredients of "violence, poverty, and other economic pressures on parents and their children, disruption of family relationships, depression, paranoia, nastiness, and alienation" (Garbarino, 1995, p. 14) as well as terrorism (Wright & Heeren, 2002).

These radical changes had an impact on the flow of different trends that emerged in relation to the families, communities, and schools. Trends consisted of work behavior, attitudes relating to gender roles, transmission of values across generations, and family circumstances such as schooling, marriage, divorce, child rearing, increased participation of women in the work force, the growth of child care, and other family practices. Some of the families experienced emotional disturbance and stress related to these changes, leading to some basic shifts in the cultural meaning of family and community life.

SOCIAL CHANGE

The rituals of daily life affected in some way the family, community, and schools. Social groups determined their social behaviors and roles that place a degree of stress in creating and supporting unity or social identity. Stress may have generated new ritual forms during social change or old ritual forms may have modified their meaning. The changes in the daily life patterns of the family and community have been causing a cultural shift in both the family and community. Families and communities assumed responsibilities as part of an entourage of partnerships. Families have modified their attitudes toward academic education. Social changes have led to an increased sense of autonomy instead of obedience as a value in children's socialization (Alwin, 1989). Transition of roles has been influenced by the change of responsibilities in the different genders. The role of women previously was to stay at home and care for the children, but changes in the labor force, especially during World War II has changed this role.

The nature of child care outside the home emerged with the growth of the labor force. Mothers of young children went to work; therefore, the percentage of children less than five years of age in child care centers increased from 6% in 1965 to 30% in 1998 (Cherlin, 1998). A fourth of all women more than 16 years of age participated in the labor force in 1940 compared to 16% in 1996. Most of them were married women with children who were younger than six-years-old in their households, which increased from 11% in 1948 to 63% in 1996 (United States Bureau of the

Census, 1997). The incidence of divorce is taking place more recently than before. It also has been having an impact in relation to the family's and community's views of divorcees. Family incidents and life series of celebrations occur in some form of acknowledgment of birthdays, marriages, and christenings. Relatives and friends from school and the community usually participate in these celebrations and other occurrences such as family funerals and other rituals taking place outside the school.

SUPPORT SYSTEM

Informational, instrumental, and emotional are the three kinds of social support that have been investigated (Cohen & Wills, 1985; House & Kahn, 1985). Informational support consists of sharing information and advising on ways to manage certain situations. Concrete help, gifts, and money are examples of instrumental support. Emotional support refers to expressions of attachment. All of these types of support were evident in the support systems that were observed in the family, community, and school. In the 1960s research and development programs identified the importance of parent involvement in the education of young children from poor and minority group backgrounds. This involvement requires much support from agencies involved.

During the last decade, an interest has emerged in family support initiatives within school and home settings. Legislative efforts have attempted to unify services for children and families and to organize discussions to assist schools in supporting parents and communities (Gadsden, 1994; United States Department of Education and United States Department of Human Services, 1993), including the intergenerational literacy nature of literacy and the individual family members' life-span development (Coleman, 1987; Smith, 1991). These endeavors motivated the development of programs with a support system. For example, Head Start, Follow Through, and other federally funded initiatives mandated parent involvement as an integral element of these programs. The programs were built on the premise that change in the lives of young children could be achieved only with concurrent changes in their parents, homes, and neighborhoods. Parent involvement in these programs often took the form of parent education. Parents acquired knowledge of child development, developed new skills in the education and raising of their children, and assisted teachers in the classrooms. In addition, parents participated in the decision-making process in the schools' parent advisory boards. They provided their input in relation to their children's educational programs and their selection of staff. Parents received the encouragement that their input was of value and that the staff wanted them to be involved; therefore, they responded with enthusiasm. Increasingly, parents were invited to participate in educational programs and became the educators' allies. In Gallagher, Maddox, and Espinosa's (1984) study a third of the parents participated in parent education and a parent support program.

About a decade ago, a new early childhood program was established to provide support to families. It was a prevention program whose major clients were the parents of young children. This early childhood program was a community-based program that was developed to provide education and support to parents in their role as socializers and caregivers. In addition, the purpose of this program was to provide these services in ways that would help parents foster their interdependence, instead of extending their helplessness and dependence. Usually, these programs offered families some type of parent education and support groups, home visitation, drop-in services, warmlines and hotlines, information and referral, lending libraries, health/nutrition services, and child care to give parents an opportunity to attend these programs. Several states (including Minnesota, Missouri, South Carolina, Kentucky, Maryland, Connecticut, and Oklahoma) have funded some of these family support programs (Stevens, 1991). This initiative may provide a path to develop a link among the family, community, and school.

CONSOLIDATION OF SERVICES

Service providers and related agencies usually have separated clients based on the type of professional expertise that is requested on their application. However, in the United States, "recent legislation, writing, and policy have reconceptualized services toward viewing clients as whole units, with interrelated needs and strengths that are not easily divided at the bureaucratic and professional boundaries that have been imposed on them" (Short & Talley, 1999, p. 195). Thus, community agencies, health care, social welfare, education, and similar organizations are required to cooperate and work together by combining their restricted resources and granting far-reaching and protective services to families (North Central Regional Educational Laboratory, NCREL, 1996). High-performance teamwork among agencies will require the intervention of professionals who have the abilities that exceed their individual career conviction.

Like human resource providers, educational disciplines also have segregated problems based on each precise specialty. In education, for example, pre-service educators learn about child development, learning theories, strategies for teaching different subject areas, and classroom management. Rarely, if ever, are the pre-professionals provided with the opportunity to consider the child within the whole situation. This procedure increases the understanding that children are more than just students, but they are also members of a family entity and a specific community. Unfortunately, this segmented procedure is duplicated in the areas of social work, criminal justice, and health care. More teamwork efforts demand strong communication between all occupations and particpatory leadership with the capacity to settle difficulty and disparities (NCREL, 1996). Thus, pre-service educators and other professionals need to develop the ability to effectively work as a team to achieve a mutual goal. Wright and Heeren (2002) suggest that interdisciplinary courses be developed (such as a course titled, "School, Community, and Family Connections") to help the students acquire the skills that will teach them to cooperate and to obtain substantial success in focusing on the combined needs of children, families and communities.

CONCLUSION

Researchers and educators need to understand the impact that the family, community, and school have on each other and the challenges that they encounter. These challenges need to be examined to better prepare pre-professionals in the areas to work together to address the challenges. Many of the sociological studies of the past two centuries and Cobb's (1992) community elements are studies searching for the cures for many of our social afflictions. Throughout the centuries, scholars have considered the community to intervene with the unresponsive intrusion of mass society; monitor the deficient segregation of the individual directed against a massive mundane equipment; create a feeling of morality, and raise the perspectives of the one above the degree of power of family ties (Redding, 2001).

Family, community, and school connections represent a disjointed problem. Presently, it is considered more important than ever for families, communities, and schools to function jointly to improve and guarantee their success in the future (NCREL, 1996). Children can profit from such collaboration even before they enter early childhood programs and at least until they leave the public schools when a bond between family, community, and school is constructed. It is important to understand the need to function synergetic with each other to approach the current and opening social controversies that influence children, families, and, finally, the community.

The literature that exists lack studies that can provide an understanding of the school–family–community partnerships, although sufficient research exists to support the value of these partnerships. The literature suggests future research to examine the complex nature of partnerships. Researchers agree that there is a lack of knowledge concerning school–family–community involvement, but they disagree on ways to justify the case for family, community, and school partnerships. Chavkin (2001) offers the following research agenda:

1. *Define the partnership terms precisely.*   Most studies are unclear about the meaning of "partnership." Another term that needs to be defined is "community." Researchers imply that they are referring to family–community–school partnership. In relation to parent involvement, studies suggest that it refers to reading to children, attending school, raising funds, or the like. It is important that there is a clear definition of optimal partnership activities and a description of the locale and range of activities that are part of a partnership.

2. *Be clear about the predicted outcomes.*   It is important that researchers clearly identify the hypothesized outcomes of the partnership effort. Researchers need to acknowledge that the outcomes are affected by the kind of activities that are provided to students, parents, and educators, especially in the short term. For example, Epstein (1996) states that working on parenting skills may first affect the interaction of families with their children and later affect the student's achievement. Gomby and Larson (1992) identify possible outcomes for the student, the school, the family, and the community, which can be used as starting points.

3. *Know the relationship between the theory of the family–community–school partnership and the partnership activities.*   A strong conceptual base needs to be provided on how partnerships work and to define the relationship of this theory to identify partnership activities. For example, Epstein (1996) proposes that examining points of transition from one grade level to the next or from one school to the next indicates the concept of change. It is essential to have a dialogue about this guiding vision with the family stakeholders and all participants to improve (Freeman & Pennckamp, 1988) the partnerships (Hooper-Briar & Lawson, 1994).

4. *Engage partnership subjects in research.*   Subjects need to be involved in the design of the study to obtain constructive criticism and suggestions about the measures and data collection process. Epstein (1996) believes that collaborating and sharing the research with educators and policymakers makes the research meaningful. Epstein (1996) refers to this process as "sharing the role of expert."

5. *Separate the individual sections of partnerships in the studies.*   In understanding the partnership role of each section in a study, it is important to separate and examine each section separately. For instance, it is important to know the independent effects of the tutoring program, mentoring program, or business involvement to understand which component of the program has improved community rela-

tions. Knapp (1995) suggests that studies should include both quantitative and qualitative analyses of the cost of these partnerships.

6. *Multiple, detailed case studies are an appropriate starting point.* Since family–community–school partnerships involve intricate relationships, which require a baseline of repeated measures. Detailed reports of both individual and partnership involvement must be recorded. These two reports are both similar and dissimilar. The individual report concentrates on individuals and families, whereas the partnership report begins with descriptive studies and case histories and continues with longitudinal and controlled studies. Knapp (1995) advocates studies that collects data over time including before participating in the partnership and during the partnership.

7. *Apply objective measures instead of self-report measures.* Studies need to use objective measures rather than self-reports of progress. Objective measures have a better reliability and validity than self-report measures. Also standardized measures and direct observations can identify the types of interactions and behavioral changes (Baker & Soden, 1997) that occur in these partnerships. Measuring changes in attitudes is different from changes in behaviors. Gomby and Larson (1992) suggest that self-report paper-and-pencil surveys are easy to administer, but they usually fail to provide the most predictive changes. However, Keir and Millea (1997) caution researchers to avoid using available data, because that data may not focus on the purpose of the study. Partnership studies must select their measures based on the purpose of the study.

8. *Focus on intervention levels.* The records of some families and community organizations may indicate a partnership, although they may not engage in partnership activities. Studies need to determine the level of implementation. Haynes and Emmons (1997) estimated the level of immersion to accurately determine the relationship of the implementation level to student outcomes. Keir and Millea (1997) suggested that studies trace the frequency of services.

9. *Identify unexpected outcomes.* A careful study of the typical practices and the conditions that support these practices in exemplary partnerships offers research new perspectives for identifying what is working (Knapp, 1995). Keir and Millea (1997) report the unforeseen gains obtained from collecting data on parent training and involvement. For example, the purpose of their study was to reach out to parents and to lure them into the project. Their surprising results showed that community members had leadership, public speaking, and advocacy skills and could administer and analyze

other surveys in their own community and assumed additional community-service responsibilities.

10. *Avoid premature research strategies.*   Several research strategies are not ready to be used. There are not sufficient studies to perform meta-analyses. Correlational research that apply factor-analytic studies are not appropriate to use with partnerships, because the collaborative design leads to many variables that are deceptive. Group-comparative experimental studies may contain errors. Studies that compare recipients and non-recipients may be invalid. Their treatment and subjects may differ (Knapp, 1995), which affect the outcomes of any study.

11. *Use groundwork from previous studies.*   The outcomes from previous studies have generated many new questions that provide the groundwork for future research with clearer questions, better data, stronger measurement models, more sophisticated analyses, more useful results, and more topics that are specially obliging and require further study. Topics may consist of (1) examining points of transition within the partnership and within schooling levels as students enter different grade units; (2) exploring the results or consequences of certain partnership activities; (3) identifying the community components; (4) exploring the students' roles in their own educational success; and (5) collaborative research with policy leaders and educators (Epstein, 1996).

Most of the problems with the gap between research and practice actually "stems from false expectations" (Kennedy, 1997, p. 10). Research does not provide clearly defined rules on time and procedures on conducting the research. The response relies on the individual partnership. Research recipes that are easy to follow do not exist, because many political, contextual, and financial issues affect the research partnerships. Most partnerships depend on soft money and the creative efforts of a small group of dedicated educators. In addition, outside elements (e.g., accreditation, funding, curriculum issues) create obstacles that influence the successes of the partnership. Actually, a strong research base that supports a family–community–school partnership does not exist. Innovative research strategies need to be developed. The traditional research methodology is inappropriate, because partnerships are complex and wreck havoc (Chavin, 2001). According to Gomby and Larson (1992), "Evaluation of school-linked service initiatives, which are characterized by great flexibility and variability, is challenging but also possible and desirable" (p. 68). It is important to proceed ahead exploring the family–community–school partnerships. Eventually, a periodical database will be available with a productive research base on the quality of family–community–school partnerships and an identification of the best research strategies (Chavin, 2001).

REFERENCES

Alwin, D. (1989). Changes in qualities valued in children in the United States, 1964–1984. *Social Science Research, 18*, 195–236.

Baker, A.J.L., & Soden, L.M. (1997).*Parent involvement in children's education: A critical assessment of the knowledge base.* New York: National Council of Jewish Women's Center for the Child.

Chavkin, N.F. (2001). Recommendations for research on the effectiveness of school, family, and community Partnerships. In S. Redding & L.G. Thomas (Eds.), *The Community of the school.* (pp. 83–96). Lincoln, IL: Academic Development Institute. [On-line] http://www.adi.org/cots.html

Cherlin, A.J. (1998, April 5). By the numbers. *The New York Magazine*, pp. 39–41.

Cobb, C.W. (1992). *Responsive schools, renewed communities.* San Francisco: ICS Press.

Cohen, S., & Wills, T.A. (1985). Stress, social support and the buffering hypothesis. *Psychological Bulletin, 98*, 310–357.

Coleman, J.S. (1987). Families and schools. *Educational Researcher, 16*, 32–38.

Epstein, J.L. (1996). Perspectives and previews on research and policy for school, family, and community partnerships. In A. Booth & J.F. Dunn (Eds.), *Family-school links: How do they affect educational outcomes?* Mahwah, NJ: Lawrence Erlbaum Associates.

Freeman, E.M., & Pennekamp, M. (1988). *Social work practice: Toward a child, family, school, community perspective.* Springfield, IL: Charles C. Thomas.

Gadsden, V.L. (1994). Understanding family literacy: Conceptual issues facing the field. *Teachers College Record, 96*(1), 58–86.

Gallagher, J., Maddox, M., & Espinosa, L. (1984). Perceptions of early childhood special education: Surveys of superintendents and parents in Washington State. *Journal of Early Intervention, 8*, 141–148.

Garbarino, J. (1995). *Educating children in a socially toxic environment.* San Francisco: Jossey-Bass.

Gomby, D.S., & Larson, C.S. (1992). Evaluation of school-linked services. *The Future of Children, 2*(1), 68–84.

Haynes, N.M., & Emmons, C.L. (1997). *Comer School Development Program effects: A ten year review, 1986–96.* New Haven, CT: Yale Child Study Center.

Hooper-Briar, K., & Larson, H.A. (1994). *Serving children, youth, and families through interprofessional collaboration and service integration.* Oxford, OH: The Danforth Foundation School, Family, and Community Partnerships and the Institute for Educational Renewal at Miami University.

House, J.S., & Kahn, R.L. (1985) Measures and concepts of social support. In S. Cohen & S.L. Syme (Eds.), *Social support and health* (pp. 83–108). Orlando FL: Academic Press.

Keir, S.S., & Millea, S. (1997). *Challenges and realities: Evaluating a school-based service project.* Austin, TX: Hogg Foundation for Mental Health.

Kennedy, M.A. (1997). The connection between research and practice. *Educational Researcher, 26*(7), 4–12.

Knapp, M.S. (1995). How shall we study comprehensive, collaborative services for children and families? *Educational Researcher, 24*(4), 5–16.

North Central Regional Educational Laboratory (NCREL). (1996, January). School-community collaboration. *New Leaders for Tomorrow's Schools, 2*(1). Retrieved on November 20, 2003, from http://www.ncrel.org/cscd/pubs/lead21/2-1a.htm

Redding, S. (2001). The community of the school. In S. Redding & L.G. Thomas (Eds.), *The Community of the school* (pp. 1–24). Lincoln, IL: Academic Development Institute.

Short, R.J., & Talley, R.C. (1999). Services integration: An introduction. *Journal of Educational and Psychological Consultation, 10*(3), 193–200.

Smith, S. (1991). Two-generation program models: A new intervention strategy. *Social Policy Reports: Society of Research in Child Development, 5,* 1–15.

Stevens, J.H. Jr. (1991). Informal social support and parenting: Understanding the mechanisms of support. In B. Spodek & O.N. Saracho (Eds.), *Yearbook of early childhood education: Issues in early childhood curriculum,* Vol. II. (pp. 152–165). New York: Teachers College Press.

United States Department of Education and United States Department of Human Services. (1993). *Together we can.* Washington, DC: United States Department of Education and United States Department of Human Services.

United States Bureau of the Census. (1997). *Statistical abstract of the United States, 1997* (117th ed.). Washington, DC: Author.

Wright, A.E., & Heeren, C. (2002). Utilizing case studies: Connecting the family, school, and community. *The School Community Journal, 12*(2), 103–115.

CHAPTER 13

ABOUT THE AUTHORS

Enrique B. Arranz Freijo is Professor of Developmental Psychology and Family Psychology at the Faculty of Psychology in the University of the Basque Country in San Sebastián, Spain. He carried out his doctoral dissertation on the subject of sibling relationships and psychological development during childhood and has published a number of books and articles within this field. His research activities are mainly focused on the influence of family context on the psychological developmental process. He currently directs a research group in collaboration with the Centre for Family Research at the University of Cambridge (United Kingdom) and the Department of Developmental Psychology at the University of Seville in Spain.

Julia M. Braungart-Rieker earned her Ph.D. in 1992 from The Pennsylvania State University, Department of Human Development and Family Studies. Currently, she is a faculty member in the Psychology Department and Associate Dean in the College of Arts and Letters at the University of Notre Dame. Her research focuses on social and emotional development during infancy and early childhood. In particular, she is interested in the development of children's abilities to regulate and manage emotions. Using longitudinal designs, she examines the extent to which children's characteristics (e.g., temperament), parenting practices, the spousal relationship, contextual factors (e.g., family earner status), and the fathers' role in the family relate to outcomes such as children's ability to manage distress, parent-child attachment security, and children's social competence. Her most current research project, which has been funded by the National Institutes of Health, is a longitudinal study that focuses on tracking individual changes

Contemporary Perspectives on Families, Communities, and Schools for Young Children, pages 257–263
Copyright © 2005 by Information Age Publishing
All rights of reproduction in any form reserved.

in infants' abilities to regulate their emotions. In particular, she and her graduate students are examining the degree to which cognitive, socio-emotional, and familial factors relate to differential patterns of change over time. Additional research projects include how parental stress is related to parents' perceptions of their children's behaviors, and the interrelationships between parenting, temperament, and early language development.

Jacqueline Bush earned a Masters degree in Clinical Psychology and is currently enrolled in the Ph.D. program in Clinical-Lifespan Psychology at the University of Victoria. She researches the role of the sibling relationship in helping children to cope with divorce. She is also a member of the Families in Motion Research and Information Group (www.uvic.ca/psyc/fmric) at the University of Victoria.

Priscilla Coleman is an Assistant Professor of Human Development and Family Studies at Bowling Green State University (BGSU) in Ohio. Dr. Coleman received her Ph.D. in Life-Span Developmental Psychology from West Virginia University in 1998. She spent four years as an Assistant Professor of Psychology and Education at the University of the South in Tennessee. Dr. Coleman's recent research has focused on attachment, parenting cognitions, and the psychological outcomes of women who have had an abortion.

Marion Ehrenberg has a Ph.D. in Clinical Psychology and is currently an Associate Professor and Director of Clinical Training in the Department of Psychology at the University of Victoria. Her research and clinical practice focuses on children and parents experiencing divorce and other family transitions. She is also a member of the Families in Motion Research and Information Group (www.uvic.ca/psyc/fmric) at the University of Victoria.

Rebecca C. Fauth is a Research Scientist at the National Center for Children and Families housed at Columbia University's Teachers College. She earned an M.S. in applied statistics from Teachers College in 2002 and a Ph.D. in developmental psychology from Columbia University in 2004. Fauth's primary research interests are the impacts of family- and neighborhood-level poverty on children's and families' well-being.

Jennifer Geisreiter recently completed her B.A. Honours degree in Psychology at the University of Victoria, focusing on young adults' relationships in light of family transitions experienced during childhood. She is also a member of the Families in Motion Research and Information Group (www.uvic.ca/psyc/fmric) at the University of Victoria.

Jeanne Brooks-Gunn is the Virginia and Leonard Marx Professor of Child Development and Education at Teachers College, Columbia University and the College of Physicians and Surgeons at Columbia University. Trained as a developmental psychologist, she specializes in policy-oriented research that focuses on family and community influences on the development of young children. Her research centers on designing and evaluating interventions and policies aimed at enhancing the well-being of children living in poverty. She is the recipient of numerous awards, including the Urie Bronfenbrenner Award for lifetime contribution to developmental psychology in the areas of science and society from the American Psychological Association, the Nicholas Hobbs Award from the American Psychological Association, the Jon B. Hill Award from the Society for Research in Child Development, and in early 2004, she was elected Margaret Mead Fellow by the American Academy of Political and Social Science. Brooks-Gunn is the author of 17 books and over 400 articles.

Charley Hare is the former American Indian–Alaska Native Collaboration Director for the American Indian–Alaska Native Program Branch of the Head Start Bureau providing partnership planning between Tribal Head Start programs and other early education systems. Hare has served as Field Operation Supervisor for the National Medical Expenditure Survey of American Indian and Alaska Natives and has served as a proposal reviewer for national Head Start research conferences.

Ashley L. Hill received her Masters degree in general psychology from the University of West Florida in 1999, where she worked on an evaluation program for children in kindergarten who had attended Head Start programs in rural areas. In 2003, Hill earned her Ph.D. at the University of Notre Dame's Department of Psychology. Her dissertation work focused on precursors and outcomes of effortful control ability in preschool aged children. Currently, Dr. Hill is a post-doctoral fellow at the University of North Carolina at Greensboro.

Laura Hubbs-Tait is Professor of Human Development and Family Science and John and Sue Taylor Professor of Human Environmental Sciences at Oklahoma State University. Her research is focused on low-income, rural families and children. Recent publications have examined parental behaviors and Head Start attendance as predictors of young children's cognitive and social competence. Between 20% and 30% of the children in her rural Oklahoma samples are American Indian or multiethnic with one or more Indian nations contributing to the child's multiethnic heritage.

Erron L. Huey is Assistant Professor of Child Development and Family Studies at West Virginia University. His research focuses on individual development and contextual influences. This currently involves work examining models of rural Head Start attendance, models of parent and community influence on individual development, and the impact of state public policy initiatives on the quality of childcare in Oklahoma.

Katherine Karraker is a professor of psychology, Associate Chair of the Department of Psychology, and Director of Graduate Training in Psychology at West Virginia University. She received her Ph.D. in Developmental Psychology from Michigan State University in 1978. Her current research interests include parent-infant relations, infant assessment, parental cognitions (including stereotypes and parenting self-efficacy), stress and coping in infancy, and the effects of maternal sleep deprivation.

Tama Leventhal is an Associate Research Scientist at the Institute for Policy Studies at Johns Hopkins University and an Assistant Professor in Population and Family Health Sciences at the Johns Hopkins Bloomberg School of Public Health. Dr. Leventhal received her Ph.D. in developmental psychology from Columbia University's Teachers College. Dr. Leventhal's primary research interest is understanding the role of neighborhood contexts in the lives of children, youth, and families.

Marei Luedemann is a Masters student in the Clinical-Lifespan Psychology program, with a special interest in the mother-daughter relationship in divorcing families. She is also a member of the Families in Motion Research and Information Group (www.uvic.ca/psyc/fmric) at the University of Victoria.

Bruce L. Mallory is Provost and Executive Vice President for Academic Affairs at the University of New Hampshire (UNH). Previously, he was Vice Provost and Dean of the Graduate School at UNH (1997–2003). Dr. Mallory has been a professor of education (early childhood and special education) since 1979; he chaired the UNH Department of Education from 1987 to 1993. Dr. Mallory received his Ph.D. in Special Education and Community Psychology from George Peabody College of Vanderbilt University. Earlier experience includes service as a public school teacher, VISTA volunteer, director of Head Start programs, and legislative researcher. His work at UNH has concentrated on the professional preparation of early childhood and special education teachers and program administrators, the development and evaluation of rural early intervention services, the analysis of social policies that affect young children with disabilities and their families, cross-cultural research in under developed and developing countries regarding disability and child care policy, and reconceptualizations of early childhood special education theory and practice. Most recently, he has been co-principal investigator of a major investigation of the socio-cultural construction of home-school relations in five Italian cities. Dr. Mallory has been a leader in school reform initiatives in New Hampshire, especially with respect to professional development of school administrators and the design of school improvement programs. Dr. Mallory directs the UNH Public Conversations Project, which fosters civic engagement and democratic participation related to public education and related social challenges. He serves on several community and national boards, including the Children's Alliance of New Hampshire, Inc. and the Topsfield Foundation.

Frances Martínez-Hancock holds an Ed.D. in early childhood education from the University of Illinois at Urbana-Champaign, where she was a Bilingual Education Fellow. In 1972, she first taught in Brownsville, Texas, and later in the innovative Child Development Associate Program at Pan American University in Edinburg, Texas. In Illinois, she directed the Champaign County Child Development Program and in California she worked for Head Start and Riverside Community College. She was an Assistant Professor of Education at Concordia University in St. Paul, Minnesota, advisory member of the State Cultural Dynamics Curriculum for Child Care, founding member of the Aurora Charter School in Minneapolis, and past President of Instituto de Arte y Cultura.

Aysegul Metindogan is a doctoral candidate in Child Dveleopment at Syracuse University. Her research interests include parent-child socialization across, social-cognitive processes in young children across cultures, paternal involvement, and early childhood education internationally.

Rebecca S. New is Associate Professor and Director of Early Childhood Teacher Education at the Eliot-Pearson Department of Child Development at Tufts University. Dr. New has over 30 years' experience in the field of early and elementary education, beginning with her work as a classroom teacher in Florida public schools. Following graduate study in Curriculum and Instruction at the University of Florida, she completed her doctoral studies in Comparative Child Development at Harvard University (1984). She currently serves as president of the Early Childhood and Child Development Special Interest Group of the American Educational Research Association. While Dr. New is perhaps best known for her role in introducing Reggio Emilia to American educators, she has been studying Italian parenting and early childhood practices for the past 25 years. Dr. New has conducted research on the cultural bases of parenting, child development, and early childhood educational policies and practices, and contributed to her critique of NAEYC guidelines for developmentally appropriate practices, as represented in the volume (edited with Bruce Mallory) on *Diversity and Developmentally Appropriate Practices: Challenges for Early Childhood Education* (Teachers College Press, 1994). Her specific knowledge of Italian social policies and early education practices led to the recent invitation to participate in the 11-nation review of early care and education sponsored by the Organization for Economic and Cooperative Development (OECD). Comparative results of this study are presented in the 2001 OECD publication, *Starting Strong*. Current activities involve a collaborative inquiry with other United States teacher education programs on the uses of Italian conceptions of documentation as it informs child assessment, curriculum planning, and home-school relations. She is also writing a book on Reggio Emilia.

Jennifer Pringle has a Masters degree in Clinical Psychology. She is currently enrolled in the Ph.D. program in Clinical-Lifespan Psychology at the University of Victoria. She is interested in support services as well as the configuration of step- and blended families. She is also a member of the Families in Motion Research and Information Group (www.uvic.ca/psyc/fmric) at the University of Victoria.

Jaipaul L. Roopnarine is Professor of Child Studies at Syracuse University. He received his Ph.D. from the University of Wisconsin. He has published extensively in the areas of childhood development and early childhood education. His research interests include fathering across cultures, play and early childhood education across cultures, globalization and childhood development, and schooling among Caribbean immigrant children. He serves on the editorial board of Fathering. His forthcoming volumes include the fourth edition to *Approaches to Early Childhood Education* (Merrill/Prentice Hall) and *Families in Global Perspectives* (Allyn & Bacon).

Olivia N. Saracho is Professor in the Department of Curriculum and Instruction at the University of Maryland at College Park. She has taught Head Start, preschool, kindergarten, and elementary classes. Her current research and writing is in the field of early childhood education. She has conducted research on children's play and family literacy. She is co-author of *Foundations of Early Childhood Education* (Prentice-Hall), *Right from the Start* (Allyn and Bacon), *Individual Differences* (Longman) and is presently co-editor of the *Handbook of Research on the Education of Young Children* (Erlbaum).

Bernard Spodek is Professor Emeritus of Early Childhood Education at the University of Illinois. He received his doctorate from Teachers College, Columbia University. His research and scholarly interests are in the areas of curriculum, teaching, and teacher education in early childhood education. He has written and edited 31 books, 48 chapters in books, and 67 scholarly articles. Dr. Spodek's most recent books are *Multiple Perspectives on Play in Early Childhood Education*, with Olivia Saracho (SUNY Press), *Issues in* *early Childhood Educational Research* (Teachers College Press), with Olivia Saracho and Anthony Pellegrini and the *Handbook of Research on the Education of Young Children* (Macmillan). Dr. Spodek has been president of the National Association for the Education of Young Children (1976–78) and is currently president of the Pacific Early Childhood Education Research Association.

David A. Tait is Assistant Professor of History at Rogers State University in Claremore, Oklahoma. His research interests include Oklahoma history and the interaction between religion and social change.